# PRACTICE TESTS
## —— IN ——
# VERBAL REASONING

Nearly 3000 Test Exercises with
Answers and Explanations

SIMBO NUGA

Order this book online at www.trafford.com
or email orders@trafford.com

Most Trafford titles are also available at major online book retailers.

© Copyright 2013 Simbo Nuga.

All rights reserved. No part of this publication may be reproduced, stored in a retrieval system, or transmitted, in any form or by any means, electronic, mechanical, photocopying, recording, or otherwise, without the written prior permission of the author.

Printed in the United States of America.

ISBN: 978-1-4669-7330-5 (sc)
ISBN: 978-1-4669-7331-2 (hc)
ISBN: 978-1-4669-7684-9 (e)

Library of Congress Control Number: 2013901169

*Trafford rev. 01/29/2013*

 www.trafford.com

North America & international
toll-free: 1 888 232 4444 (USA & Canada)
phone: 250 383 6864 ♦ fax: 812 355 4082

To my father,
Christopher O. Otubushin
and in memory of my mother,

Esther O. Odufuwa

Thank you for your love and the priceless gift of education.


Education is not the filling of a pail, but the lighting of a fire.

—William Butler Yeats

# CONTENTS

Foreword .................................................................................................. vii
Preface ..................................................................................................... ix
Acknowledgment ...................................................................................... xi

**SECTION 1: INTRODUCTION** ................................................................ 1
  The Purpose of Testing ........................................................................... 1
  About This Book ..................................................................................... 3

**SECTION 2: TIMED TESTS** .................................................................... 4
  VERBAL REASONING TESTS ................................................................ 5
  Verbal Usage ........................................................................................... 5
    Meaning of a Word ............................................................................... 5
    Correct Spelling of a Word ................................................................. 19
    Words Spelled Incorrectly ................................................................. 29
    Missing Letters .................................................................................. 36
    Compound Words ............................................................................. 41
    Prefixes ............................................................................................. 47
    Palindrome ........................................................................................ 54
    Word Recognition ............................................................................. 56
  Verbal Comprehension ......................................................................... 60
    Grammar (Sentence Completion) ..................................................... 60
    Ambiguities and Confusable Words .................................................. 71
    Correct Use of a Word ...................................................................... 80
    Similes .............................................................................................. 92
    Collective Nouns ............................................................................... 95
    Grammar (Sentence Errors) ............................................................ 101
    Mixed Sentences ............................................................................ 104
  Verbal Application ............................................................................... 107
    Logical Reasoning .......................................................................... 107
    Place in Alphabetical Order ............................................................ 110

- Alphabetical Position of Words .................................................................. 113
- Word Pyramid ................................................................................................ 118
- Letter Sequence ........................................................................................... 125
- Number Sequence ........................................................................................ 127
- Checking ....................................................................................................... 129
- Code ............................................................................................................. 133
- Algebra ......................................................................................................... 135
- Crosswords ................................................................................................... 138
- Addition and Subtraction .............................................................................. 146

Verbal Analysis .................................................................................................... 150
- Problem Solving ........................................................................................... 150

Verbal Analogy .................................................................................................... 155
- Relationship Between Words ....................................................................... 155
- Pairs of Words .............................................................................................. 160
- Synonyms and Antonyms ............................................................................. 170
- Odd One Out ................................................................................................ 208
- Anagrams ..................................................................................................... 217
- Letter Moved From One Word To Another .................................................. 219

CRITICAL VERBAL REASONING TESTS ........................................................... 222
- Decision Making ........................................................................................... 222

SECTION 3: ANSWERS AND EXPLANATIONS .................................................. 237

SECTION 4: FURTHER INFORMATION ............................................................... 271
- Success: Hints and Tips ............................................................................... 271
- CV Writing Tips ............................................................................................. 276

Appendix A: List of Test Providers and Suppliers ................................................ 279
Appendix B: List of Useful Websites .................................................................... 281
Appendix C: General Careers Information .......................................................... 284
Appendix D: Additional Answer Sheet ................................................................. 287
Appendix E: Sample Study Planner ..................................................................... 291
Appendix F: Spelling Practice Sheet .................................................................... 292
Notes .................................................................................................................... 293
References ........................................................................................................... 294

# FOREWORD

In an economic environment where employment opportunities are limited, constructive self-help books based on sound principles, such as this one, are an invaluable tool for job-seekers, employers, and HR professionals.

Every type of business needs cogent, clear messages, and serious readers of this book will be well-placed to deliver these.

Alison Broadbent BA (Hon.) DM, MA, FCIS
Retired Director of Membership and Education
Chartered Institute of Secretaries and Administrators (ICSA)

---

National boundaries are diminishing because of globalization. Employers are now able to employ the most resourceful employees. Most employers reward such employees generously because they appreciate the significance of a knowledgeable employee to their businesses. Employers invest in their human resources because they are aware that their best assets are their employees.

This book is the catalyst required by employees to sharpen their skills in the competitive business world we live in. The advancement of technology and the availability of other resources in our modern era make it essential for everyone to excel in whatever discipline they are in.

This book has been well thought through, and it is very practical. You can learn how to improve your skills by reading and using this workbook. The reader will learn how to improve his or her confidence and the ability to innovate and make quick and precise decisions. This book is a brain sharpener because the benefits to the reader cannot be quantified. I am encouraged by the efforts by the author in making the book very practical and user-friendly.

I highly recommend this book to every employer, employee, and every person who is aspiring to improve his or her skills and intellect.

Charles Ampofo
Founder and Chairman
Kampac International PLC
HQ Dubai

# PREFACE

In the last twenty years, we have truly become a global economy. Technology has brought us closer together with greater opportunities to interact and exchange information. Budget travel has opened the door for more people to seek work and life abroad. Migration has provided enrichment and new challenges for greater understanding and integration. But above all, educational standards have improved, making the international job market more competitive than ever.

In India, the number of those making up the brightest 25 percent of pupils equals the total of the whole of the UK population. This figure takes no account of other emerging economies where educational attainment has become the fastest and most successful route out of poverty.

So imagine an employer today, faced with the high standards of university degrees and a wealth of experience from candidates seeking employment. In this highly competitive global economy, employers must find new ways to test for personality, sharpness, intelligence, and mental agility. The psychometric test has found its place as a further way to select the best from the many.

Psychometric tests are becoming an increasingly popular tool for those recruiting because they seek to add a better understanding of the personality and mental agility of the candidates. But if interviews can be stressful the psychometric test transports you back to your worst moments at school when you are sitting in the examination hall, waiting to turn the paper over.

But it need not be like that. There is a secret to preparing for the tests and for achieving the best results. As they say, "Practice makes perfect." Well, it might not always deliver you that much-wanted job, but there is no doubt that preparing well and understanding the nature of the tests will stand you in good stead.

## PRACTICE TESTS IN VERBAL REASONING

This book is a great way to support that preparation. With a series of tests with varying degrees of difficulty, the book is an invaluable handbook for the types of questions that could appear. Getting your mind in tune to the format of tests will be the best preparation that you can make. The success of this book is based on the ability to be able to redo tests at your convenience. Through practice, you can improve your score and improve your chance of getting that job.

Good luck and happy testing.

Clare Ward
Member of Parliament
Parliamentary Undersecretary of State at the Ministry of Justice

# ACKNOWLEDGMENT

I would like to thank Jacqueline Scully, Benjamin Nuga, Tara Scully, and Julianne Nuga for their unflinching and enthusiastic support during the writing of this book. I would also like to express my appreciation to Gazey Unmeni, Rita Akwetey and Olu Ajayi for their friendship, support and words of wisdom.

I am grateful to the following people for being a source of encouragement: Oluneye Oshin, Teniola Onabajo, Yemisi and Marilyn Otubushin, Gbuyi and Stella Otubushin, Abiodun Otubushin, Abayomi Otubushin, Dele John, Wasiu and Abiola Jimoh, Bukola Jimoh, Adedeji and Damola Kuye, Christia Otubushin, Michael Otubushin, Adewale Otubushin, Gbenga Otubushin, Kemi Otubushin, Banke Otubushin, Bunmi Otubushin, Adebowale Otubushin, Tejumade Otubushin, Yemi Orija, Oyin Oshikanlu, Oyinkansola Otubushin, Alfred and Kehinde Aruya, Val and Buki Okoh, Shola Osinowo, Tunde John, Emmanuel John, Ireti John, Titomi Kuye, Juwon Kuye, Tofunmi Banjoh, Timehin Banjoh, Bose Onabajo, Nike Kujore, Linda Haye, Deola Aminu, Remi and Taiwo Omotoye, Iyare and Gazey Umweni, Yinka and Edna Adegbite, Michael and Cathy Shambler, David and Claudia Oliver, Kayode and Gail Fapohunda, Vince and Edna Waname, Eddie and Lydia Creppy, James and Rita Akwetey, Toks and Yetunde Princewill, Myriam Ba, Roger and Safi Mohila, Kemi Tob-Ogu, Wemimo Adama, Folake Adama, Julie Cramer, Debbie Peters, Teresa Sheridan, Paul Hughes and Lorna Bevan, Seyi and Yemisi Osinowo, Lameen and Lili Abdul-Malik, Bimbo Aridegbe, Marie Heraty, Jay and Rupa Jayawickrama, Maxine Alison, Patricia Blankson, Babara Hoffmann, Andrew Watson, Dawn Watson, Steve and Ann McKenzie, Grace Joseph, Tayo and Funmi Buraimoh, Christopher and Patricia Monney, Lizzie Davedas, Sam and Kenan Maciel, Opoku and Janet Sarkodi, Gbola and Bisola Osinowo, Jonathan and Marsha Brandon, Yemi and Leye Osilaja, Adrian Wallace, Susie Arellano, Jamie Smith and Emma Nappier-Smith, Vijay and Tanuja Malaparthi, Jenni Williams, Phil and Stella Osagie, Sierra Kariyawasam, Ruscoe and Shiromi Philomin, Michel and Rosalie Miambanzila, Nicolas and Elodie Couture, Denis Arday, Thandi Haruperi, Tomi Coker, Herbert and Remi Macaulay, Solomon Igein, Uwamai and Doreen Igein, Gislain and Christian Matingou,

## PRACTICE TESTS IN VERBAL REASONING

Roch and Wende Miambanzila, Frank-Hecto and Sylvie Yoba, Betty Miller, Xaviere Marie, Claire Gardener and Chidi Okemadu. Some of these people are not aware of the motivation and assistance they provided, which, in one way or another, contributed to this book being completed.

Special thanks to the families of Gbenga Osinowo, Sesby Banjoh, and Abiodun and Labo Aminu for all their love and support over the years.

Thanks also to Richard Hill for being a support in the past and for his example as an exceptional investor in people.

Thanks to Alison Broadbent for her inspiration and encouragement, and to Liz Rushton, Sheila Selwood, Gwyneth Lawson, Gill Grogan, Declan O'Farrel, and the other members of the board of governors of West Herts College for their professionalism, dedication to duty, and understanding during the writing of the book.

My thanks to Bruce Woodcock of the Careers Advisory Service at the University of Kent–Canterbury for giving me the permission to reproduce practice test numbers 34, 54, and 72. They own the copyright to these three sets of questions. I would also like to express my thanks to Roy Davis and Tony Mays of Saville and Holdsworth (SHL) for the permission granted to reproduce practice test number 71.

My love to my darling husband and children, Julius, Benjamin, and Julianne. I thank them for enriching my life and for the various experiences and memories we continue to share.

All the people mentioned above have helped me firm up, consolidate, reinforce, adapt, and make improvements to the book.

# SECTION 1
# INTRODUCTION

## The Purpose of Testing

*I hear and I forget, I see and I remember, I do and I understand.*
—*Confucius*

Organizations use tests to diagnose and assess different attributes because they provide a measure of objectivity and standardization to the selection process. Some people first come across verbal reasoning tests after applying for employment with an organization. It is difficult to prepare for these tests when there are no past papers or copies of the test available from the employer. This lack of information, coupled with the fact that most people do not like being tested, can cause doubt to creep in about a person's ability to pass verbal reasoning tests. In fact, all that is required is a lot of practice. The proverb quoted above and this saying by Francis Bacon are very relevant: "Natural abilities are like plants that need pruning by study." You should choose to be confident because you can pass. Simulate test conditions, assess your performance, and the more you practice, your scores will improve.

Most of us, at an early age, have taken one test or another. Society regards education as being very important, and passing tests is seen as one of the ways of confirming that knowledge has been acquired. Some of us also expect that when we finish school or graduate from higher education, we would no longer have to sit for tests. The reality, however, is that we continue to be assessed for various purposes and at various stages in our lives. Tests are there to challenge us, and in most cases, we only have one shot at passing or failing them. This is why you have to always be prepared to pass any test that you are about to take. Tests are necessary tools used by organizations providing college placements, great employment, and career opportunities. Sadly, some people choose to keep passing over opportunities repeatedly (POOR) because they have to take a test. By reading and practicing the tests in this book, you have chosen to take the challenge, understand the requirements, and plan for success. The saying "If you fail to plan, you plan to fail" is very relevant to passing tests or examinations.

Tests are also used to evaluate the fitness for purpose of an individual to a task, role, or situation. Football players, racing drivers, and astronauts are people we expect to go through stringent selection processes. The fact is that in education, employment, and business, similar tests are becoming increasingly applicable. It is now common knowledge that the suitability of an applicant for a role does not merely depend on a curriculum vitae (CV) and an interviewer's subjective perception of an applicant. Businesses understand the importance of an individual's competence and are therefore increasingly dedicating themselves to improving their human resource selection processes.

The necessity for you to take tests as a requirement of getting a much-desired role should not put you off applying for that job. There are so many wise sayings, songs, stories from different cultures encouraging us to be our best. There are also many examples of inspirational people in various walks of life, some close to us and others who are famous for their achievements. Being our best takes determination and dedication, and what sets the people we admire apart is that they believed in themselves; they practice and assess the improvements being made. They review their technique and practice some more. These people are aware that "a winner never whines" (Paul Brown). This mindset is required in order to pass any test.

The most commonly used tests are termed psychometric tests. Psychometric testing is supported by science, and it is a standard way of measuring an aspect of mental performance. There are three types of psychometric testing. These are aptitude testing, ability testing, and personality questionnaires. These tests include numerical reasoning, data interpretation, verbal reasoning, and diagrammatic reasoning. The most commonly used types of psychometric tests are aptitude tests that concentrate on verbal reasoning and numeracy. Psychometric tests are usually timed and come in various formats.

Verbal reasoning, critical verbal reasoning, numerical reasoning, and diagrammatical reasoning tests are generally multiple choice in format. Practice is the key to passing these tests. It is also important to have a good vocabulary, command of grammar, and ability to solve mechanical problems. You will be expected to reason with numbers and follow instruction. While psychometric testing is very versatile, it cannot be expected to test everything. There are some qualities such as loyalty, dedication to duty, and enthusiasm that it does not claim to measure accurately.

# About This Book

People buy people first, so businesses are looking for people who would promote their business and brand. They require friendly, confident, enthusiastic, and capable employees. All these qualities are fundamental elements of good communication, both written and spoken. Assessing this important skill is the purpose of verbal reasoning tests.

This is a verbal reasoning practice book. You are to use it as a workbook. It has over two thousand five hundred practice questions with differing levels of difficulty. The tests are very similar to the kinds of tests you will face in exams or assessment centers. Some of the tests have been provided by two renowned test publishers, Saville and Holdsworth (SHL) and the University of Kent Careers Advisory Service. This book will enable you to thoroughly prepare for your verbal reasoning tests. In the words of Francis Bacon, "some books are to be tasted, others to be swallowed, and some few to be chewed and digested." This book is to be chewed and digested.

The tests have been categorized into two main types: verbal reasoning and critical verbal reasoning tests. The verbal reasoning questions are the first type, followed by the critical verbal reasoning questions. Verbal reasoning tests generally focus on word comprehension, spelling, and grammar. Accuracy and speed are essential to successfully complete these tests . There is a self-assessment grid after each test for your use. Critical verbal reasoning tests are used in the selection process for managerial roles in order to test the decision-making, business-planning, and project-management abilities of the applicant. The tests in this section are those provided by SHL and the University of Kent Careers Advisory Service.

This book is designed to be instructive and user-friendly. You will learn some new words, and you are encouraged to have a dictionary handy. It will provide you with an opportunity to increase your vocabulary so that you are better prepared for verbal reasoning tests. The questions will come in the various commonly used formats. Explanations of the various formats will be provided along with the answers to the questions. The book is divided into the following sections: timed tests, answers, and further information. Each type of test begins with a brief introductory paragraph, sample questions, followed by the practice tests.

This book is a comprehensive, practical, and fun book and will be useful to anyone about to take a verbal reasoning and critical verbal reasoning test. Anyone interested in improving his or her word power will also find this book fit for purpose. It will help you ace your tests.

# SECTION 2

# TIMED TESTS

This section provides examples of the various kinds of verbal and critical verbal reasoning tests. There is a brief description of each type of test, an example, followed by the practice tests. Under test conditions, you are usually expected to complete 80 questions in 50 minutes or 50 questions in 30 minutes. Use these times as your guide when taking the tests. Practice as many times as possible, and try to reduce the time it takes you to complete the test with each attempt. The tests are generally in sets of 20, 30, 40, and 50 questions, so aim to complete the respective set within 10, 15, 20, and 25 minutes or less. You should aim to have some time to review your answers.

The first sets of tests are verbal reasoning tests, and the second section of the tests consists of critical verbal reasoning tests. The verbal reasoning tests have been further categorized into five main subsections, which are verbal usage, verbal comprehension, verbal application, verbal analysis, and verbal analogies. There are no subsections in the critical verbal reasoning section.

The aim of the book is to provide you with ample opportunity to practice in order to pass verbal reasoning tests. It is a workbook, so you are encouraged to write your answer in the box or space provided in pencil because this allows you to do and redo the questions if necessary. Use the self-assessment grid below each test to record your progress, and remember that "energy and persistence conquer all things" (Benjamin Franklin).

# 1. Verbal Usage

The tests in this section aim to assess the extent of your word power or vocabulary. The dictionary definition of *vocabulary* is the "words that a person knows or all the words in a language." A good dictionary is an essential resource, so ensure that the dictionary you have is up to date and that it comprehensively explains words with many meanings. It should also include phrases, idioms, and slangs that are used in daily conversations. Your dictionary should provide cross-references to relevant and related words and also information and guidance on plural forms, hyphenation, capitalization, and spelling variations.

A lot of people prefer to communicate by e-mail, word processors, and by sending text messages. These methods of communication are less formal and encourage you to rely on spelling being corrected automatically. By doing the tests in this section, you will be able to rectify any spelling mistakes you make. The words chosen in the test reflect some of the words used professionally and socially, which you should be able to spell. Some of the words are used by advanced speakers of English, but if English is not your first language and you are not familiar with any word, refer to a dictionary and regard this as a learning opportunity.

Here now follows examples of verbal usage questions and some practice tests.

## SAMPLE TEST 1: MEANING OF A WORD

What is the correct meaning of the words in capitals? Write your answer in the space provided.

|  | A | B | C | D | Answer |
|---|---|---|---|---|---|
| PAROXYSM | scared | an outburst, a fit | redundant | height, scale | <u>B</u> |

The answer is *B*.

Now do the test below.

## Practice Test 1 (Answer on page 237)

What is the correct meaning of the words in capitals? Write your answer in the space provided.

## PRACTICE TESTS IN VERBAL REASONING

|    |              | A                                        | B                                       | C                           | D                                      |     |
|----|--------------|------------------------------------------|-----------------------------------------|-----------------------------|----------------------------------------|-----|
| 1  | ABERRATION   | to depart from the normal                | pharmacist                              | nearly asleep               | group of animals                       | A   |
| 2  | DUODENARY    | calculating by ten                       | a system of computing by twelve         | marching up and down        | to appear small                        | B   |
| 3  | AMORTIZE     | use a sinking fund to pay off debt gradually | forbid                              | walk leisurely              | make bigger                            | A   |
| 4  | CAJOLE       | ingot                                    | infringe                                | inquest                     | coax                                   | D   |
| 5  | ACCRUE       | malign                                   | to increase by addition or growth       | nagana                      | pochard                                | B   |
| 6  | SCARCE       | reside                                   | hard to find                            | extreme                     | constant                               | B   |
| 7  | ENORMOUS     | victory                                  | vivid                                   | consume                     | huge                                   | D   |
| 8  | CATERPILLAR  | grub                                     | score                                   | abide                       | temple                                 | a   |
| 9  | ANALGESIC    | analogue                                 | anecdote                                | a pain-relieving drug       | angelic behavior                       | C   |
| 10 | FAMISHED     | very hungry                              | bounty                                  | factory                     | windmill                               | A   |
| 11 | JURISPRUDENT | lawyer                                   | leery                                   | lecithin                    | levity                                 | A   |
| 12 | COMICAL      | pluperfect                               | funny                                   | Roquefort                   | plebeian                               | B   |
| 13 | AFFIDAVIT    | risible                                  | samarium                                | sahib                       | a written statement made on oath       | D   |
| 14 | PARR         | sain                                     | valgus                                  | young salmon                | usurp                                  | C   |

6

PRACTICE TESTS IN VERBAL REASONING

|    |              | A                              | B                           | C                      | D                            |     |
|----|--------------|--------------------------------|-----------------------------|------------------------|------------------------------|-----|
| 15 | FARINACEOUS  | starchy food                   | parsec                      | taffeta                | facula                       | A   |
| 16 | HEXAGON      | extol                          | a flat shape with six sides | porpoise               | anile                        | B   |
| 17 | LUNATIC      | faille                         | retsina                     | teletype               | mad person                   | D   |
| 18 | ACQUIESCE    | to agree without protest       | tautog                      | tauton                 | anbury                       | A   |
| 19 | BRUTISH      | coarse                         | bugle                       | celt                   | comfrey                      | A   |
| 20 | COLLOP       | slice of meat                  | druid                       | ratafia                | pelisse                      | A   |
| 21 | PERENNIAL    | perpetual                      | stamina                     | chafe                  | initial                      | A   |
| 22 | FECUND       | herbal                         | fauna                       | fertile                | fetid                        | C   |
| 23 | HEROINE      | okapi                          | darts                       | brave woman or girl    | hertz                        | C   |
| 24 | ACUMEN       | hemmer                         | deep insight                | cordon                 | angora                       | B   |
| 25 | AVARICE      | excessive greed                | chortle                     | feckless               | feudal                       | A   |
| 26 | DAWDLE       | to loiter                      | darn                        | dainty                 | prehistoric                  | A   |
| 27 | AMIABLE      | deodorant                      | scented candle              | friendly               | grasshopper                  | C   |
| 28 | MAGNIFICENT  | humorous                       | splendid                    | negative               | logistic                     | B   |
| 29 | ACQUIESCE    | customer of famous shop        | soprano                     | relative               | to agree without protest     | D   |
| 30 | LIMBER       | bond                           | lime                        | flexible               | delirious                    | C   |

7

# PRACTICE TESTS IN VERBAL REASONING

|    |              | A                              | B             | C                                              | D        |     |
|----|--------------|--------------------------------|---------------|------------------------------------------------|----------|-----|
| 31 | FEIGN        | nudge                          | noose         | pretend                                        | ramrod   | C   |
| 32 | RANKLE       | Zouave                         | to fester     | zucchini                                       | xylem    | B   |
| 33 | AGNOSTIC     | dryad                          | duckbill      | one who does not believe in the existence of God | viburnum | C |
| 34 | THAW         | tease                          | to melt       | tackle                                         | tenor    | B   |
| 35 | EMPOISON     | taint                          | dark          | viable                                         | viscacha | A   |
| 36 | VISCID       | glutinous                      | Druse         | yamen                                          | xenon    | A   |
| 37 | ADAMANT      | inflexible and rigid           | vibe          | enamel                                         | centaur  | A   |
| 38 | MACKINTOSH   | ramose                         | raincoat      | realgar                                        | tempura  | B   |
| 39 | ACUITY       | sharpness of thought or vision | xanthine      | mundane                                        | texture  | A   |
| 40 | TERSE        | vial                           | concise       | calm                                           | emu      | B   |
| 41 | ALLUDE       | fellow                         | to refer to something indirectly | amount                       | viol     | B   |
| 42 | NIGHTMARE    | thatch                         | testis        | frightening dream                              | expect   | C   |
| 43 | FEBRILE      | chamois                        | feverish      | bequeath                                       | bergamot | B   |
| 44 | ACRIMONIOUS  | bitterness of manner or language | berceuse    | bezoar                                         | biaxial  | A   |
| 45 | DOZE         | map                            | cot           | nap                                            | cape     | C   |

PRACTICE TESTS IN VERBAL REASONING

|    |              | A        | B              | C        | D                |     |
|----|--------------|----------|----------------|----------|------------------|-----|
| 46 | AUBURN       | dawn     | reddish brown  | shine    | perm             | b   |
| 47 | FARRAGO      | quest    | tame           | connect  | jumble           | D   |
| 48 | ATTIC        | dome     | globe          | Braille  | a garret         | D   |
| 49 | ASYLUM       | caravan  | a refuge       | grave    | import           | B   |
| 50 | PECULIAR     | odd      | advert         | proclaim | a Christian sect | a   |

### Record Your Progress

| Number of Times You Have Taken the Test | Record | | | Record Your Completion Time |
|---|---|---|---|---|
| | Number of Questions Completed | Your Total Score | Total No. of Questions | |
| 1 | | | | |
| 2 | | | | |
| 3 | | | | |
| 4 | | | | |
| 5 | | | | |

## Practice Test 2 (Answer on page 237)

What is the correct meaning of the words in capitals? Write your answer in the space provided.

|   |               | A        | B       | C        | D       |   |
|---|---------------|----------|---------|----------|---------|---|
| 1 | PERPENDICULAR | clench   | civic   | upright  | a clerk | C |
| 2 | AUDACIOUS     | jaundice | daring  | plaster  | plan    | B |
| 3 | ENJOYABLE     | rewind   | rift    | pleasant | slash   | C |
| 4 | LIBERAL       | ample    | slang   | likely   | rhyme   | A |

9

## PRACTICE TESTS IN VERBAL REASONING

|    |              | A                 | B              | C          | D           |     |
|----|--------------|-------------------|----------------|------------|-------------|-----|
| 5  | JAB          | jar               | to poke        | hide       | hey         | B   |
| 6  | POUCH        | effort            | budget         | small bag  | elect       | C   |
| 7  | CONFINE      | restrict          | acacia         | accord     | emblem      | A   |
| 8  | VALUABLE     | elope             | beach          | precious   | bangle      | C   |
| 9  | CONVALESCE   | berry             | demote         | get better | grow up     | C   |
| 10 | EGOCENTRIC   | group             | self-centered  | void       | devalue     | B   |
| 11 | ENCHASE      | to emboss         | crime          | warm       | wart        | B   |
| 12 | ATTEST       | ulcer             | to certify     | ulna       | tire        | D   |
| 13 | ENSIGN       | serpent           | save           | a flag     | fowl        | C   |
| 14 | CIRCUMSPECT  | freak             | cautious       | saber      | foster      | B   |
| 15 | JUBILANT     | just              | triumphant     | jury       | joiner      | B   |
| 16 | ATELIER      | account           | invoice        | statement  | a workshop  | A   |
| 17 | ITINERARY    | marketing         | covet          | route      | acclaim     | D   |
| 18 | COMBUST      | carbon            | to burn        | to carry   | radiation   | C   |
| 19 | JOURNAL      | chisel            | diary          | demure     | fluttery    | A   |
| 20 | LEDGER       | accounting record | bribe          | forceps    | flux        | B   |
| 21 | DEMURE       | guardian          | goldsmith      | absurd     | reserved    | C   |
| 22 | SINCERE      | grumpy            | delight        | honest     | puncture    | D   |
| 23 | APPOSITE     | royalty           | intent         | rake       | appropriate | C   |
| 24 | JOVIAL       | cheerful          | query          | prepayment | foxtrot     | B   |

10

PRACTICE TESTS IN VERBAL REASONING

|    |              | A          | B            | C            | D                  |     |
|----|--------------|------------|--------------|--------------|--------------------|-----|
| 25 | SUPPLEMENTAL | echo       | whiskey      | militant     | additional         | A   |
| 26 | ASCETIC      | regular    | acidic       | austere      | potent             | B   |
| 27 | ASSIDUITY    | diligence  | careless     | reward       | assign             | A   |
| 28 | JUST         | tango      | impartial    | lima         | alpha              | b   |
| 29 | EPISTYLE     | furnace    | receipt      | an architrave| niece              | a   |
| 30 | SKYSCRAPER   | finance    | tattoo       | balcony      | very tall building | c   |
| 31 | COPIOUS      | personnel  | nursery      | abundant     | ladder             | a   |
| 32 | EXPRESSWAY   | clutch     | motorway     | rapid        | raucous            | c   |
| 33 | FERVENCY     | ardor      | zodiac       | amicable     | courtship          | a   |
| 34 | COLOSSAL     | tolerate   | gigantic     | ballot       | mnemonic           | a   |
| 35 | ANNEAL       | to bake    | whimsy       | tunic        | brilliant          | B   |
| 36 | FIDDLING     | genuine    | petty        | privacy      | breeze             | a   |
| 37 | OVERWHELM    | reliance   | irresistible | faculty      | embryo             |     |
| 38 | FLUMMOX      | scholarship| quack        | perplex      | logical            |     |
| 39 | FLAUTIST     | triangle   | flute player | exotic       | tamarind           |     |
| 40 | CONTE        | futile     | short story  | slouch       | essential          |     |
| 41 | NOCUOUS      | hurtful    | successive   | refurbish    | exhibition         |     |
| 42 | NULL         | yawn       | equity       | invalid      | fiscal             |     |
| 43 | SKELETON     | bagpipes   | holistic     | swollen      | bones in the body  |     |
| 44 | CORDATE      | survey     | prestige     | heart-shaped | almanac            |     |

PRACTICE TESTS IN VERBAL REASONING

|    |            | A         | B          | C          | D        |      |
|----|------------|-----------|------------|------------|----------|------|
| 45 | INDICT     | to write  | verdict    | dividend   | merger   | ____ |
| 46 | PILLAGE    | plunder   | dignitary  | wharf      | quitting | ____ |
| 47 | OPULENT    | horizon   | luxuriant  | hardship   | iris     | ____ |
| 48 | DERIDE     | scorn     | elect      | rosy       | mead     | ____ |
| 49 | CORDWAINER | slang     | shoemaker  | ignition   | pageant  | ____ |
| 50 | INDOCILE   | rage      | chiropodist| unteachable| cease    | ____ |

### Record Your Progress

| Number of Times You Have Taken the Test | Record | | | Record Your Completion Time |
|---|---|---|---|---|
| | Number of Questions Completed | Your Total Score | Total No. of Questions | |
| 1 | | | | |
| 2 | | | | |
| 3 | | | | |
| 4 | | | | |
| 5 | | | | |

## Practice Test 3 (Answer on page 238)

What is the correct meaning of the words in capitals? Write your answer in the space provided.

|   |            | A          | B          | C         | D       |      |
|---|------------|------------|------------|-----------|---------|------|
| 1 | ELOQUENT   | articulate | supremo    | allergic  | remark  | ____ |
| 2 | SMUDGE     | repent     | grill      | smear     | sense   | ____ |
| 3 | CONTIGUOUS | cenotaph   | myopic     | adjoining | beret   | ____ |
| 4 | PLAUSIBLE  | inmate     | reasonable | weal      | assail  | ____ |

PRACTICE TESTS IN VERBAL REASONING

|    |              | A            | B           | C          | D                 |      |
|----|--------------|--------------|-------------|------------|-------------------|------|
| 5  | PRECIOUS     | thrift       | tactic      | beloved    | alcove            | ____ |
| 6  | THORN        | lethargy     | prickle     | flier      | to omit           | ____ |
| 7  | ERUDITE      | learned      | limp        | gabble     | pastel            | ____ |
| 8  | PUNCTUAL     | on time      | adequate    | dilute     | gherkin           | ____ |
| 9  | PREDICAMENT  | random       | plight      | serenade   | repertoire        | ____ |
| 10 | ARBOREOUS    | synagogue    | wooded      | tarpaulin  | ulcer             | ____ |
| 11 | GENUINE      | snooker      | lactose     | ajar       | real              | ____ |
| 12 | REIMBURSE    | wicket       | to repay    | burglar    | unison            | ____ |
| 13 | PULLOVER     | sentry       | eclipse     | jersey     | tremble           | ____ |
| 14 | ANNIHILATE   | pilfer       | wren        | sponge     | completely destroy | ____ |
| 15 | DISCARD      | maggot       | essay       | to reject  | to sign           | ____ |
| 16 | RENEGADE     | inferno      | meteor      | artery     | a deserter        | ____ |
| 17 | DOUBTING     | remain       | skeptical   | alight     | recorder          | ____ |
| 18 | CONSTRUE     | system       | interpret   | Everest    | package           | ____ |
| 19 | ILLUSTRIOUS  | rivet        | renowned    | inertia    | instance          | ____ |
| 20 | PYTHON       | enslave      | large snake | profane    | launch            | ____ |
| 21 | AUTOMATOUS   | spontaneous  | precede     | wreath     | wilt              | ____ |
| 22 | DEPRAVITY    | sighted      | sombrero    | magpie     | turpitude         | ____ |
| 23 | CONSENSUS    | impudent     | addict      | inaccurate | general agreement | ____ |
| 24 | GUARDIANSHIP | tutelage     | thatch      | miserly    | soaring           | ____ |

# PRACTICE TESTS IN VERBAL REASONING

|    |              | A          | B                | C               | D          |       |
|----|--------------|------------|------------------|-----------------|------------|-------|
| 25 | HYPOCRITICAL | pledge     | tapestry         | two-faced       | stagger    | _____ |
| 26 | CONSECUTIVE  | tyranny    | tease            | logical sequence | epicure   | _____ |
| 27 | UNCOMMON     | ovule      | rare             | famine          | breastbone | _____ |
| 28 | ARROGANT     | corroded   | stereo           | crypt           | uppity     | _____ |
| 29 | WARFARE      | umbrella   | conflict         | conspicuous     | abdomen    | _____ |
| 30 | DISTORTED    | blanch     | plinth           | warped          | enforce    | _____ |
| 31 | WHIMSICAL    | molest     | unusual          | precede         | wheelbarrow | _____ |
| 32 | RESPECTABLE  | retailer   | worth admiring   | rivet           | oboe       | _____ |
| 33 | BENEFICIAL   | burn       | earnest          | advantageous    | decorate   | _____ |
| 34 | DISOBEDIENT  | coup       | tremor           | unruly          | enormity   | _____ |
| 35 | OFFENSIVE    | propel     | protocol         | distasteful     | bracelet   | _____ |
| 36 | COMMENT      | tramp      | remark           | critical        | pitied     | _____ |
| 37 | ENTHUSIASTIC | hydrometer | wholehearted     | laundry         | aristocracy | _____ |
| 38 | INTROVERTED  | fertile    | caper            | octopus         | withdrawn  | _____ |
| 39 | VARIETY      | erode      | assortment       | roundabout      | polar      | _____ |
| 40 | CONNIVE      | to plot    | peruse           | twig            | collateral | _____ |
| 41 | DOGGEDNESS   | tenacity   | density          | enfold          | partial    | _____ |
| 42 | TENUOUS      | demon      | geology          | flimsy          | machete    | _____ |
| 43 | DOCTRINE     | tenet      | aperture         | ruminate        | accustom   | _____ |
| 44 | ABRUPT       | ignorant   | throb            | sudden          | nostalgia  | _____ |

PRACTICE TESTS IN VERBAL REASONING

|    |             | A          | B          | C         | D         |     |
|----|-------------|------------|------------|-----------|-----------|-----|
| 45 | CONSTERNATE | to dismay  | adrift     | smear     | diligent  | ___ |
| 46 | REQUIRE     | diverge    | to need    | mumps     | weird     | ___ |
| 47 | SAPLING     | young tree | lent       | yearning  | multitude | ___ |
| 48 | SANGUINE    | hopeful    | infantry   | raise     | garrison  | ___ |
| 49 | PROMPT      | pillow     | confederate| immediate | exhale    | ___ |
| 50 | PROHIBIT    | to prevent | abysmal    | adjacent  | umpire    | ___ |

| Record Your Progress |||||
|---|---|---|---|---|
| Number of Times You Have Taken the Test | Record |||  Record Your Completion Time |
|  | Number of Questions Completed | Your Total Score | Total No. of Questions |  |
| 1 |  |  |  |  |
| 2 |  |  |  |  |
| 3 |  |  |  |  |
| 4 |  |  |  |  |
| 5 |  |  |  |  |

## Practice Test 4 (Answers on page 238)

What is the correct meaning of the words in capitals? Write your answer in the space provided.

|   |            | A          | B          | C         | D           |     |
|---|------------|------------|------------|-----------|-------------|-----|
| 1 | FASTIDIOUS | very tired | very fast  | to fast   | overcritical| ___ |
| 2 | DEHYDRATED | scene      | desiccated | crisis    | cordial     | ___ |
| 3 | ABANDONED  | fraction   | fibula     | desuetude | disdain     | ___ |

15

# PRACTICE TESTS IN VERBAL REASONING

|    |              | **A**         | **B**              | **C**       | **D**      |      |
|----|--------------|---------------|--------------------|-------------|------------|------|
| 4  | CLANDESTINE  | linoleum      | secret             | curry       | valance    | ____ |
| 5  | HANDSOME     | evolution     | fine               | cozy        | opaque     | ____ |
| 6  | FEALTY       | loyalty       | sauna              | instinct    | gypsy      | ____ |
| 7  | UNEMPLOYED   | cripple       | idle               | croquet     | quango     | ____ |
| 8  | INFINITE     | applaud       | scissors           | polyester   | boundless  | ____ |
| 9  | ABROAD       | commission    | course             | overseas    | parsley    | ____ |
| 10 | EQUANIMITY   | appoint       | calmness of temper | resident    | pride      | ____ |
| 11 | ASPIRING     | septic        | guard              | ambitious   | trap       | ____ |
| 12 | PERMEATE     | penetrate     | psychology         | starter     | meter      | ____ |
| 13 | CRUCIAL      | crier         | vital              | seat        | storm      | ____ |
| 14 | DEXTRAL      | right-handed  | wipe               | allow       | grocer     | ____ |
| 15 | FOUNDATION   | institute     | license            | processor   | ware       | ____ |
| 16 | ANTITHETICAL | opposite      | group              | berry       | ache       | ____ |
| 17 | OVERHEAD     | gage          | above              | tennis      | probe      | ____ |
| 18 | KNOWINGLY    | mate          | charm              | consciously | pinch      | ____ |
| 19 | INHERENT     | inborn        | prompt             | guerilla    | satellite  | ____ |
| 20 | GLOOMY       | topic         | permit             | somber      | brush      | ____ |
| 21 | DEVOTION     | dedication    | prose              | navel       | please     | ____ |
| 22 | APPROPRIATE  | scent         | quench             | apt         | cautious   | ____ |
| 23 | STANDARD     | speak         | kite               | slide       | criterion  | ____ |

PRACTICE TESTS IN VERBAL REASONING

|    |              | A          | B                | C          | D         |        |
|----|--------------|------------|------------------|------------|-----------|--------|
| 24 | UNIQUE       | cautious   | distinctive      | stairwell  | basic     | _____ |
| 25 | GUSTO        | poverty    | zest             | morale     | proceed   | _____ |
| 26 | RESILIENCE   | influence  | concern          | elasticity | isolate   | _____ |
| 27 | NEGLECT      | infancy    | role             | assume     | abandoned | _____ |
| 28 | SUGGESTION   | unanimous  | insinuation      | dullness   | monopoly  | _____ |
| 29 | EQUIPMENT    | slipper    | leniency         | bondage    | kit       | _____ |
| 30 | DIDACTIC     | favor      | inclined to teach| wealthy    | literate  | _____ |
| 31 | VACILLATE    | yeast      | waver            | acquire    | lanky     | _____ |
| 32 | SLOT         | Spaniard   | to groove        | dialect    | colony    | _____ |
| 33 | STATUS       | directive  | autumn           | rank       | explore   | _____ |
| 34 | ASCEND       | climb      | brick            | courier    | cockerel  | _____ |
| 35 | EXTRACT      | mince      | essence          | directive  | grand     | _____ |
| 36 | CURIOUS      | particular | squid            | inquisitive| propel    | _____ |
| 37 | CEREMONY     | Accra      | exact            | rescue     | ritual    | _____ |
| 38 | MEDIOCRE     | spinal     | average          | huddles    | macho     | _____ |
| 39 | COLLAPSE     | quit       | vendor           | skipper    | slump     | _____ |
| 40 | COMPELLING   | spectator  | obligatory       | piglet     | colossal  | _____ |
| 41 | CONVEY       | impart     | vintage          | wallet     | cipher    | _____ |
| 42 | FEASIBILITY  | official   | marble           | chores     | possibility | _____ |
| 43 | ENLIGHTEN    | to instruct| linen            | asset      | bracelet  | _____ |

17

PRACTICE TESTS IN VERBAL REASONING

|    |                | A        | B           | C            | D        |     |
|----|----------------|----------|-------------|--------------|----------|-----|
| 44 | CARGO          | windfall | freight     | pottery      | hammer   | ___ |
| 45 | CEMENT         | harvest  | timely      | recite       | concrete | ___ |
| 46 | MARK           | nanny    | sign        | mortar       | crescent | ___ |
| 47 | BANQUET        | pestle   | fragment    | platform     | feast    | ___ |
| 48 | IDENTIFICATION | poem     | recognition | servant      | rural    | ___ |
| 49 | BASE           | tutorial | ignoble     | rattle       | lounge   | ___ |
| 50 | BENEFICIAL     | escort   | flawed      | advantageous | scared   | ___ |

| Record Your Progress |||||
|---|---|---|---|---|
| Number of Times You Have Taken the Test | \multicolumn{3}{c|}{Record} | Record Your Completion Time |
| | Number of Questions Completed | Your Total Score | Total No. of Questions | |
| 1 | | | | |
| 2 | | | | |
| 3 | | | | |
| 4 | | | | |
| 5 | | | | |

PRACTICE TESTS IN VERBAL REASONING

# SAMPLE TEST 2: CORRECT SPELLING OF A WORD

What is the correct spelling of this word?

| A | B | C | D |
|---|---|---|---|
| continually | contenualy | continualy | countinually |

The correct answer is *continually*, so write A in the box.

Now do the following practice tests. Remember to refer to your dictionary after you have done the test if you provided an incorrect answer.

## Practice Test 5 (Answers on page 238)

What is the correct spelling of this word? Write your answer in the box.

| | A | B | C | D | |
|---|---|---|---|---|---|
| 1 | aliteration | alliterasion | alliteration | alieteration | C |
| 2 | albatross | allbatrose | allbartrose | albartrous | |
| 3 | budgerigar | budgeriga | bugerigar | burdgerigar | |
| 4 | ignominous | ignominious | ignomenious | ignomenous | |
| 5 | plyerss | pliears | plieres | pliers | D |
| 6 | inteligence | intelligence | intellegence | intelegence | B |
| 7 | akward | hawkward | awkward | awkword | C |
| 8 | contradictry | contradectory | cuntradictory | contradictory | |
| 9 | diligent | deligent | dilegent | deligeant | |
| 10 | creavice | crevice | creivice | crevise | B |
| 11 | acknoledge | acknowleging | acknowledging | acknowleding | C |

19

# PRACTICE TESTS IN VERBAL REASONING

|    | A | B | C | D | |
|----|---|---|---|---|---|
| 12 | herbalist | herbaleast | haberlist | herberlist | A |
| 13 | silables | syllables | sylables | sylabbles | B |
| 14 | bolderdash | baldadash | balderdash | balderdarsh | |
| 15 | moustache | musstache | moustash | mustash | A |
| 16 | hipochrondriac | hypochondriac | hypochrondyiac | hipochrondyiac | |
| 17 | lumberjack | lumbajack | lomberjack | lumbarjack | A |
| 18 | flowride | floryde | fluoride | fluoryde | C |
| 19 | insomniac | insomeniac | insoumniac | isnomiac | A |
| 20 | Cadilac | Cadillac | Cardillac | Cardilac | |
| 21 | afrodisiac | aprodissiac | aphrodisiac | aphrodiciac | C |
| 22 | jackal | jackle | jacall | jackall | A |
| 23 | oulfactory | olfaktory | olfactory | ollfactorey | A |
| 24 | encounter | encountar | encounta | encounttar | A |
| 25 | riefract | reffract | refract | refrarch | C |
| 26 | autobiographycal | autobiofical | autobiographycle | autobiographical | D |
| 27 | protagonist | prontagonist | pronttagonist | protagoniste | A |
| 28 | sarddlebag | saddlebag | sadlebag | saddlebarg | B |
| 29 | dispot | disspot | despot | dispott | C |
| 30 | miunicipality | municiparlity | munisiparlity | municipality | |
| 31 | neutrality | neutriality | nutrality | neutrallity | A |

PRACTICE TESTS IN VERBAL REASONING

|    | A | B | C | D |    |
|----|---|---|---|---|----|
| 32 | epygram | epigramme | epigram | epigrarm | |
| 33 | parallelogram | parrallelogram | parallelograme | parallelowgram | A |
| 34 | electriocardiogram | electrocardiogram | ellectrocadiograme | electrocardeogram | |
| 35 | superficiality | suparficiality | supperficiality | surparficiality | |
| 36 | diephrame | diaphragme | diaphragm | diaphraigm | C |
| 37 | aerodynamic | aerodiemamic | aerodymanic | aerowdynamic | A |
| 38 | pommegranate | pormegranate | pomegranate | pomigranatte | C |
| 39 | hinterland | hintterland | hynterland | hinterlarnde | |
| 40 | cobblar | cobbler | corbler | corbbler | B |
| 41 | missanthropest | missantropiste | misanthropist | miessanthropist | |
| 42 | candor | candouw | carndour | canddour | |
| 43 | sallamander | sarlarmander | salamander | salamamdar | C |
| 44 | quardrangle | quadranggle | quadrangel | quadrangle | |
| 45 | askance | askiance | askanse | askancee | |
| 46 | Bizantynee | Byzantine | Bizzantyne | Bizhantyne | |
| 47 | Harwaian | Hawarian | Hawaiane | Hawaiian | |
| 48 | shrapnelle | shrapnel | schrapnel | scrapnell | |
| 49 | tarragon | taragone | traraghone | taragune | |
| 50 | perculiariety | parculiarity | peculiarity | percoliarite | |

21

PRACTICE TESTS IN VERBAL REASONING

| Record Your Progress ||||
|---|---|---|---|---|
| Number of Times You Have Taken the Test | Record ||| Record Your Completion Time |
|  | Number of Questions Completed | Your Total Score | Total No. of Questions |  |
| 1 |  |  |  |  |
| 2 |  |  |  |  |
| 3 |  |  |  |  |
| 4 |  |  |  |  |
| 5 |  |  |  |  |

## Practice Test 6 (Answers on page 239)

What is the correct spelling of this word? Write your answer in the box.

|    | A | B | C | D |  |
|----|---|---|---|---|---|
| 1  | audacity | oudacity | ordacity | audercity | |
| 2  | inncapercitate | incarpacitate | incapacitate | incapercitate | |
| 3  | sagacity | sagarcity | sargarcite | sargercity | |
| 4  | entusiaste | enthursiastte | enthusiastte | enthusiast | |
| 5  | quvier | quiver | quivare | quiverre | |
| 6  | panache | parnache | pernache | panarche | |
| 7  | abradde | abrade | abraide | abraide | |
| 8  | potuberrance | protubarance | protuberance | protwoberance | |
| 9  | rottweiler | rotweiller | rotwailer | ruttwhyler | |
| 10 | phibular | fibula | phybular | fibullar | |

22

PRACTICE TESTS IN VERBAL REASONING

|    | A | B | C | D |  |
|----|---|---|---|---|---|
| 11 | konstabulary | consterbulary | constabulary | constarbulary | |
| 12 | desalination | disalinnation | deserlination | desirlination | |
| 13 | corpulenght | corpulent | curpullent | corpullente | |
| 14 | tarpaulin | terpauline | tapaulline | tappaulyne | |
| 15 | pilaice | playce | plaice | plaicce | |
| 16 | pliable | plyaible | pliabel | plaibbel | |
| 17 | parasit | parasite | parisite | paracite | |
| 18 | litiracy | literacy | lateracy | literacie | |
| 19 | iconeic | iconicque | iconic | eyeconique | |
| 20 | regulation | regullation | regulasion | regullasion | |
| 21 | metteor | meteor | meatteor | mettoere | |
| 22 | vellian | villain | vyllian | velain | |
| 23 | repertoire | repetoire | repartoire | repartoise | |
| 24 | essecudo | escudo | escudoe | escudow | |
| 25 | mineature | miniature | menetature | meneatoire | |
| 26 | decorum | deccorum | dercorum | dercorrume | |
| 27 | anniahalate | annahyalate | annihilate | anniahlyate | |
| 28 | rhubarb | rubbarbe | rhuebarb | rhruebarb | |
| 29 | narcissus | nercissus | nercessus | narcissusse | |
| 30 | pedestrian | perdestriane | perdestrine | pardestriane | |

# PRACTICE TESTS IN VERBAL REASONING

|    | A | B | C | D |    |
|----|---|---|---|---|----|
| 31 | stupefy | stupify | stopify | stupifie | |
| 32 | zepeline | zeppelin | zerpelline | zerperlline | |
| 33 | spinnet | spinet | spinnete | spiienet | |
| 34 | linnient | lenient | leniente | lennient | |
| 35 | cynic | cenique | cynique | ceinique | |
| 36 | tankarde | tankcarde | tankard | tancarde | |
| 37 | eminent | emenent | eminnent | erminente | |
| 38 | meager | megar | meiger | meegre | |
| 39 | meenuet | myenuet | minuet | mienuet | |
| 40 | premonition | primonition | premonision | primonetion | |
| 41 | quintet | queentet | queintet | quintete | |
| 42 | tryplicate | treeplicate | triplycate | triplicate | |
| 43 | epoch | eporch | eporche | epurshe | |
| 44 | cargoule | cagoule | cergoulle | carggoule | |
| 45 | clairvoyant | clarevoyante | clarevoryant | clairvoryant | |
| 46 | scalpel | scarelpel | scarpel | scarepel | |
| 47 | amiabble | armyable | amiable | armiabbel | |
| 48 | rhubella | rubella | roubellar | ruberller | |
| 49 | adjudecator | adjudicator | adjudecateur | adjudecatore | |
| 50 | boisteirus | boisterous | boysterious | boysterious | |

PRACTICE TESTS IN VERBAL REASONING

| Number of Times You Have Taken the Test | Record |  |  | Record Your Completion Time |
|---|---|---|---|---|
|  | Number of Questions Completed | Your Total Score | Total No. of Questions |  |
| 1 |  |  |  |  |
| 2 |  |  |  |  |
| 3 |  |  |  |  |
| 4 |  |  |  |  |
| 5 |  |  |  |  |

## Practice Test 7 (Answers on page 239)

What is the correct spelling of this word? Write your answer in the box.

|    | A | B | C | D |
|----|---|---|---|---|
| 1  | notoriety | nottoriety | notorietie | notorriaety |
| 2  | margnamemous | magnanimous | magnernimous | magnarnimouse |
| 3  | vynyl | vinyl | vinyle | vineyle |
| 4  | tuat | taut | taute | taurte |
| 5  | corgnac | cognac | cogniac | cognaic |
| 6  | ranceed | ransced | rancid | ranncide |
| 7  | aeisthetically | aesthetically | aeistheticalie | aesthertically |
| 8  | lauriate | lariat | laureatte | laurieatt |
| 9  | seissmology | seismologie | siesmology | seismology |
| 10 | pyromaniac | piromaniac | piromeiniac | pyroemaniac |

PRACTICE TESTS IN VERBAL REASONING

|    | A | B | C | D |
|----|---|---|---|---|
| 11 | beret | berrett | berete | berret |
| 12 | snokell | snorkel | snorkell | snorklee |
| 13 | aporthy | apathy | apatic | apethie |
| 14 | tommahawk | tomerhawk | tomahawk | tomarhawk |
| 15 | kaleidoscope | kaledoscope | kalideoscope | kaleadoscope |
| 16 | dadodile | dadordile | darffodill | daffodil |
| 17 | emit | emet | emeat | emett |
| 18 | therapeutic | therrapeutic | therapeutique | therarpeutique |
| 19 | septet | serptet | serptete | serptett |
| 20 | gurlible | gurlible | gurleble | gullible |
| 21 | whippet | wheppet | whipette | wephette |
| 22 | amnesia | armnesia | amnesea | amneisia |
| 23 | terapine | terrarpin | terrapin | terrapine |
| 24 | diedeme | diaderme | diadem | diardeme |
| 25 | blancmange | blanchmange | blanchemange | bluncmange |
| 26 | caterstrophe | catastrophe | catasttrophe | catastrophie |
| 27 | couldrone | cauldron | cauldrone | caulldrone |
| 28 | phynomenal | phenomenal | phenormenal | phenomerna |
| 29 | nauseate | norsiate | nausiate | nurssiatte |
| 30 | camouflage | carmorflage | carmurflagge | carmouflarge |

PRACTICE TESTS IN VERBAL REASONING

|    | A | B | C | D |    |
|----|---|---|---|---|----|
| 31 | skifle | sciflle | skiffe | skiffle | |
| 32 | scrumpy | scromppy | schrumpie | schrompie | |
| 33 | roulette | rullete | roullete | ruolete | |
| 34 | amfibious | amphibous | amphibious | amphybiouse | |
| 35 | frankfurter | franckfuter | frunckfuter | frankfurtter | |
| 36 | octogernarian | octorgenerian | oktogernarean | octogenarian | |
| 37 | plectrum | plecktruim | plektrume | plekruim | |
| 38 | parculator | percolator | percollator | perculateur | |
| 39 | flippant | flypant | flipante | flipphant | |
| 40 | inauspeceous | inauspycious | inauspicious | inauspecious | |
| 41 | cyanide | syanade | cyaniade | cianide | |
| 42 | asparagus | asperagus | asparaguse | aspharagus | |
| 43 | averecious | avarecious | avaricious | avariciouse | |
| 44 | kerosene | kerrosene | kherosene | keroscene | |
| 45 | inebriated | inebrated | inebrieated | inebryated | |
| 46 | ararbesqe | arabisque | arabesque | arabessque | |
| 47 | portmanteau | portemanteau | portmantaue | portmanthur | |
| 48 | whymsicale | whimisicale | whemsicalle | whimsical | |
| 49 | stalactite | starlactite | starlactyte | startactite | |
| 50 | excerpt | excarpt | excirpte | exscerpt | |

PRACTICE TESTS IN VERBAL REASONING

| Record Your Progress |||||
|---|---|---|---|---|
| Number of Times You Have Taken the Test | Record |||  Record Your Completion Time |
|  | Number of Questions Completed | Your Total Score | Total No. of Questions |  |
| 1 |  |  |  |  |
| 2 |  |  |  |  |
| 3 |  |  |  |  |
| 4 |  |  |  |  |
| 5 |  |  |  |  |

PRACTICE TESTS IN VERBAL REASONING

## SAMPLE TEST 3: WORDS SPELLED INCORRECTLY

Which of these words is spelled incorrectly?

|   A    |    B    |   C    |     D     |
|--------|---------|--------|-----------|
| Dinning | uniform | sucess | necessary |

The answer is *C*. The correct spelling of the word is *success*. All the others were spelled correctly.

Now answer the following questions.

## Practice Test 8 (Answers on page 239)

Which of these words is spelled incorrectly?

Write your answer in the box provided.

|    | A | B | C | D |
|----|---|---|---|---|
| 1  | opportunity | candidate | approachable | intransigient |
| 2  | penitentiarie | extremely | initiative | sensible |
| 3  | purrl | leadership | interesting | interview |
| 4  | recruiting | thimmble | requirement | confidence |
| 5  | millineier | cheating | advance | prepared |
| 6  | ilated | personality | productive | discussion |
| 7  | whether | individual | confedant | incredibly |
| 8  | scanning | concentration | terrappine | different |
| 9  | separate | multiple | unanswered | intriegue |
| 10 | valuable | unscrupulouse | through | progressing |
| 11 | consumption | epaullet | encounter | dedicate |

# PRACTICE TESTS IN VERBAL REASONING

|    | A | B | C | D | |
|---|---|---|---|---|---|
| 12 | ability | parllour | mechanical | spatial | |
| 13 | comprehension | numerical | tardpole | constraint | |
| 14 | Aphroditte | appropriate | accurately | familiar | |
| 15 | brigaydier | suggested | technique | deliberate | |
| 16 | clerical | grammar | presented | pummice | |
| 17 | measure | painting | diaborlicale | contained | |
| 18 | juggernautte | strictly | phrase | weakness | |
| 19 | kellp | organization | experience | employment | |
| 20 | hemartolorgy | obviously | encourage | applicants | |
| 21 | plaques | infringed | facilities | carjolled | |
| 22 | gnorme | permanent | qualified | beneficial | |
| 23 | desarlinaetion | evaluate | assistant | administrative | |
| 24 | oreyx | according | freedom | societies | |
| 25 | improve | amarlgam | select | argument | |
| 26 | policy | expectation | xernorphobia | education | |
| 27 | logically | appropriate | pleasantness | phlergmatique | |
| 28 | lymphartick | stickers | furthermore | automatically | |
| 29 | apprentices | technical | idiosyncraetic | material | |
| 30 | seismorgraphe | relevant | efficiency | fuelled | |
| 31 | reactors | auditory | tactile | fuserlarge | |
| 32 | paraphernaeliar | stimuli | senses | decommission | |

30

PRACTICE TESTS IN VERBAL REASONING

|    | A | B | C | D |   |
|----|---|---|---|---|---|
| 33 | disputes | barluestrade | uranium | economic | |
| 34 | disparities | kamiekarze | bombarded | compute | |
| 35 | concentration | journals | baricarde | maneuver | |
| 36 | scrabble | influence | analytical | kleptormaniak | |
| 37 | polyuretayne | specifically | chronicle | analysis | |
| 38 | million | luccent | financial | mathematical | |
| 39 | performance | abstract | intellectual | strateficaition | |
| 40 | halucinaition | occupation | supervisory | sequence | |
| 41 | diagram | research | altered | bruskue | |
| 42 | dillineate | measures | horizontally | square | |
| 43 | programming | exornnerate | systematic | debugging | |
| 44 | symbols | tracking | prolertariate | blackening | |
| 45 | veriegatted | immediately | architecture | publishing | |
| 46 | manipulate | immediately | innuiendou | illustration | |
| 47 | leuiternante | electronic | difficulty | labyrinth | |
| 48 | identical | development | scintiellaiting | orientated | |
| 49 | dermisemequaver | dimensional | draughts | visualize | |
| 50 | software | pattern | excherquer | reassemble | |

PRACTICE TESTS IN VERBAL REASONING

| Record Your Progress |||||
|---|---|---|---|---|
| Number of Times You Have Taken the Test | Record ||| Record Your Completion Time |
| | Number of Questions Completed | Your Total Score | Total No. of Questions | |
| 1 | | | | |
| 2 | | | | |
| 3 | | | | |
| 4 | | | | |
| 5 | | | | |

## Practice Test 9 (Answers on page 240)

Which of these words is spelled incorrectly? Write your answer in the box provided.

| | A | B | C | D | |
|---|---|---|---|---|---|
| 1 | ambled | insurrance | cabaret | ugliness | |
| 2 | tongue | calmness | confort | drunk | |
| 3 | gather | originality | minuscule | reasure | |
| 4 | haughtiness | untidiness | drunk | intenssive | |
| 5 | paper | pamper | especialy | lure | |
| 6 | nustalgic | variant | minuscule | tournament | |
| 7 | personal | makeshift | pernetential | maladroit | |
| 8 | lunary | oficious | lockspit | fresh | |
| 9 | vacuum | construction | Bizantine | difficulty | |
| 10 | pernultimate | diagnosis | accuracy | tackling | |
| 11 | desrupt | original | delivered | separate | |

PRACTICE TESTS IN VERBAL REASONING

|    | A              | B              | C            | D              |   |
|----|----------------|----------------|--------------|----------------|---|
| 12 | burstal        | electronics    | appropriate  | schemes        |   |
| 13 | somewhere      | concentration  | calous       | corresponding  |   |
| 14 | intellectual   | underneath     | foresttation | disturbed      |   |
| 15 | quotient       | consignement   | comical      | capricious     |   |
| 16 | broccolli      | uncanny        | whimsical    | September      |   |
| 17 | eightine       | obscure        | severe       | obstinate      |   |
| 18 | osetrogen      | visible        | conspicuous  | apparent       |   |
| 19 | surveilance    | disturbed      | encourage    | indeterminable |   |
| 20 | endorse        | heterogenous   | orchestra    | abandon        |   |
| 21 | occupy         | attempt        | catarh       | tourist        |   |
| 22 | jolity         | halt           | tasteful     | invest         |   |
| 23 | begruge        | gallery        | curator      | opposite       |   |
| 24 | government     | elswhere       | army         | battlefield    |   |
| 25 | surreptitious  | opposite       | correcttness | potential      |   |
| 26 | hexagon        | submarine      | suspicous    | restaurant     |   |
| 27 | guarantee      | indeterminable | advice       | arogance       |   |
| 28 | choriographer  | blackmailer    | florist      | available      |   |
| 29 | solicitor      | ephimeral      | sycophant    | ruffian        |   |
| 30 | handshake      | scored         | fraigile     | preferred      |   |
| 31 | questionnaires | genuine        | belithe      | interviewed    |   |
| 32 | publisher      | probably       | aspects      | reperttory     |   |

33

PRACTICE TESTS IN VERBAL REASONING

|    | A | B | C | D |
|---|---|---|---|---|
| 33 | professional | aserted | eliminate | unsuitable |
| 34 | particular | popular | rettrospective | typical |
| 35 | conflicts | enlivine | talkative | resolves |
| 36 | mechanism | fielarea | limitation | sophisticated |
| 37 | inconsistent | hindouism | intuitive | energetically |
| 38 | typically | personality | epittome | honestly |
| 39 | intangeble | colleagues | procedures | brilliant |
| 40 | cancel | hundred | guagge | discover |
| 41 | insurscepteble | liaison | imminence | immittance |
| 42 | haptic | jurydical | gizzard | gladden |
| 43 | erump | lacteale | easel | detonator |
| 44 | devastation | deuce | gastroenomie | detersive |
| 45 | irriedescent | detoxify | cumin | consequence |
| 46 | caïque | liseback | Cajun | courteous |
| 47 | couscous | leturgicale | disaffect | gattine |
| 48 | marlassimiliation | hister | lilac | quench |
| 49 | ilk | kedney | locket | margravine |
| 50 | marinade | margarine | margistrate | martlet |

| \multicolumn{4}{c|}{**Record Your Progress**} |
| --- | --- | --- | --- |
| Number of Times You Have Taken the Test | \multicolumn{3}{c|}{Record} | Record Your Completion Time |
| | Number of Questions Completed | Your Total Score | Total No. of Questions | |
| 1 | | | | |
| 2 | | | | |
| 3 | | | | |
| 4 | | | | |
| 5 | | | | |

# PRACTICE TESTS IN VERBAL REASONING

## SAMPLE TEST 4: MISSING LETTERS

You have been provided with a word with missing letters. From the meaning provided, fill in the gaps and identify this word:

    a_ _u_n          the season between summer and winter

The answer is *autumn*.

Now answer the following questions.

## Practice Test 10 (Answers on page 240)

From the meaning provided, fill in the gaps and identify the word:

| | | |
|---|---|---|
| 1 | v_ _bose | using an unnecessary number of words |
| 2 | _ _ icure | a person whose main concern is sensual pleasure |
| 3 | _m_ _ _tus | honorably discharged from service |
| 4 | _ _rt_ _t_ _ _ | produced by chance, accidental |
| 5 | _ u_b _nd_ _ | administration and management of a household, domestic economy |
| 6 | m_s_ _ _ery | the carrying of a message or errand |
| 7 | d_ ff_ _ _nt | lack of confidence in one's ability or worth, timid |
| 8 | _m_i_ote_ _ | having unlimited or very great power, force, or influence |
| 9 | _i_ _ag | a line having a series of abrupt alternate right and left turns |
| 10 | m_gal_m_ _ia | delusions of grandeur or self-importance |
| 11 | u_e_ _i_oca_ | plain, unmistakable |
| 12 | _t_er_ _se | if not, else, in other ways or by other means |
| 13 | _ur _ _ | a painting executed directly on a wall |
| 14 | f_l_ _ _ ate | issue formal censures, utter formal denunciation |
| 15 | d_ l_ _or_ | characterized by delay, slow, tardy, having purpose to gain time |
| 16 | m_d_ _ te | take a moderate position, settle or soothe a dispute |
| 17 | v_r_f_ _ _ _ion | the action of proving something to be true by evidence or testimony |
| 18 | _y_ _op | an aromatic, bitter-tasting labiate herb |
| 19 | _o_ _rot | a pace with short steps, as in changing from trotting to walking |
| 20 | em_ _ _ ient | makes skin soft or supple |
| 21 | _l_l_ _ _ on | the action of a cry, howl, or other sound so produced |
| 22 | _ og _ | a steward, bailiff, or similar official in Germany |
| 23 | _ab_r_ _ th_n_ | intricate, complicated, involved, pertaining to the labyrinth or inner ear |

| | | |
|---|---|---|
| 24 | _ _ e_o_ _ c | intended or designed to aid the memory, code |
| 25 | d_ l _ tt_n_e | a lover of fine arts |
| 26 | _st_ _ t_ t_o_s | pretentious and showy, intending to attract attention or admiration |
| 27 | u_b_ _ ge | shade or shadow cast by trees, giving shade, a reason for suspicion |
| 28 | _i _ _ ay | the middle of the day, when the sun is at its highest point |
| 29 | l_m_ _ _ n | a virulent or scurrilous satire against a person |
| 30 | l_ _ g_ _ fr_ _ca | any language serving as a medium between different nations |

<table>
<tr><th colspan="4">Record Your Progress</th></tr>
<tr><th rowspan="2">Number of Times You Have Taken the Test</th><th colspan="2">Record</th><th rowspan="2">Record Your Completion Time</th></tr>
<tr><th>Number of Questions Completed</th><th>Your Total Score</th><th>Total No. of Questions</th></tr>
<tr><td>1</td><td></td><td></td><td></td><td></td></tr>
<tr><td>2</td><td></td><td></td><td></td><td></td></tr>
<tr><td>3</td><td></td><td></td><td></td><td></td></tr>
<tr><td>4</td><td></td><td></td><td></td><td></td></tr>
<tr><td>5</td><td></td><td></td><td></td><td></td></tr>
</table>

## Practice Test 11 (Answers on page 240)

From the meaning provided, fill in the gaps and identify the word:

| | | |
|---|---|---|
| 1 | m_n_ _ a_ist | an advocate or practitioner of monetarism |
| 2 | _ag_r_ | a wandering or devious journey, an excursion, a ramble |
| 3 | d_sc_ _ _ ode | put to inconvenience, disturb, trouble |
| 4 | _o_ | a solemn promise to observe a specified state or condition |
| 5 | od_ _ _o_ _gy | a branch of anatomy that deals with the structure and development of teeth |
| 6 | i_id_s_ _nce | a glittering play of changing colors |
| 7 | i_t_ _ n_ _ c | by its very nature, inherent, essential, not superficial |
| 8 | _o _ a | the smallest or a very small part or quantity |
| 9 | _ath_ _ | a froth or foam made by the agitation of a mixture of soap and water |
| 10 | l_ _ i_e | establish communication or cooperation |
| 11 | u_f_ _ _ se_n | unpredictable |

PRACTICE TESTS IN VERBAL REASONING

| 12 | d_f_ _it_on | a precise statement of the nature, properties, scope, or qualities of a thing |
| 13 | o_ci_ _ a_e | swing or move to and fro between two points |
| 14 | _u_ere_ _ | pertaining to or appropriate to a funeral, gloomy, dismal, mournful |
| 15 | _n_nc_ _ te | pronounce, articulate, state publicly, express in definite terms |
| 16 | m_ _ us | a faultfinder, a carping critic |
| 17 | o_ _ ro_r_ um | disgrace attached to conduct considered shameful |
| 18 | h_p_rt_r_al | of a branch of a bronchus situated below the pulmonary artery |
| 19 | d_ _g_ _ n | resentment, a feeling of anger or offence |
| 20 | u_to_ _rd | difficult to manage, awkward to deal with, unruly, perverse |
| 21 | v_rn_ _ _ lar | a language or dialect spoken as a mother tongue of a country or district |
| 22 | m_ _c_ _ _ry | a person who works merely for money, a hired soldier |
| 23 | s_ _p_ic | a person who doubts the truth or validity of accepted beliefs of a particular subject |
| 24 | m_ _ at_ri_m | deliberate temporary suspension or postponement of some activity |
| 25 | dr_g_et | a coarse woven fabric used for floor and table coverings |
| 26 | _ea_ ot | a fanatical enthusiast |
| 27 | s_o_ _ e | thick, tenacious mud or soil; stiff, starchy food |
| 28 | m_ _ c_ _ en_ _ion | the mixing of people considered to be of different racial types |
| 29 | f_r_ r | enthusiastic admiration, uproar, fuss |
| 30 | _o_tr_ _ _ _ | a book or instruction on a subject such as religion |

| Record Your Progress |||||
|---|---|---|---|---|
| Number of Times You Have Taken the Test | Record |||  Record Your Completion Time |
| | Number of Questions Completed | Your Total Score | Total No. of Questions | |
| 1 | | | | |
| 2 | | | | |
| 3 | | | | |
| 4 | | | | |
| 5 | | | | |

# Practice Test 12 (Answers on page 241)

From the meaning provided, fill in the gaps and identify the word:

| | | |
|---|---|---|
| 1 | s _ _ or _ _ic | inducing or tending to produce sleep, very tedious or boring |
| 2 | m _ _t _ _a r _ o _ s | having a great variety of diversity |
| 3 | ep _ _ _on | an animal that lives on the surface of another as a parasite |
| 4 | _ _ ip _ _ _t | treating serious matters lightly, disrespectful, playful |
| 5 | _e _ _ _e | a person's spirit or courage, the quality of a person's disposition |
| 6 | m_nc _ _ _te | a card game derived from tarot |
| 7 | _u_d_n_m | the first portion of the small intestine immediately beyond the stomach |
| 8 | m _ _ _ty | a lesser share of something, a half, either of two equal parts |
| 9 | me _z _ _ine | a floor beneath the stage from which the traps are worked |
| 10 | f_t_l_ _y | tendency to be occupied with trivial matters, ineffective, uselessness |
| 11 | _ri_l_y | a small sum of money, small debt |
| 12 | v_l _ _ i _y | rapidity of motion, operation, or action; swiftness or speed |
| 13 | _a_ue | the worth of a thing |
| 14 | t _ _ b _ _ _ nt | characterized by violent disturbance or commotion |
| 15 | r _ _ e _l _ _ | move from one area of activity to another or transfer to another function |
| 16 | s_b_t_n _ _ _s | hastily produced or constructed |
| 17 | p _ _ p _ _ t_ | a thing or things belonging to a person or persons |
| 18 | t _ _ v _ l | a stick for stirring porridge or anything cooked in a pot |
| 19 | p_e_e _ _ b _ _ | to be chosen rather than another |
| 20 | o_e _ _om_ | get the better of, defeat or prevail |
| 21 | s_a_u_e | a law or decree made by a monarch or legislative authority |
| 22 | _ st _ _ _h | a very large, swift, flightless bird |
| 23 | _y _ _ on | a huge serpent or monster |
| 24 | _ q _ _l_d | foul through neglect or lack of cleanliness |
| 25 | p _ _m _ _ _ve | having a quality associated with early or ancient period or stage |

PRACTICE TESTS IN VERBAL REASONING

26   _ _ b_ ds_ an         an official appointed to investigate complaints by individuals against maladministration by public authorities
27   n_m _ _ a_e           to appoint a person by name to hold some office or discharge some duty
28   _ _ ir_               a basic monetary unit of Nigeria
29   r_c_pe_ _ te          to recover or regain health, something mislaid or lost
30   o_ _ _e_ e            a dish of beaten eggs cooked in a frying pan, served plain or with a savory or sweet filling

| | Record Your Progress | | | |
|---|---|---|---|---|
| Number of Times You Have Taken the Test | Record | | | Record Your Completion Time |
| | Number of Questions Completed | Your Total Score | Total No. of Questions | |
| 1 | | | | |
| 2 | | | | |
| 3 | | | | |
| 4 | | | | |
| 5 | | | | |

# SAMPLE TEST 5: COMPOUND WORDS

You have been presented with the first part of a compound word, and you are required to select the second part of the word from the options provided and write your answer in the space provided. Here is an example.

|  | | A | B | C | D | |
|---|---|---|---|---|---|---|
| FAIR | | way | thyme | lamp | nail | __A__ |

The answer is A, so you write A in the space provided as shown above.

Now do the following practice tests.

## Practice Test 13 (Answers on page 241)

You have been presented with the first part of a compound word, and you are required to select the second part of the word from the options provided and write your answer in the space provided

|  |  | A | B | C | D |  |
|---|---|---|---|---|---|---|
| 1 | LIFE | chew | dine | time | lunch | _____ |
| 2 | GRAND | snack | mother | nosh | wolf | _____ |
| 3 | PASS | our | carry | port | buy | _____ |
| 4 | CARPET | read | could | bagger | carry | _____ |
| 5 | SUN | just | flower | word | page | _____ |
| 6 | BASKET | enjoy | ball | look | may | _____ |
| 7 | MOON | best | run | light | tie | _____ |
| 8 | FOOT | cup | ball | crepe | wine | _____ |
| 9 | EARTH | pasta | opera | quake | Rome | _____ |
| 10 | EVERY | thing | Cannes | early | wild | _____ |
| 11 | MEAN | blaze | days | time | drink | _____ |
| 12 | BACK | morn | praise | wake | ward | _____ |
| 13 | FOOT | little | wake | bloom | prints | _____ |
| 14 | BACK | that | apple | done | bone | _____ |
| 15 | PEPPER | early | again | spirit | mint | _____ |
| 16 | AIR | their | style | port | write | _____ |
| 17 | BUTTER | towel | fax | flies | buds | _____ |
| 18 | SCHOOL | dot | seed | house | touch | _____ |

# PRACTICE TESTS IN VERBAL REASONING

|    |         | A       | B       | C       | D       |     |
|----|---------|---------|---------|---------|---------|-----|
| 19 | UP      | tulip   | stream  | motor   | radio   | ___ |
| 20 | ANY     | egg     | body    | blot    | boot    | ___ |
| 21 | BY      | wheels  | pass    | door    | potter  | ___ |
| 22 | SPEAR   | clue    | due     | mint    | ducks   | ___ |
| 23 | THROW   | won     | they    | test    | back    | ___ |
| 24 | SKATE   | cup     | circle  | yellow  | board   | ___ |
| 25 | CROSS   | clutch  | after   | walk    | kind    | ___ |
| 26 | SUPER   | each    | mine    | market  | teeth   | ___ |
| 27 | WEATHER | love    | band    | man     | draw    | ___ |
| 28 | RATTLE  | seed    | boot    | bout    | snake   | ___ |
| 29 | THERE   | engine  | active  | score   | fore    | ___ |
| 30 | SUPER   | face    | fake    | human   | wall    | ___ |
| 31 | SPEAR   | battle  | usual   | head    | their   | ___ |
| 32 | NORTH   | down    | nest    | crest   | east    | ___ |
| 33 | SILVER  | derby   | grand   | summer  | smith   | ___ |
| 34 | WATCH   | each    | maker   | red     | coin    | ___ |
| 35 | BOOT    | draw    | strap   | pop     | head    | ___ |
| 36 | DISH    | laugh   | washer  | plug    | phone   | ___ |
| 37 | POP     | glass   | pitch   | corn    | net     | ___ |
| 38 | SPOKES  | wait    | book    | person  | read    | ___ |
| 39 | HONEY   | search  | very    | dew     | best    | ___ |
| 40 | PACE    | over    | cash    | knit    | maker   | ___ |

| Record Your Progress |||||
|---|---|---|---|---|
| Number of Times You Have Taken the Test | Record |||  Record Your Completion Time |
| | Number of Questions Completed | Your Total Score | Total No. of Questions | |
| 1 | | | | |
| 2 | | | | |
| 3 | | | | |
| 4 | | | | |
| 5 | | | | |

PRACTICE TESTS IN VERBAL REASONING

## Practice Test 14 (Answers on page 241)

You have been presented with the first part of a compound word, and you are required to select the second part of the word from the options provided and write your answer in the space provided

|    |         | A       | B       | C       | D       |          |
|----|---------|---------|---------|---------|---------|----------|
| 1  | HOME    | season  | square  | ignite  | town    | _____ |
| 2  | BLUE    | dean    | leek    | coin    | fish    | _____ |
| 3  | THUNDER | prince  | jaws    | storm   | what    | _____ |
| 4  | HAM     | pail    | lace    | burger  | hill    | _____ |
| 5  | HOUSE   | rank    | fox     | fair    | hold    | _____ |
| 6  | RIVER   | stilts  | feast   | small   | banks   | _____ |
| 7  | TOUCH   | jewel   | skin    | down    | thrash  | _____ |
| 8  | LIME    | found   | loafer  | stone   | skate   | _____ |
| 9  | HEAD    | topic   | locket  | wedge   | quarters| _____ |
| 10 | SHADY   | them    | fool    | side    | corn    | _____ |
| 11 | UNDER   | beige   | rust    | ground  | swing   | _____ |
| 12 | SAND    | path    | leek    | stone   | vase    | _____ |
| 13 | TOOTH   | genius  | name    | sack    | paste   | _____ |
| 14 | HOUSE   | clog    | bowl    | spread  | keeper  | _____ |
| 15 | COMMON  | elder   | paste   | almond  | place   | _____ |
| 16 | SEA     | coach   | change  | shore   | Cain    | _____ |
| 17 | KEY     | hope    | actors  | board   | golf    | _____ |
| 18 | BABY    | meat    | stone   | sitter  | sand    | _____ |
| 19 | TOOTH   | eyes    | plug    | fence   | pick    | _____ |
| 20 | ANY     | snip    | pen     | more    | alarm   | _____ |
| 21 | BOOK    | pillow  | paper   | keeper  | rub     | _____ |
| 22 | FORK    | mobile  | dress   | lift    | blouse  | _____ |
| 23 | UNDER   | board   | age     | bag     | trip    | _____ |
| 24 | NOISE   | tripe   | maker   | bath    | glass   | _____ |
| 25 | BACK    | dull    | log     | toy     | face    | _____ |
| 26 | WATER   | mend    | finger  | fall    | case    | _____ |
| 27 | ANY     | cross   | dark    | where   | nose    | _____ |
| 28 | WATCH   | grease  | nine    | dog     | wall    | _____ |
| 29 | SOME    | had     | bake    | them    | how     | _____ |
| 30 | UNDER   | tire    | brooch  | photo   | belly   | _____ |
| 31 | BOOK    | singer  | caramel | slope   | worm    | _____ |

PRACTICE TESTS IN VERBAL REASONING

|    |       | A      | B       | C        | D       |     |
|----|-------|--------|---------|----------|---------|-----|
| 32 | LOW   | swing  | land    | master   | south   | ___ |
| 33 | BACK  | ten    | hand    | diva     | hill    | ___ |
| 34 | SUPER | camel  | script  | east     | dinner  | ___ |
| 35 | UNDER | bird   | charge  | prince   | nail    | ___ |
| 36 | SUN   | shine  | jaws    | jade     | bench   | ___ |
| 37 | BOOK  | shelf  | belt    | swim     | quit    | ___ |
| 38 | FORE  | pierce | finger  | typist   | shower  | ___ |
| 39 | WIND  | sweat  | lick    | mill     | kick    | ___ |
| 40 | SEA   | mover  | mule    | triangle | side    | ___ |

| Record Your Progress |||||
|---|---|---|---|---|
| Number of Times You Have Taken the Test | \multicolumn{3}{c|}{Record} | Record Your Completion Time |
|  | Number of Questions Completed | Your Total Score | Total No. of Questions |  |
| 1 |  |  |  |  |
| 2 |  |  |  |  |
| 3 |  |  |  |  |
| 4 |  |  |  |  |
| 5 |  |  |  |  |

## Practice Test 15 (Answers on page 242)

You have been presented with the first part of a compound word, and you are required to select the second part of the word from the options provided and write your answer in the space provided

|   |       | A       | B       | C      | D       |     |
|---|-------|---------|---------|--------|---------|-----|
| 1 | SUPER | quench  | place   | sonic  | jaws    | ___ |
| 2 | BACK  | ditch   | jumper  | easy   | breaker | ___ |
| 3 | CROSS | quail   | dizzy   | make   | over    | ___ |
| 4 | SIDE  | ten     | noun    | kick   | very    | ___ |
| 5 | AIR   | disrupt | diver   | field  | disk    | ___ |
| 6 | BACK  | pest    | either  | queen  | drop    | ___ |

|   | | A | B | C | D | |
|---|---|---|---|---|---|---|
| 7 | TEXT | egg | book | early | flick | _____ |
| 8 | BACK | fizz | firm | bite | flea | _____ |
| 9 | UNDER | inside | install | Koran | arm | _____ |
| 10 | MILE | knee | koala | stone | kilt | _____ |
| 11 | FORE | ledge | laugh | leg | least | _____ |
| 12 | SOFT | myth | mutter | ball | mussel | _____ |
| 13 | BACK | peril | pebble | pear | ground | _____ |
| 14 | UP | pedal | rely | room | tight | _____ |
| 15 | SUN | seen | bathe | bark | scrub | _____ |
| 16 | KEY | sober | stroke | soap | snap | _____ |
| 17 | BLACK | sniff | berries | threw | thick | _____ |
| 18 | LOOP | thigh | even | hole | bounce | _____ |
| 19 | FRIEND | boss | brag | pen | ship | _____ |
| 20 | UP | topic | wallet | biscuit | bringing | _____ |
| 21 | WHITE | group | wash | bent | peak | _____ |
| 22 | BLACK | slope | jack | turn | their | _____ |
| 23 | PAN | lace | highly | cake | seat | _____ |
| 24 | BRAIN | kind | child | pimple | pot | _____ |
| 25 | DEAD | brown | guitar | line | guilt | _____ |
| 26 | RAIN | weep | quench | bow | flip | _____ |
| 27 | WATER | bread | melon | film | peas | _____ |
| 28 | DAY | sage | dream | grass | fruit | _____ |
| 29 | PIG | let | run | seal | write | _____ |
| 30 | STORE | room | rust | rumble | kid | _____ |
| 31 | PIN | swing | stripe | slope | skate | _____ |
| 32 | UNDER | tenor | achieve | score | tire | _____ |
| 33 | WALL | bra | bow | paper | Nike | _____ |
| 34 | EYE | admit | then | sore | divert | _____ |
| 35 | FISH | west | skirt | coin | pond | _____ |
| 36 | TAX | rapid | repeat | payer | shirt | _____ |
| 37 | TEAM | margin | mobile | work | shake | _____ |
| 38 | GRAND | mosaic | parent | rapport | baker | _____ |
| 39 | UP | ointment | shot | case | talk | _____ |
| 40 | BLACK | out | bad | avenue | axle | _____ |

PRACTICE TESTS IN VERBAL REASONING

PRACTICE TESTS IN VERBAL REASONING

| Record Your Progress |||||
|---|---|---|---|---|
| Number of Times You Have Taken the Test | Record ||| Record Your Completion Time |
| | Number of Questions Completed | Your Total Score | Total No. of Questions | |
| 1 | | | | |
| 2 | | | | |
| 3 | | | | |
| 4 | | | | |
| 5 | | | | |

# SAMPLE TEST 6: PREFIXES

You are presented with words that begin with the same letters. You are required to find the missing preceding letters and then write the answer in the space provided. Here is an example.

What two letters go before each of these words to make a word? Write your answer in the space provided.

|   | A | B | C |   |
|---|---|---|---|---|
| 1 | lace | joy | grave | _____ |

The answer is *en*. The words will then be *enlace*, *enjoy*, and *engrave*.

Now answer the following similar questions. You are required to write the two, three, four, and five letters that go before the listed in the space provided.

## Practice Test 16 (Answers on page 242)

What *two* letters go before each of these to make a word? Write your answer in the space provided.

| | | | | |
|---|---|---|---|---|
| 1 | ways | together | so | _____ |
| 2 | blood | bow | tail | _____ |
| 3 | joy | tangle | case | _____ |
| 4 | compose | form | code | _____ |
| 5 | vice | where | way | _____ |
| 6 | tension | voice | supportable | _____ |
| 7 | half | gun | head | _____ |
| 8 | unite | member | sign | _____ |
| 9 | ray | read | it | _____ |
| 10 | gross | due | join | _____ |
| 11 | verse | verb | vise | _____ |
| 12 | fair | fix | fluent | _____ |
| 13 | ate | ile | ape | _____ |
| 14 | at | am | an | _____ |
| 15 | raid | forest | flux | _____ |
| 16 | ready | right | pine | _____ |
| 17 | crow | chew | cape | _____ |

PRACTICE TESTS IN VERBAL REASONING

| 18 | opt | ore | coastal | _____ |
| 19 | set | say | sign | _____ |
| 20 | pear | part | pease | _____ |
| 21 | long | low | loved | _____ |
| 22 | son | row | ray | _____ |
| 23 | tune | torn | test | _____ |
| 24 | ill | one | edge | _____ |
| 25 | code | claim | compress | _____ |
| 26 | oxide | ode | late | _____ |
| 27 | ink | own | ape | _____ |
| 28 | sure | sort | size | _____ |
| 29 | are | and | each | _____ |
| 30 | vine | verse | van | _____ |
| 31 | have | gin | half | _____ |
| 32 | way | word | path | _____ |
| 33 | tray | under | sent | _____ |
| 34 | form | mate | secure | _____ |
| 35 | oat | ink | end | _____ |
| 36 | press | print | prison | _____ |
| 37 | continent | credible | corrupt | _____ |
| 38 | prove | proper | pure | _____ |
| 39 | apt | audible | bred | _____ |
| 40 | door | complete | dispose | _____ |

| Record Your Progress ||||
| --- | --- | --- | --- | --- |
| Number of Times You Have Taken the Test | Record ||| Record Your Completion Time |
|  | Number of Questions Completed | Your Total Score | Total No. of Questions |  |
| 1 |  |  |  |  |
| 2 |  |  |  |  |
| 3 |  |  |  |  |
| 4 |  |  |  |  |
| 5 |  |  |  |  |

# Practice Test 17 (Answers on page 242)

What *three* letters go before each of these to make a word? Write your answer in the space provided.

| | | | | |
|---|---|---|---|---|
| 1 | side | coat | spin | _____ |
| 2 | bull | stop | fall | _____ |
| 3 | grove | handle | hole | _____ |
| 4 | less | lift | lock | _____ |
| 5 | hive | line | keeper | _____ |
| 6 | net | den | age | _____ |
| 7 | craft | port | flow | _____ |
| 8 | snip | son | take | _____ |
| 9 | mill | dust | fish | _____ |
| 10 | post | bug | room | _____ |
| 11 | lass | throat | let | _____ |
| 12 | light | break | book | _____ |
| 13 | appear | agree | allow | _____ |
| 14 | powder | fire | boat | _____ |
| 15 | space | lock | borne | _____ |
| 16 | politics | physics | metric | _____ |
| 17 | sent | service | similar | _____ |
| 18 | maker | less | giver | _____ |
| 19 | shot | sight | brow | _____ |
| 20 | cover | count | obey | _____ |
| 21 | lay | fit | take | _____ |
| 22 | head | less | mother | _____ |
| 23 | poise | ridge | table | _____ |
| 24 | strip | tight | way | _____ |
| 25 | about | by | man | _____ |
| 26 | fume | form | cent | _____ |
| 27 | soil | most | coat | _____ |
| 28 | lead | place | print | _____ |
| 29 | close | credit | cord | _____ |
| 30 | light | bag | works | _____ |
| 31 | sense | plus | entity | _____ |
| 32 | chief | carry | conceive | _____ |

PRACTICE TESTS IN VERBAL REASONING

| Record Your Progress |||||
| --- | --- | --- | --- | --- |
| Number of Times You Have Taken the Test | Record ||| Record Your Completion Time |
|  | Number of Questions Completed | Your Total Score | Total No. of Questions |  |
| 1 |  |  |  |  |
| 2 |  |  |  |  |
| 3 |  |  |  |  |
| 4 |  |  |  |  |
| 5 |  |  |  |  |

## Practice Test 18 (Answers on page 242)

What *four* letters go before each of these to make a word? Write your answer in the space provided.

| 1  | come     | load    | seas      | _____ |
|----|----------|---------|-----------|------------|
| 2  | pin      | less    | cut       | _____ |
| 3  | hold     | town    | way       | _____ |
| 4  | dynamic  | space   | plane     | _____ |
| 5  | dote     | body    | cyclone   | _____ |
| 6  | bone     | ache    | drop      | _____ |
| 7  | cast     | awe     | all       | _____ |
| 8  | back     | faced   | foot      | _____ |
| 9  | fight    | lock    | frog      | _____ |
| 10 | log      | stroke  | lash      | _____ |
| 11 | christ   | biotic  | clockwise | _____ |
| 12 | sight    | dose    | due       | _____ |
| 13 | charge   | sized   | take      | _____ |
| 14 | tail     | roach   | pit       | _____ |
| 15 | date     | fire    | bite      | _____ |
| 16 | right    | hold    | book      | _____ |
| 17 | age      | wagon   | stand     | _____ |
| 18 | field    | flakes  | flour     | _____ |
| 19 | log      | climax  | node      | _____ |

| 20 | pack | gammon | yard | _____ |
| --- | --- | --- | --- | --- |
| 21 | man | mat | stop | _____ |
| 22 | mark | stall | worm | _____ |
| 23 | stairs | cast | beat | _____ |
| 24 | perspirant | septic | social | _____ |
| 25 | place | proof | man | _____ |
| 26 | way | knob | step | _____ |
| 27 | slide | side | stage | _____ |
| 28 | stone | staff | ship | _____ |
| 29 | it | master | width | _____ |
| 30 | man | front | bear | _____ |
| 31 | grade | hill | pour | _____ |
| 32 | see | head | court | _____ |
| 33 | hardy | scalp | proof | _____ |
| 34 | bird | like | ship | _____ |
| 35 | long | boat | line | _____ |
| 36 | arm | wood | fly | _____ |
| 37 | fisher | pin | ship | _____ |
| 38 | lady | mass | slide | _____ |
| 39 | land | mast | frame | _____ |
| 40 | beam | struck | stone | _____ |

| Record Your Progress |||||
| --- | --- | --- | --- | --- |
| Number of Times You Have Taken the Test | Record |||  Record Your Completion Time |
|  | Number of Questions Completed | Your Total Score | Total No. of Questions |  |
| 1 |  |  |  |  |
| 2 |  |  |  |  |
| 3 |  |  |  |  |
| 4 |  |  |  |  |
| 5 |  |  |  |  |

PRACTICE TESTS IN VERBAL REASONING

**Practice Test 19 (Answers on page 243)**

What *five* letters go before each of these to make a word? Write your answer in the space provided.

| | | | | |
|---|---|---|---|---|
| 1 | fold | spot | alley | _____ |
| 2 | shave | math | birth | _____ |
| 3 | age | head | release | _____ |
| 4 | wash | piece | watering | _____ |
| 5 | mat | tennis | mountain | _____ |
| 6 | break | burn | felt | _____ |
| 7 | shade | mare | shirt | _____ |
| 8 | cross | breed | grade | _____ |
| 9 | proud | master | bound | _____ |
| 10 | box | stick | maker | _____ |
| 11 | club | dress | fall | _____ |
| 12 | word | bow | way | _____ |
| 13 | bird | board | jack | _____ |
| 14 | melon | shed | well | _____ |
| 15 | word | wind | walk | _____ |
| 16 | boat | hold | breaker | _____ |
| 17 | child | father | master | _____ |
| 18 | ache | land | beat | _____ |
| 19 | thought | wards | taste | _____ |
| 20 | scope | phone | wave | _____ |
| 21 | pants | take | ware | _____ |
| 22 | bar | bow | fire | _____ |
| 23 | wife | maid | work | _____ |
| 24 | stone | wood | land | _____ |
| 25 | pick | paste | brush | _____ |
| 26 | marry | national | face | _____ |
| 27 | house | weight | ship | _____ |
| 28 | fall | gown | cap | _____ |
| 29 | house | national | marry | _____ |
| 30 | copy | fit | graph | _____ |

52

## Record Your Progress

| Number of Times You Have Taken the Test | Record | | | Record Your Completion Time |
|---|---|---|---|---|
| | Number of Questions Completed | Your Total Score | Total No. of Questions | |
| 1 | | | | |
| 2 | | | | |
| 3 | | | | |
| 4 | | | | |
| 5 | | | | |

# PRACTICE TESTS IN VERBAL REASONING

## SAMPLE TEST 7: PALINDROME

Palindrome may be described as words or sentences that are spelled the same forward or backward. You are presented with a set of words, and one of the words is a palindrome. You are required to identify the word and write your answer in the space provided. Here is an example.

| A | B | C | D | |
|---|---|---|---|---|
| deer | dead | deed | dial | --- |

The answer is *C*. The word *deed* is spelled the same forward and backward. Now answer the following similar questions.

## Practice Test 20 (Answers on page 243)

You are required to identify the word that is spelled the same forward and backward from the list of words. Write your answer in the space provided.

| | A | B | C | D | |
|---|---|---|---|---|---|
| 1 | seconds | high | murdrum | willow | ____ |
| 2 | sips | paste | syringe | level | ____ |
| 3 | rotator | expenditure | kipper | knurl | ____ |
| 4 | evitative | joker | joist | holt | ____ |
| 5 | redder | kick | flank | Koran | ____ |
| 6 | human | devoved | keck | grunt | ____ |
| 7 | rigor | scruple | terret | sclera | ____ |
| 8 | gusset | folktale | reviver | raider | ____ |
| 9 | fluid | sips | stats | flute | ____ |
| 10 | jeopardy | kink | aibohphobia | monotype | ____ |
| 11 | deified | monkfish | prominent | tagliatelle | ____ |
| 12 | dewed | tact | systole | throes | ____ |
| 13 | thrust | thresh | moorcock | reifier | ____ |
| 14 | numerate | obligee | nurture | tenet | ____ |
| 15 | kayak | treat | clock | paper | ____ |
| 16 | tacit | minim | craft | origami | ____ |
| 17 | crayon | account | peeweep | kapok | ____ |
| 18 | assets | redder | always | projects | ____ |

PRACTICE TESTS IN VERBAL REASONING

|    | A         | B         | C          | D          |   |
|----|-----------|-----------|------------|------------|---|
| 19 | slogans   | sagas     | hatch      | heavy      |   |
| 20 | study     | signs     | signet     | lemel      |   |
| 21 | design    | tablet    | exist      | refer      |   |
| 22 | taint     | habit     | squirrels  | Hannah     |   |
| 23 | business  | departed  | question   | detartrated |   |
| 24 | ewe       | quarter   | missing    | tacet      |   |
| 25 | repaper   | knack     | amass      | provide    |   |
| 26 | solos     | slow      | suits      | gross      |   |
| 27 | alula     | benign    | inform     | grape      |   |
| 28 | tackle    | wow       | fluff      | eradicate  |   |
| 29 | growth    | Malayalam | endanger   | message    |   |
| 30 | orange    | refer     | rumor      | spread     |   |
| 31 | knight    | honor     | radar      | natural    |   |
| 32 | outdoor   | knock     | madam      | karate     |   |
| 33 | invests   | deleveled | tennis     | insurance  |   |
| 34 | visitors  | available | sports     | civic      |   |
| 35 | racecar   | govern    | enroll     | benefit    |   |
| 36 | fleet     | keek      | contagious | stress     |   |
| 37 | testset   | arrive    | retreat    | sequence   |   |
| 38 | crosswords| subjects  | sexes      | aligned    |   |
| 39 | rotor     | sentence  | seven      | registrar  |   |
| 40 | escort    | pop       | painted    | dotted     |   |

| \multicolumn{5}{c}{**Record Your Progress**} |||||
|---|---|---|---|---|
| Number of Times You Have Taken the Test | \multicolumn{3}{c}{Record} | Record Your Completion Time |
|   | Number of Questions Completed | Your Total Score | Total No. of Questions |   |
| 1 |   |   |   |   |
| 2 |   |   |   |   |
| 3 |   |   |   |   |
| 4 |   |   |   |   |
| 5 |   |   |   |   |

PRACTICE TESTS IN VERBAL REASONING

# SAMPLE TEST 8: WORD RECOGNITION

For this test, you are provided with the definition of a word and the letters of the word. The letters have been jumbled up, so you are required to spell the word correctly. Here is an example.

| Word | Meaning | Answer |
|---|---|---|
| ihsmelb | a flaw or defect, as a spot | blemish |

The answer is *blemish*. Now provide the answer to the following tests.

## Practice Test 21 (Answers on page 243)

Each of the following is a word with its letters jumbled up. Using the clue, rearrange the letters and write the correct word in the space provided.

| | Word | Meaning | Answer |
|---|---|---|---|
| 1 | koanbbce | the bones going down your back | _____ |
| 2 | unmtau | the season between summer and winter | _____ |
| 3 | tibaaecr | tiny creature that can cause disease | _____ |
| 4 | mobb | a weapon that explodes and causes damage | _____ |
| 5 | ublb | the round glass part of an electric light | _____ |
| 6 | ronac | a small nut that grows on oak trees | _____ |
| 7 | litetrb | hard, but easy to break | _____ |
| 8 | ascospm | an instrument with a needle that always points north | _____ |
| 9 | rbeeicg | a very large lump of ice that floats in the sea | _____ |
| 10 | unolge | a room in your house where you can rest and watch TV | _____ |
| 11 | usrhb | You smooth your hair with it. | _____ |
| 12 | cukl | good or unpleasant things that happen by chance | _____ |
| 13 | iiwk | a type of bird from New Zealand that cannot fly | _____ |
| 14 | eqeaaudt | just enough | _____ |
| 15 | echmain | something with parts that move together to do a job | _____ |
| 16 | kferaatsb | first meal of the day that you eat in the morning | _____ |
| 17 | henlai | to breathe in | _____ |
| 18 | hovnacy | a small fish with a salty taste | _____ |
| 19 | derdal | a frame with steps used to climb up to reach things | _____ |
| 20 | ioccm | a magazine with pictures that tell a story, popular with children | _____ |

PRACTICE TESTS IN VERBAL REASONING

|    | Word     | Meaning                                                              | Answer |
|----|----------|----------------------------------------------------------------------|--------|
| 21 | adlb     | with no hair on your head                                            | _____ |
| 22 | lwho     | to make a loud noise like a baby                                     | _____ |
| 23 | aiffnru  | somewhere outside with games and things to ride on                   | _____ |
| 24 | imaardl  | an important person in the navy who is in charge of a group of ships | _____ |
| 25 | nayhe    | a wild animal that looks like a dog                                  | _____ |
| 26 | zaime    | a tall plant with big yellow seeds that people eat                   | _____ |
| 27 | rdeang   | a male goose                                                         | _____ |
| 28 | fbnoeir  | a big fire that you make outside                                     | _____ |
| 29 | rlcgai   | a plant like a little onion with a very strong taste                 | _____ |
| 30 | htpeblaa | all the letters of a language                                        | _____ |

### Record Your Progress

| Number of Times You Have Taken the Test | Record | | | Record Your Completion Time |
|---|---|---|---|---|
| | Number of Questions Completed | Your Total Score | Total No. of Questions | |
| 1 | | | | |
| 2 | | | | |
| 3 | | | | |
| 4 | | | | |
| 5 | | | | |

## Practice Test 22 (Answers on page 244)

Each of the following is a word with its letters jumbled up. Using the clue, rearrange the letters and write the correct word in the space provided.

|   | Word      | Meaning                                             | Answer |
|---|-----------|-----------------------------------------------------|--------|
| 1 | rlaat     | a special table used in religious ceremonies        | _____ |
| 2 | jtseaym   | a name used when speaking to a king or queen        | _____ |
| 3 | ninoaaimxte | a test of someone's knowledge                     | _____ |
| 4 | halmeecon | a lizard that can change color                      | _____ |
| 5 | ddbistuh  | someone who believes in the religion of the Buddha  | _____ |
| 6 | eatrcbia  | tiny creatures that can cause disease               | _____ |

PRACTICE TESTS IN VERBAL REASONING

|    | Word       | Meaning                                                                  | Answer |
|----|------------|--------------------------------------------------------------------------|--------|
| 7  | oaeswme    | an informal way of saying *excellent*                                    |        |
| 8  | ciletar    | something that someone has written in a newspaper or magazine            |        |
| 9  | slosrbtaa  | a big white seabird with very long wings                                 |        |
| 10 | bthxieiino | an event where people show things such as paintings                      |        |
| 11 | ffeidertn  | not like someone or something                                            |        |
| 12 | gettoca    | a little house in the country                                            |        |
| 13 | llaoaimrd  | an animal with a long nose and tail and a very hard shell                |        |
| 14 | toobllaf   | a game where two teams kick a ball to score goals                        |        |
| 15 | nldaom     | a type of flat, pale nut that tastes slightly sweet                      |        |
| 16 | pelmaex    | something that shows what you mean                                       |        |
| 17 | nnievecotn | good and useful because it makes things easier                           |        |
| 18 | nigritnahdw| the way someone writes with a pen or pencil                              |        |
| 19 | iderlg     | a light plane that has no engine                                         |        |
| 20 | ybdeoog    | a word you say to someone when you leave them                            |        |
| 21 | thriiemtac | the skill of adding, subtracting, multiplying, and dividing numbers      |        |
| 22 | uosrhc     | part of a song that you can sing between each verse                      |        |
| 23 | uummnlia   | a silver-colored metal that is not very heavy                            |        |
| 24 | llaiogr    | a very big and strong ape that lives in Africa                           |        |
| 25 | skphosticc | thin sticks used to eat Chinese food                                     |        |
| 26 | bkgdonucar | the back part of a picture or scene                                      |        |
| 27 | simepgl    | a very quick look at something or someone                                |        |
| 28 | tcarniof   | a tiny amount of something                                               |        |
| 29 | tedloasi   | far away from anything else                                              |        |
| 30 | ttlongu    | someone who eats too much                                                |        |

| Record Your Progress ||||| 
|---|---|---|---|---|
| Number of Times You Have Taken the Test | Record ||| Record Your Completion Time |
| | Number of Questions Completed | Your Total Score | Total No. of Questions | |
| 1 | | | | |
| 2 | | | | |
| 3 | | | | |
| 4 | | | | |
| 5 | | | | |

# 2. Verbal Comprehension

The use of words is important in our everyday life, so the inability to write or speak effectively can be a hindrance. It takes time and effort to acquire a better grasp of any language, but it is worth remembering that good communication is a vital social skill that can increase self-confidence in personal relationships and can also improve efficiency at work. The extent of our word power, for example, affects our ability to express facts, opinions, and emotions; write letters, memoranda, proposals; draft contracts; respond to emails; and write blogs. Our comprehension of the written and spoken word is therefore influenced by the extent of our knowledge. It is very rewarding to spend time to improve your vocabulary and grammar.

The tests in this section will focus on assessing the correct use of words. These types of verbal reasoning questions also come in various formats. In order to logically arrange the material, each sample test will be followed by the related practice tests.

## SAMPLE TEST 9: GRAMMAR (SENTENCE COMPLETION)

Choose the pairs of words that best completes the sentence.

Amy, the sales representative, uses her _____ skills _____ when selling used cars.

| A | B | C | D |
|---|---|---|---|
| negotiation | negottiation | sensory | presence |
| effectively | principle | practical | primary |

The correctly spelled pair of words are *negotiation* and *effectively*, so A is the answer. Now write the two words in the blank spaces in the sentence.

Now try the following questions:

## Practice Test 23 (Answers on page 244)

Choose the pairs of words that best completes each sentence. Write your answer in the space provided.

1   I'll never get this _____ if you keep _____ me!      _____

| A | B | C | D |
|---|---|---|---|
| finish | finished | granded | finish |
| sparkling | interrupting | interrupt | interrupting |

PRACTICE TESTS IN VERBAL REASONING

2  Do you share any _____ or _____ with your husband?    _____

| A | B | C | D |
|---|---|---|---|
| licks | likes | like | likes |
| dislike | dislikes | dislickes | non likes |

3  Can you _____ yourself as a TV _____?    _____

| A | B | C | D |
|---|---|---|---|
| look | Imagine | views | impress |
| reporter | reporter | report | reporte |

4  That _____ is _____ everywhere she goes.    _____

| A | B | C | D |
|---|---|---|---|
| celebrate | celebrity | celebrity | stars |
| known | recognized | secret | recognized |

5  In English grammar, an _____ can be followed by a _____.    _____

| A | B | C | D |
|---|---|---|---|
| oxen | verb | adjective | gerund |
| diet | activities | preposition | soldier |

6  Kemi, the cheerful nurse, works _____ hours without _____.    _____

| A | B | C | D |
|---|---|---|---|
| unsocial | unsociable | unhappy | insociable |
| companies | complaining | places | complaning |

7  The _____ runner said that winning the gold medal felt _____.    _____

| A | B | C | D |
|---|---|---|---|
| famous | reknown | shame | famous |
| shiver | shinning | wonderful | wonderful |

8  The man is rich enough to _____ in the _____.    _____

| A | B | C | D |
|---|---|---|---|
| appear | appease | appear | appear |
| documentary | program | document | documentery |

PRACTICE TESTS IN VERBAL REASONING

9  The young boy quickly _____ his coat and _____ out.

| A | B | C | D |
| --- | --- | --- | --- |
| pull on | put in | put out | put on |
| rushed | rashed | risked | rushed |

10  Millions of _____ all over the world watch the opening _____ of the games.

| A | B | C | D |
| --- | --- | --- | --- |
| views | viewers | people | persons |
| ceremony | cerimony | ceremony | mass |

11  An _____ in Europe spends a lot of time playing _____ games.

| A | B | C | D |
| --- | --- | --- | --- |
| teenagger | adolescence | adolescent | adolecent |
| computer | computer | computer | computer |

12  That family _____ is a record of a _____ event.

| A | B | C | D |
| --- | --- | --- | --- |
| photographe | photograph | fotograph | photo |
| memorable | memorable | memory | laughter |

13  Julianne is very _____ and this is why she is _____.

| A | B | C | D |
| --- | --- | --- | --- |
| conscientious | meticuluse | conscientiouse | conscientious |
| painfully | success | successful | successful |

14  Let us look for the _____ and _____ between those twin brothers.

| A | B | C | D |
| --- | --- | --- | --- |
| similarities | similarities | similar | similarity |
| differences | different | difference | different |

15  Celine is so _____ that she always wants to _____.

| A | B | C | D |
| --- | --- | --- | --- |
| ambition | ambitiouse | ambitious | ambitious |
| win | win | wins | win |

16  The _____ thinks that _____ is easy, so it should be an optional subject. _____

| A | B | C | D |
|---|---|---|---|
| statistican | statistical | statistician | statistician |
| mathematics | mathmatics | mathmatics | mathematics |

17  Efu would like to go to Dubai to do some _____ and _____. _____

| A | B | C | D |
|---|---|---|---|
| sightseeing | sightsee | siteseeing | siteseaing |
| painting | painting | painting | painting |

18  Wayne had to _____ every _____ in the essay before the tutor arrived. _____

| A | B | C | D |
|---|---|---|---|
| rewrite | written | rewrite | rewrit |
| sentence | sentense | sentence | sentence |

19  The _____ have developed a new _____ for moving along the roof of the cave. _____

| A | B | C | D |
|---|---|---|---|
| cavers | cavars | caveers | cavers |
| technique | technik | techmique | technik |

20  The employees _____ the freezing _____ to go to work. _____

| A | B | C | D |
|---|---|---|---|
| braived | braved | braved | braved |
| temperatures | temperatures | tempratures | termperatures |

21  Charlie was a very _____ and _____ grandfather. _____

| A | B | C | D |
|---|---|---|---|
| generus | generous | generous | gernerous |
| caring | carring | caring | careing |

22  There is now a _____ salt stock in the county because of the _____ weather conditions. _____

| A | B | C | D |
|---|---|---|---|
| lemited | limited | limited | lemited |
| extreme | extreme | extrime | extremely |

PRACTICE TESTS IN VERBAL REASONING

23  The brave swimmer was badly _____ in her effort to _____ the koala. _____

| A | B | C | D |
|---|---|---|---|
| bruced | bruised | bruised | brused |
| rescue | resque | rescue | resque |

24  A _____ is necessary before planning _____ is given to the project. _____

| A | B | C | D |
|---|---|---|---|
| consultation | consultetion | consultertion | consultation |
| permission | permision | permission | parmission |

25  The youth _____ seeks to _____ the voice of young people. _____

| A | B | C | D |
|---|---|---|---|
| paliarment | parliament | paliament | parliament |
| represent | represent | represent | represent |

26  There were many people _____ in organizing the _____ day. _____

| A | B | C | D |
|---|---|---|---|
| involved | innvolved | involved | involved |
| eventfull | eventful | eventful | evantful |

27  Dealing with _____ parking by parents has been a _____ for the local police. _____

| A | B | C | D |
|---|---|---|---|
| iresponsible | irresponsible | irresponsible | iresponsible |
| priority | prioty | priority | prioritie |

28  An _____ to the building has been _____. _____

| A | B | C | D |
|---|---|---|---|
| extention | extension | extention | extension |
| proposed | propossed | propossed | proposed |

29  The politician's _____ tears over the need to combat social _____ was not acceptable. _____

| A | B | C | D |
|---|---|---|---|
| crocodile | cocodile | croccodile | crocodile |
| exclusion | exclusion | exclusion | exclution |

64

30  Mrs. Rowland and her two _____ live in a hut in Togo.  _____

| A | B | C | D |
|---|---|---|---|
| teenage daughters | tinage daughters | teenage daugters | tinage daugthers |

### Record Your Progress

| Number of Times You Have Taken the Test | Number of Questions Completed | Your Total Score | Total No. of Questions | Record Your Completion Time |
|---|---|---|---|---|
| 1 | | | | |
| 2 | | | | |
| 3 | | | | |
| 4 | | | | |
| 5 | | | | |

## Practice Test 24 (Answers on page 244)

Choose the pairs of words that best completes each sentence. Write your answer in the space provided.

1  The government has introduced tax on _____ in order to combat global _____.  _____

| A | B | C | D |
|---|---|---|---|
| emmission warming | emission worming | emission warmming | emission warming |

2  The _____ are investing a lot in this area because land is cheaper.  _____

| A | B | C | D |
|---|---|---|---|
| commercial developers | commercial divelopers | commarcial developers | cormercial developers |

65

PRACTICE TESTS IN VERBAL REASONING

3   The priest thanked all the _____ for all their _____.  _____

| A | B | C | D |
|---|---|---|---|
| parisioners | parishioners | parishioners | parissioners |
| contribution | contrebution | contribution | contribution |

4   The _____ were called to _____ the fire in Banjul.  _____

| A | B | C | D |
|---|---|---|---|
| firefighters | firefighter | firefirghter | firefihgter |
| extinguish | exteenguish | extinguishe | extinguish |

5   Charitable organizations are always _____ for _____.  _____

| A | B | C | D |
|---|---|---|---|
| appealing | apealing | appealing | apealing |
| volonteers | volunteers | volunteers | vorluneers |

6   The bowling club will receive a _____ to pay for _____ to their green.  _____

| A | B | C | D |
|---|---|---|---|
| grant | grant | grant | grants |
| inprovement | improvements | inpruvment | improvements |

7   She _____ dresses quite _____.  _____

| A | B | C | D |
|---|---|---|---|
| usally | usually | usualy | usualy |
| casually | casually | casually | casualy |

8   He is rather _____ to be a qualified _____.  _____

| A | B | C | D |
|---|---|---|---|
| inexperienced | inexperenced | inexpirienced | inexperienced |
| coach | coacher | coach | coache |

9   She is an _____ and _____ lady.  _____

| A | B | C | D |
|---|---|---|---|
| enthusiastic | enthuseastic | enthusiastic | enthusiastic |
| reliable | reliable | reliarble | relieable |

PRACTICE TESTS IN VERBAL REASONING

10  What do you think _____ to the lady in the _____?  _____

| A | B | C | D |
|---|---|---|---|
| happened | happened | harppened | harpened |
| picture | pickture | picture | picture |

11  Andrew's mom said he always _____ like an angry _____ first thing in the morning.  _____

| A | B | C | D |
|---|---|---|---|
| looks | lukes | looks | lookes |
| hegehog | hedgehog | hedgehog | hedgehog |

12  Sleep is _____ by _____ chemicals in the body.  _____

| A | B | C | D |
|---|---|---|---|
| controlled | controled | controlled | controlled |
| certain | certain | cartain | certein |

13  You should not feel _____ to _____ the business opportunity.  _____

| A | B | C | D |
|---|---|---|---|
| embarrassed | embarased | embarassed | embarrased |
| recommend | recommend | recommend | recommend |

14  In that _____ monastery, silence must be _____ at all times.  _____

| A | B | C | D |
|---|---|---|---|
| paticular | perticular | particular | peticuler |
| observed | observed | observed | observed |

15  The qualified _____ carried out the work on the _____.  _____

| A | B | C | D |
|---|---|---|---|
| electrecial | electrician | electrician | electricean |
| appliance | appliance | apliance | appliance |

16  The last family _____ was on the _____ of Father's birthday.  _____

| A | B | C | D |
|---|---|---|---|
| garthering | gathering | gerthering | gathering |
| occasion | occassion | occassion | occasion |

67

# PRACTICE TESTS IN VERBAL REASONING

**17** It is _____ to have a _____ and drink beer in Australia. _____

| A | B | C | D |
|---|---|---|---|
| customary | customery | curstomary | customary |
| barbecue | barbecue | barbecue | berbacue |

**18** It is _____ that you eat the _____ as soon as it is served. _____

| A | B | C | D |
|---|---|---|---|
| esential | essential | essential | esenteal |
| mill | meal | meale | meal |

**19** Sean had a _____ left leg, which is _____ treated by the doctor. _____

| A | B | C | D |
|---|---|---|---|
| fractured | fractured | fractured | fractured |
| being | bean | been | bin |

**20** The man is being questioned in _____ with the _____ in the area. _____

| A | B | C | D |
|---|---|---|---|
| conection | connection | conection | connection |
| bulgaries | ballgaries | bolgaries | burglaries |

**21** I would suggest that you _____ him to focus on developing his _____. _____

| A | B | C | D |
|---|---|---|---|
| encourage | encorage | encourage | encourage |
| talent | talent | tallent | tarlent |

**22** The airport baggage _____ went into the luggage _____ to collect the last bag. _____

| A | B | C | D |
|---|---|---|---|
| handler | handlar | handler | handler |
| compartment | compartment | compatment | compartmente |

**23** The financial _____ informed her of the relevant financial _____ of the investment. _____

| A | B | C | D |
|---|---|---|---|
| plannar | plannar | planner | planer |
| considerations | consideration | considerations | considerations |

24  Every year, a few unlucky _____ have their _____ stolen.  _____

| A | B | C | D |
|---|---|---|---|
| travellers | travelers | travellers | travelers |
| valuables | valuables | varluables | varluable |

25  I would _____ that you go and see the _____ before leaving a deposit.  _____

| A | B | C | D |
|---|---|---|---|
| suggest | sugests | sugests | surggest |
| accommodation | acomodotion | accomodation | acomodotion |

26  The _____ lives in a _____ in the town center.  _____

| A | B | C | D |
|---|---|---|---|
| musician | musiciean | musician | misiciean |
| skyscraper | skycraper | skysraper | skysraper |

27  People's lives are _____ by a variety of _____.  _____

| A | B | C | D |
|---|---|---|---|
| govarned | gorverned | governed | governed |
| restrictions | restrictions | restrictions | restricsion |

28  Stephen has an _____ acrobatic _____.  _____

| A | B | C | D |
|---|---|---|---|
| exseptional | exceptional | exceptional | exceptionale |
| ability | ability | arbility | ability |

29  Some banks have _____ video cameras as part of their _____ system.  _____

| A | B | C | D |
|---|---|---|---|
| instaled | installed | installed | instaled |
| security | security | seacurty | seccurity |

30  A large number of the _____ are suffering from _____.  _____

| A | B | C | D |
|---|---|---|---|
| porpulation | population | population | popurlation |
| malnutrition | malnutricion | malnutrition | malnutrition |

| Record Your Progress |||||
|---|---|---|---|---|
| Number of Times You Have Taken the Test | Record ||| Record Your Completion Time |
| | Number of Questions Completed | Your Total Score | Total No. of Questions | |
| 1 | | | | |
| 2 | | | | |
| 3 | | | | |
| 4 | | | | |
| 5 | | | | |

PRACTICE TESTS IN VERBAL REASONING

# SAMPLE TEST 10: AMBIGUITIES AND CONFUSABLE WORDS

Ambiguities are words that are often confused with each other. They are sometimes referred to as homophones. The following tests will assess your ability to identify and use such words correctly. There are many words that sound alike and are often confused, one for the other. In this section, you are required to identify the correct usage of the words. You are required to place the correct word in the gap in the sentence below.

The winner of the race between the chicken and the _____ will receive a valuable prize.

| hair | hare |
|---|---|

The answer is *hare*. Now attempt the questions below.

## Practice Test 25 (Answers on page 244)

Place the correct word into the gaps in the sentences below:

1. The widow in the village has seven _____.

   | dependents | dependants |
   |---|---|

2. The flood disaster _____ lots of lives.

   | effected | affected |
   |---|---|

3. The postal strike will delay the delivery of the _____.

   | mail | male |
   |---|---|

4. There was a major accident on the _____ carriageway

   | duel | dual |
   |---|---|

5. The large and tall plant has been there for _____ years.

| tree | three |

6. Xaviere stepped on the _____ to make an emergency stop.

| break | brake |

7. Amelie Oliver likes a lot of _____ products.

| dairy | diary |

8. Joseph was surprised, but happy, that Mark got his just _____.

| deserts | desserts |

9. Please note that only employees will be granted _____ to the backstage.

| excess | access |

10. Doreen, the thief, was _____ red-handed.

| caught | cut |

11. Nigel promised to _____ the letter of apology to his mother.

| write | right |

12. Angel needs a _____ to complete the project.

| lone | loan |

13. The _____ hive has been in the compound for generations.

| be | bee |

14. Julianne has paid for her _____ -arranging course.

| flour | flower |

15. _____ approach to life is different to yours.

| There | Their |

16. Sophie informed James that the two issues were quite _____.

| discreet | discrete |

17. Nathan said that he would _____ the material.

| die | dye |

18. I really like the _____ on her scarf.

| brooch | broach |

19. Despite the rain, the match was _____ to continue.

| allowed | aloud |

20. This is not a time for _____ but of celebration.

| morning | mourning |

PRACTICE TESTS IN VERBAL REASONING

21. The _____ is located in the middle of the country.

| dam | damn |

22. Benjamin acknowledged that he was _____ in the topic being discussed.

| disinterested | uninterested |

23. Jacqui is unable to attend _____ to official commitments.

| dew | due |

24. It is very inappropriate to _____.

| his | hiss |

25. There was a _____ in the plan.

| flaw | floor |

26. The pictures have been saved on the six giga_____ memory stick.

| byte | bite |

27. The pencil is on the desk, along with the relevant _____.

| stationery | stationary |

28. Shelly's behavior _____ from her excellent academic achievement.

| distracted | detracted |

29. The trolley raced down the _____.

| isle | aisle |

30. I have to _____ the dough.

| need | knead |

| Record Your Progress ||||||
| --- | --- | --- | --- | --- | --- |
| Number of Times You Have Taken the Test | | Record ||| Record Your Completion Time |
| | Number of Questions Completed | Your Total Score | Total No. of Questions | | |
| 1 | | | | | |
| 2 | | | | | |
| 3 | | | | | |
| 4 | | | | | |
| 5 | | | | | |

## Practice Test 26 (Answers on page 245)

Place the correct word into the gaps in the sentences below

1. There is a worm in the _____.

| hole | whole |

2. The dress was dark _____ in color.

| blew | blue |

PRACTICE TESTS IN VERBAL REASONING

3. Craig must have cleaned up. I know he _____.

| deed | did |

4. The optician requires you to remain _____ .during the eye test.

| still | steal |

5. The doctor said you should _____ down and put your feet up.

| sit | seat |

6. Tania's mom reminded her that she needs to be home _____ 6:00 p.m.

| by | bye |

7. I have _____ that very interesting book. It is a best seller.

| read | red |

8. You have given me _____ much to eat.

| too | two |

9. My _____ will be sixty years old next year.

| aunt | ant |

10. During the expedition, a _____ came to the camp at night.

| boar | bore |

11. I like _____ with boiled vegetables.

| sole | soul |
|---|---|

12. You need to send in your application form if you want to be considered for the _____.

| coarse | course |
|---|---|

13. I can only imagine what it must be like to be on the _____ of Mount Everest.

| peak | pick |
|---|---|

14. My right _____ was swollen after my visit to the dentist.

| chick | cheek |
|---|---|

15. Chloe's _____ school jumper is made of wool and cashmere.

| new | knew |
|---|---|

16. The development plan for the _____ needs to be brought to the board for discussion.

| site | sight |
|---|---|

17. When I was on holiday in America, I ate _____ with mustard nearly every day.

| steak | stake |
|---|---|

18. Please ensure that you diligently perform your _____ as a project leader.

| roll | role |
|---|---|

19. You are very _____ to me; I hope you know that.

| dear | dare |
|---|---|

20. Jenny cannot wait to _____ with her friends and tell them all about her holiday.

| meet | meat |
|---|---|

21. Joyce is a very _____ and beautiful baby.

| sweet | suite |
|---|---|

22. He was _____ doing nothing on the island for six months.

| bored | board |
|---|---|

23. You need to insure your home, especially in the _____ global economic climate.

| currant | current |
|---|---|

24. I will request to be sent a _____ of covenant.

| did | deed |
|---|---|

25. I have learned that it is wise to shop around for the best price before you _____ anything.

| ensure | insure |
|---|---|

26. Darren spoke to his boss and took his _____.

| advice | advise |

27. The satellite navigation showed the _____ to our destination.

| root | route |

28. Daniel _____ open the door.

| pries | prize |

29. Marie Heraty is the _____ of the school.

| principle | principal |

30. I think coffee is a _____ because it keeps me awake.

| stimulus | stimulant |

## Record Your Progress

| Number of Times You Have Taken the Test | Record ||| Record Your Completion Time |
|---|---|---|---|---|
| | Number of Questions Completed | Your Total Score | Total No. of Questions | |
| 1 | | | | |
| 2 | | | | |
| 3 | | | | |
| 4 | | | | |
| 5 | | | | |

PRACTICE TESTS IN VERBAL REASONING

## SAMPLE TEST 11: CORRECT USE OF A WORD

You are required to identify the best possible word to complete the sentence. Write your answer in the space provided. Here is an example.

1     The race was made _____ more difficult by the injury of their best player.

     A  unique
     B  outstanding
     C  infinitely
     D  operational

The answer is C.

Now answer the following questions.

## Practice Test 27 (Answers on page 245)

Identify the best possible word to complete the sentence. Write your answer in the space provided.

1     He has _____ to laugh at himself.

     A  taught
     B  bought
     C  caught
     D  learned

2     It is difficult to always be _____ when you are at the top of the league.

     A  consistent
     B  hesitant
     C  resistant
     D  inefficient

3     We need to assess his _____ thoroughly.

     A  substantial
     B  casualty
     C  credentials
     D  discount

4    You need to be careful how you spend because there are _____ times ahead.

   A  balancing
   B  challenging
   C  defiant
   D  comfort

5    The lady has begun the _____ task of managing change in the company.

   A  peace
   B  arduous
   C  disturbance
   D  retirement

6    The situation was enough to make anyone feel _____.

   A  hamper
   B  disenchanted
   C  council
   D  gossip

7    I am not afraid of the big _____ ahead of us.

   A  motivation
   B  casual
   C  goodwill
   D  challenge

8    That gambler was _____ himself in mind games.

   A  revolving
   B  recuperate
   C  indulging
   D  parading

9    The employee was absent on _____ leave due to an illness in his family.

   A  display
   B  overtime
   C  compassionate
   D  holiday

10  The tennis player is technically very good, but there is a lot of room for _____.

A ransom
B school
C improvement
D good-bye

11  Please remember that you are _____ to your opinion on the issue.

A entitled
B disagreeable
C pleasant
D argument

12  Victory for the Togolese team would _____ their position in the championship.

A consolidate
B convalesce
C school
D transparent

13  We need to wait and see how his _____ will do things.

A employment
B suspension
C wage
D successor

14  The opponents seem to sometimes be very _____.

A combined
B communication
C engagement
D aggressive

15  I think there needs to be an _____ pay league for bankers in the public domain.

A overwhelming
B development
C executive
D commitment

16   There is a _____ concern about his ability to lead the team.

   A  solution
   B  presentation
   C  lingering
   D  unconscious

17   Those two chemistry students had a _____.

   A  liberation
   B  authentication
   C  disagreement
   D  departmental

18   You are much too young to _____ retiring.

   A  lecture
   B  busy
   C  consider
   D  notice

19   The rich businessman _____ potential property investors.

   A  professional
   B  ability
   C  entertained
   D  talent

20   We are all _____ that Mr. Chin would be the one chosen to lead that project.

   A  radiant
   B  transparent
   C  speculating
   D  organization

21   The most popular _____ would be for the bid to be successful.

   A  payment
   B  scenario
   C  designer
   D  song

22  It has finally been decided that the injured man should be _____.

   A illuminated
   B experienced
   C subject
   D compensated

23  The snooker player struggled initially, but after he changed _____, he won the game.

   A negotiation
   B mouth
   C tactics
   D desk

24  It was great to see the young boy being rescued from the rubble of the _____ building.

   A demanding
   B essential
   C collapsed
   D flexible

25  The evidence provided was a bit _____.

   A talented
   B multiple
   C ambiguous
   D grammar

26  Joshua's legal _____ alleged that she was unfairly dismissed.

   A disguise
   B representative
   C cloak
   D culture

27  The meeting between Charlie and Bernard was the most _____ match in the second week of the tournament.

   A allegation
   B internal
   C intriguing
   D gnome

28  Davina's mum looked on proudly and _____ during the graduation ceremony.

   A  permanent
   B  tremendous
   C  project
   D  applauded

29  It is essential that you are fulfilled as a parent, so aim to have a healthy _____ between work and family.

   A  clock
   B  sound
   C  balance
   D  business

30  The politician has _____ qualities and skills, so we will vote for her.

   A  responsibility
   B  transferred
   C  exceptional
   D  clarity

| Record Your Progress ||||| 
|---|---|---|---|---|
| Number of Times You Have Taken the Test | Record ||| Record Your Completion Time |
|  | Number of Questions Completed | Your Total Score | Total No. of Questions |  |
| 1 |  |  |  |  |
| 2 |  |  |  |  |
| 3 |  |  |  |  |
| 4 |  |  |  |  |
| 5 |  |  |  |  |

## Practice Test 28 (Answers on page 245)

Identify the best possible word to complete the sentence. Write your answer in the space provided.

1. It is _____ that you are absolutely punctual for the appointment.

   A simple
   B working
   C essential
   D masked

2. Her _____ French has improved considerably.

   A activity
   B reinforcement
   C conversational
   D central

3. Your salesmen need to work on delivering a _____ service.

   A mason
   B reliable
   C mission
   D dry-clean

4. The sick man who was _____ has now been discharged.

   A external
   B champion
   C hospitalized
   D reduced

5. Sally, the mayor, has lost a lot of _____ because of her involvement in the scandal we exposed.

   A activity
   B credibility
   C senior
   D function

**6** I was _____ by the scenes I saw in Thailand.

A vacant
B injected
C appalled
D qualified

**7** The _____ temperatures have brought further isolation and illness to older people.

A lost
B plummeting
C competitive
D market

**8** Despite their _____ hardship, they remain joyful.

A financial
B target
C watchful
D trade

**9** I don't feel comfortable _____ the subject with the professor.

A qualified
B discussing
C ejecting
D during

**10** The local council pledged to tackle the increasing burglaries and robberies in the _____.

A butcher
B attraction
C neighborhood
D duplicate

**11** Her standard _____ each year is to lose weight, and it generally fails to last beyond January.

A independence
B resolution
C paper
D hospital

PRACTICE TESTS IN VERBAL REASONING

12  The Brooklyn is a superb _____ restaurant that offers fine dining in an elegant setting at the fraction of the price you would pay elsewhere.

A  public
B  training
C  mergers
D  accurate

13  Scientists in Canada have _____ a unique beaked, plant-eating dinosaur.

A  boast
B  drudge
C  eclipse
D  discovered

14  Please be informed that every dress in our shop is truly _____ and tailored to your requirements.

A  subject
B  individual
C  sitting
D  compute

15  The scenery is very quaint and _____.

A  metallic
B  blossom
C  burrow
D  picturesque

16  The marketing expert stated that the best way of increasing product awareness in various countries is by involving local public _____ specialists.

A  friends
B  relations
C  photographs
D  intrigue

17  The valuable painting was found by chance by a local _____.

A  van
B  taxidermist
C  bravo
D  history

88

18   That shop that sells _____ jewelry is located in that village.

   A   cake
   B   exquisite
   C   tension
   D   dry

19   Nathan was _____ by the resourcefulness of the people in Banjul.

   A   central
   B   flabbergasted
   C   tense
   D   durable

20   There is a tangible sense of _____ as we are soon to go on an adventurous journey in Africa.

   A   service
   B   taste
   C   membership
   D   anticipation

21   Salt is important to human life. This is probably a reason why it appears _____ in the history of superstition.

   A   uncomfortable
   B   superb
   C   frequently
   D   heavy

22   Ola finds Doreen's myopic mentality very _____.

   A   document
   B   off-putting
   C   divorce
   D   formula

23   Craig thinks that the admission policy in that school is _____ elitist.

   A   easel
   B   brazenly
   C   fortunate
   D   disgraceful

# PRACTICE TESTS IN VERBAL REASONING

24  It is important for young married men to be better informed about _____ and be provided with tips so that they can better support their partners.

   A  dynamic
   B  fatherhood
   C  informal
   D  formation

25  The _____ that their daughter was involved in the incident horrified her parents.

   A  poster
   B  revelation
   C  instant
   D  silence

26  The research shows that most grounded and confident children grew up in happy and _____ families.

   A  club
   B  monogamous
   C  gnarled
   D  fossil

27  The future of our planet and our requirement to reduce pollution is of _____ importance.

   A  grasping
   B  foster
   C  wrinkle
   D  prime

28  Be careful because there is an _____ motive behind her actions.

   A  postman
   B  lovely
   C  twinkle
   D  ulterior

29  The _____ influx of immigrants to New Guinea was unexpected.

   A  unprecedented
   B  crumble
   C  master
   D  untidy

**30** There were some _____ claims in the report.

A obstacle
B vapor
C exaggerated
D warmth

| Record Your Progress |||||
|---|---|---|---|---|
| Number of Times You Have Taken the Test | Record ||| Record Your Completion Time |
| | Number of Questions Completed | Your Total Score | Total No. of Questions | |
| 1 | | | | |
| 2 | | | | |
| 3 | | | | |
| 4 | | | | |
| 5 | | | | |

# SAMPLE TEST 12: SIMILES

A *simile* is a figure of speech, and it is useful to understand them. Some similes are clichés, and anyone can make one up. The similes in this section are commonly used phrases. Here is a sample of a simile: as red as a beetroot. Similes are used to compare two dissimilar entities and are usually linked by *as* or *like*, just like in the example above. This type of question is not very common, but it is worth knowing these clichés. You now have the opportunity to assess your knowledge.

You are provided with the first part of commonly used similes, and you are required to provide the missing elements.

1   As beautiful as_____          The answer is *nature*.

2   As agile as a _____          The answer here is *monkey*.

3   As big as an _____           The answer is *elephant*.

Now do the test and write your answer in the space provided.

## Practice Test 29 (Answers on page 246)

Complete the following phrases by writing your answer in the space provided.

1   As proud as _____

2   As plain as _____

3   As old as _____

4   As quick as _____

5   As slippery as _____

6   As slow as _____

7   As sound as _____

8   As solid as _____

9   As thin as _____

10  As smooth as _____

11  As white as _____

12  As pure as _____

13  As sharp as _____

14  As wise as _____

15  As sour as _____

16  As tall as _____

17  As mad as _____

18  As poor as _____

19  As scarce as _____

20  As quiet as _____

21  As safe as _____

22  As timid as _____

23  As tough as _____

24  As strong as _____

25  As busy as _____

26  As calm as _____

27  As bald as _____

28  As blind as _____

29  As clear as _____

30  As deaf as _____

PRACTICE TESTS IN VERBAL REASONING

**31** As dry as _____

**32** As easy as _____

**33** As hard as _____

**34** As hungry as _____

**35** As innocent as _____

**36** As light as _____

**37** As large as _____

**38** As brave as _____

**39** As bright as _____

**40** As stubborn as _____

| Record Your Progress |||||
|---|---|---|---|---|
| Number of Times You Have Taken the Test | Record ||| Record Your Completion Time |
| | Number of Questions Completed | Your Total Score | Total No. of Questions | |
| 1 | | | | |
| 2 | | | | |
| 3 | | | | |
| 4 | | | | |
| 5 | | | | |

# SAMPLE TEST 13: COLLECTIVE NOUNS

These are nouns that stand for a group of things or animals, but they are used in many other contexts as well. These tests are to assess your knowledge of collective nouns. Examples of collective nouns are *a den of lions*, *a school of fish*, and *a flock of sheep*. These questions are not very common in verbal reasoning, but they will help to assess your knowledge of collective nouns. Now do the following practice tests.

## Practice Test 30 (Answers on page 246)

Complete the following phrases by writing your answer in the space provided.

1. a babble of _____

2. an ostentation of _____

3. an army of _____

4. an ambush of _____

5. an aurora of _____

6. a band of _____

7. a battery of _____

8. an ascension of _____

9. a barrel of _____

10. a bask of _____

11. a barn of _____

12. a bew of _____

13. a bevy of _____

14. a bike of _____

15. a bloodstock of _____

PRACTICE TESTS IN VERBAL REASONING

16. a blessing of _____

17. a chaos of _____

18. a cask of _____

19. a bunch of _____

20. a bushel of _____

21. a crackle of _____

22. a caravan of _____

23. a business of _____

24. a choir of _____

25. a chatter of _____

26. a chime of _____

27. a coalition of _____

28. a cloud of _____

29. a colony of _____

30. a colony of _____

31. a congregation of _____

32. a diligence of _____

33. a cuddle of _____

34. a dazzle of _____

35. a field of _____

36. a flamboyance of _____

PRACTICE TESTS IN VERBAL REASONING

37. a drift of _____

38. a drove of _____

39. a fever of _____

40. a flight of _____

41. an exaltation of _____

42. a flock of _____

43. a hive of _____

44. a host of _____

45. a huddle of _____

46. a litter of _____

47. a parliament of _____

48. a pride of _____

49. a school of _____

50. a shoal of _____

| Record Your Progress |||||
| --- | --- | --- | --- | --- |
| Number of Times You Have Taken the Test | Record ||| Record Your Completion Time |
| | Number of Questions Completed | Your Total Score | Total No. of Questions | |
| 1 | | | | |
| 2 | | | | |
| 3 | | | | |
| 4 | | | | |
| 5 | | | | |

PRACTICE TESTS IN VERBAL REASONING

## Practice Test 31 (Answers on page 247)

Complete the following phrases by writing your answer in the space provided.

1. a squadron of _____

2. a swarm of _____

3. a tuft of _____

4. a walk of _____

5. a board of _____

6. a yoke of _____

7. a zeal of _____

8. a zoo of _____

9. a caravan of _____

10. a company of _____

11. a crowd of _____

12. a class of _____

13. a crew of _____

14. a dynasty of _____

15. a batch of _____

16. an album of _____

17. an archipelago of _____

18. a basket of _____

19. a bouquet of _____

20. a bunch of _____

21. a block of _____

22. a bowl of _____

23. a cloud of _____

24. a bundle of _____

25. a chest of _____

26. a cloud of _____

27. a constellation of _____

28. a column of _____

29. a compendium of _____

30. a flight of _____

31. a clump of _____

32. a harvest of _____

33. a grove of _____

34. a hedge of _____

35. a fall of _____

36. a necklace of _____

37. a mass of _____

38. a list of _____

39. a library of _____

40. a heap of _____

PRACTICE TESTS IN VERBAL REASONING

41. a fleet of _____

42. a quiver of _____

43. a pencil of _____

44. a range of _____

45. a row of _____

46. an outfit of _____

47. a ream of _____

48. a suite of _____

49. a series of _____

50. a set of _____

| Record Your Progress ||||
|---|---|---|---|
| Number of Times You Have Taken the Test | Record ||| Record Your Completion Time |
| | Number of Questions Completed | Your Total Score | Total No. of Questions | |
| 1 | | | | |
| 2 | | | | |
| 3 | | | | |
| 4 | | | | |
| 5 | | | | |

# SAMPLE TEST 14: GRAMMAR (SENTENCE ERRORS)

You are required to identify the correct option in terms of spelling, grammar, and punctuation. You are then to put a tick under *Right* or *Wrong* in the space provided. Here is an example.

|  | Right | Wrong |
|---|---|---|
| Clara and me are going to the meeting. | _____ | _____ |

The answer is *Wrong* because the word *I* should be used instead of *me*. Now do the following tests.

## Practice Test 32 (Answers on page 248)

You are required to identify the correct option in terms of spelling, grammar, and punctuation. You should then put a tick under *Right* or *Wrong* in the space provided.

| | | Right | Wrong |
|---|---|---|---|
| 1 | In London, the manager don't know how operate machinery | _____ | _____ |
| 2 | Claudia, the hardresser, said it have to do | _____ | _____ |
| 3 | Goverment is looking at tougher requirements to disclose company finance. | _____ | _____ |
| 4 | The famous supermarket chain seen off their competitors take over build. | _____ | _____ |
| 5 | The planning will at its early stages at the school office. | _____ | _____ |
| 6 | Sally is considering a major inveesment that plans its UK launch. | _____ | _____ |
| 7 | She'll be a millionaire by the time she was fifty. | _____ | _____ |
| 8 | James decorated the house in a tasteful combination of colors. | _____ | _____ |
| 9 | Could you please stop interrupting me whenever I speak? | _____ | _____ |
| 10 | We will have to stop the plan because of the lack of funds. | _____ | _____ |
| 11 | It seems to me that nobody is in control of the children in that class. | _____ | _____ |
| 12 | It's time we sold our flat and bought a house. | _____ | _____ |
| 13 | The remains are said to be over a thousand years old. | _____ | _____ |
| 14 | As soon as I went into the room, I switched on the light. | _____ | _____ |
| 15 | Cherri didn't want the children to laugh at her. | _____ | _____ |

|  |  | Right | Wrong |
|---|---|---|---|
| 16 | I think you better leave now. It's getting late, and it will snow. | _____ | _____ |
| 17 | You will have to change your washing machine soon. | _____ | _____ |
| 18 | I will learn Spanish by borrowing books and tapes from my local library. | _____ | _____ |
| 19 | Jane blamed her husband's job for his ill health. | _____ | _____ |
| 20 | I mostn't forget to go on the charity walk. | _____ | _____ |
| 21 | Alicia must really stop smoking in the building. | _____ | _____ |
| 22 | Jenni said that she will feel in the enrolment form. | _____ | _____ |
| 23 | Geoff was offered that fantastic job whereas his poor qualification | _____ | _____ |
| 24 | Aimee handed in her reputation after the disagreement with her boss. | _____ | _____ |
| 25 | We need to extent the house because we require more bedrooms. | _____ | _____ |
| 26 | Dorothea is a very domesticated young lady. | _____ | _____ |
| 27 | Norma was very upset because James cheat her. | _____ | _____ |
| 28 | Cassandra is the shotest girl in the class. | _____ | _____ |
| 29 | Walk straight ahead den turn left and you should see the office block. | _____ | _____ |
| 30 | He left hiss jacket in the lavatory. | _____ | _____ |
| 31 | India was given a laptop for her eighteenth birthday. | _____ | _____ |
| 32 | The children were educated at home by there mother | _____ | _____ |
| 33 | Let us go on a tripe to Bradford. | _____ | _____ |
| 34 | Do let me know if you have any more suggestions to make. | _____ | _____ |
| 35 | Grace apologized for been inefficient. | _____ | _____ |
| 36 | How much acquaintances do you have. | _____ | _____ |
| 37 | Encourage her to be more positive, and find out why she is so pessimistic. | _____ | _____ |
| 38 | Ask the waiter to provide you with the master key. | _____ | _____ |
| 39 | Please turn the volume down because I connot hear Christopher. | _____ | _____ |
| 40 | Elsa still remembers the memorable time she spent with her cousins last summer. | _____ | _____ |

PRACTICE TESTS IN VERBAL REASONING

| Number of Times You Have Taken the Test | Record | | | Record Your Completion Time |
|---|---|---|---|---|
| | Number of Questions Completed | Your Total Score | Total No. of Questions | |
| 1 | | | | |
| 2 | | | | |
| 3 | | | | |
| 4 | | | | |
| 5 | | | | |

**Record Your Progress**

# SAMPLE TEST 15: MIXED SENTENCES

In mixed sentence tests, you are required to identify two words that have been swapped so that the sentences no longer make sense. Ensure that you always read the sentences carefully, identify the two misplaced words, and underline them. Here is an example.

Underline the words to be interchanged or the pair that correctly completes the sentence.

1. Being a doctor can be problems because some patients come to see them with their personal challenging.

Answer: The two words to be interchanged are *problems* and *challenging*.

Now attempt the following questions.

## Practice Test 33 (Answers on page 248)

1. Sticks and stones bones break my may.

2. There is a new life about the film of the famous ballet dancer

3. The credited was payment to the account.

4. A predatory is a lynx cat.

5. Those badly were treated people for doing right.

6. All the pirates galleon the Spanish invaded.

7. Carnivorous sharks are hammerhead.

8. We all amazement in watched as he won the race.

9. Don't tie your door in a revolving laces.

10. The annual is being inaugurated at the president parade.

11. Level take a chance at a never crossing.

12. I told him not to give into pressure peer when he goes.

13. Favorite is my absolute math subject.

14. Glasses opticians gave me designer the for my eyes.

15. We are attend to required lectures if we expect to pass.

16. I need help with the complicated extremely quiz.

17. The MOT really needed an Volkswagen at the mechanic.

18. Intricate is an extremely chess game.

19. Hyphenation can help with writing complicated.

20. The trip to the memorable was a zoo experience.

21. Gatwick Airport overcrowded was by late passengers.

22. A dictionary is used for finding definitions words of.

23. I know safari live in the area close to where we went on the African wildebeests.

24. Jewel is a priceless green emerald.

25. Child grotto is a Santa's friendly and fun experience.

26. Carbon is monoxide a poisonous gas.

27. Fulham against a football match played Arsenal.

28. Country is the capital city of Jamaica, a Caribbean Kingston.

29. James's birthday celebration was a success complete.

30. A parrot is an mimic bird that can intelligent speech.

PRACTICE TESTS IN VERBAL REASONING

| Record Your Progress |||||
|---|---|---|---|---|
| Number of Times You Have Taken the Test | Record ||| Record Your Completion Time |
| | Number of Questions Completed | Your Total Score | Total No. of Questions | |
| 1 | | | | |
| 2 | | | | |
| 3 | | | | |
| 4 | | | | |
| 5 | | | | |

# 3. Verbal Application

These types of questions vary significantly in format and requirement. The tests sometimes include numerical, crosswords, and word sequence, to name a few. The questions are used to assess applicants for administrative, clerical, graduate, and even managerial roles. The speed at which you correctly complete these tests is critical to your success. Each sample question will also be followed by practice tests. Remember to time yourself and continue to use the standard time-to-number of questions ratio provided in the beginning of the book to assess your performance.

## SAMPLE TEST 16: LOGICAL REASONING

This test involves letter sequences and assesses your ability to think logically and analytically. Some employers use similar tests as part of their selection procedures, and this test will give you some idea of what to expect.

A B C D E F G H I J K L M N
O P Q R S T U V W X Y Z

The alphabet above is provided to help you with the following questions. You are required to look at the sequence and work out which of the five options below is the next member of the sequence. Write your answer is the space provided.

H G ? E D          options are          a b c f l _____

The answer is *f*. This is the next letter in the sequence. This is the logical answer because the letters of the alphabet have been written in reverse order.

Now attempt the following questions.

## Practice Test 34 (Answers on page 249)

| A | B | C | D | E | F | G | H | I | J | K | L | M | N |
|---|---|---|---|---|---|---|---|---|----|----|----|----|----|
| 1 | 2 | 3 | 4 | 5 | 6 | 7 | 8 | 9 | 10 | 11 | 12 | 13 | 14 |

| O | P | Q | R | S | T | U | V | W | X | Y | Z |
|----|----|----|----|----|----|----|----|----|----|----|----|
| 15 | 16 | 17 | 18 | 19 | 20 | 21 | 22 | 23 | 24 | 25 | 26 |

# PRACTICE TESTS IN VERBAL REASONING

The alphabet above is provided to help you with the following questions. You are required to look at the sequence and work out which of the five options below is the next member of the sequence. Write your answer is the space provided.

| Question No. | Sequence | | | | | | | | OPTIONS | | | | |
|---|---|---|---|---|---|---|---|---|---|---|---|---|---|
| 1  | a | d | B | b | ? | c |   |   | a | b | c | d | e |
| 2  | c | c | D | ? | e | f | g | g h | b | c | d | e | f |
| 3  | a | z | B | ? | c | x |   |   | b | c | w | x | y |
| 4  | f | g | e | h | d | i | c | ? | a | b | j | k | l |
| 5  | r | q | p | r | q | p | ? |   | o | p | q | r | s |
| 6  | b | e | h | k | n | ? | t |   | o | p | q | r | s |
| 7  | y | e | w | g | u | i | ? |   | s | t | r | k | l |
| 8  | x | ? | p | l | h |   |   |   | r | s | q | o | t |
| 9  | c | c | d | f | i | ? |   |   | j | k | l | m | n |
| 10 | j | g | d | k | ? | e | l |   | h | f | i | m | g |
| 11 | a | b | d | h | ? |   |   |   | l | m | n | o | p |
| 12 | b | g | d | i | ? | k | h |   | j | e | c | f | g |
| 13 | a | d | i | ? |   |   |   |   | p | n | o | l | m |
| 14 | g | ? | d | i | j | d | k l | d | f | e | c | h | d |
| 15 | p | q | q | ? | s | s | t | u | r | t | s | u | q |
| 16 | g | g | k | k | o | o | ? |   | q | s | r | o | t |
| 17 | y | e | u | i | q | m | ? |   | m | n | j | k | o |
| 18 | v | s | p | w | t | q | ? |   | r | u | x | v | y |
| 19 | a | b | k | c | d | k | e | ? | f | g | k | e | h |
| 20 | q | r | k | s | t | i | u v | ? | v | y | h | x | g |
| 21 | c | j | q | x | e | ? | s |   | j | l | n | g | p |
| 22 | y | d | j | w | f | l | u | h ? | m | o | n | s | j |
| 23 | m | o | n | n | o | m | p | ? | l | p | m | n | o |
| 24 | c | d | c | d | d | d | e d | e ? | d | e | f | g | h |
| 25 | a | b | b | c | f | d | ? |   | e | f | g | h | i |
| 26 | b | c | e | g | k | ? | q | s | l | m | n | o | p |
| 27 | m | n | o | o | ? | p | p | p | r | p | q | n | o |

108

PRACTICE TESTS IN VERBAL REASONING

| Record Your Progress |||||
|---|---|---|---|---|
| Number of Times You Have Taken the Test | Record ||| Record Your Completion Time |
| | Number of Questions Completed | Your Total Score | Total No. of Questions | |
| 1 | | | | |
| 2 | | | | |
| 3 | | | | |
| 4 | | | | |
| 5 | | | | |

PRACTICE TESTS IN VERBAL REASONING

# SAMPLE TEST 17: PLACE IN ALPHABETICAL ORDER

Some tests require that you put words in alphabetical order. An example of such tests is illustrated below.

Put the following words in alphabetical order. Write the answer in the space provided.

|   A   |   B   |    C    |       |       |         |
|-------|-------|---------|-------|-------|---------|
| queen | glaze | radiator | <u>glaze</u> | <u>queen</u> | <u>radiator</u> |

The answer is *glaze*, *queen*, and *radiator*, so you write these words in the each of the space provided.

Now do the following practice tests.

## Practice Test 35 (Answers on page 249)

Put the following words in alphabetical order according to their first letter. Write your answer in the space provided.

|    | A      | B      | C       |
|----|--------|--------|---------|
| 1  | dog    | cat    | fox     |
| 2  | pig    | humane | bull    |
| 3  | place  | south  | choir   |
| 4  | scale  | lose   | vote    |
| 5  | future | center | town    |
| 6  | horrid | mean   | locust  |
| 7  | months | zenith | ghosts  |
| 8  | flood  | help   | advice  |
| 9  | reason | about  | public  |
| 10 | chart  | thump  | month   |
| 11 | order  | event  | waste   |
| 12 | earth  | text   | golden  |
| 13 | emerge | wrap   | paste   |
| 14 | view   | first  | data    |
| 15 | styles | horn   | reason  |
| 16 | lode   | king   | firm    |
| 17 | camel  | fooled | snoop   |
| 18 | loop   | pull   | lined   |
| 19 | light  | snip   | lecture |

PRACTICE TESTS IN VERBAL REASONING

|    | A       | B       | C      |          |          |          |
|----|---------|---------|--------|----------|----------|----------|
| 20 | antler  | fine    | cart   | _____ | _____ | _____ |
| 21 | jewel   | sky     | naught | _____ | _____ | _____ |
| 22 | possess | caught  | love   | _____ | _____ | _____ |
| 23 | nip     | hurt    | bite   | _____ | _____ | _____ |
| 24 | hip     | vow     | shoot  | _____ | _____ | _____ |
| 25 | short   | regular | long   | _____ | _____ | _____ |
| 26 | cry     | sweat   | heat   | _____ | _____ | _____ |
| 27 | struck  | dumb    | pole   | _____ | _____ | _____ |
| 28 | greet   | hello   | arise  | _____ | _____ | _____ |
| 29 | stomp   | car     | call   | _____ | _____ | _____ |
| 30 | lovely  | fast    | homely | _____ | _____ | _____ |

| | Record Your Progress ||||
|---|---|---|---|---|
| Number of Times You Have Taken the Test | Record ||| Record Your Completion Time |
| | Number of Questions Completed | Your Total Score | Total No. of Questions | |
| 1 | | | | |
| 2 | | | | |
| 3 | | | | |
| 4 | | | | |
| 5 | | | | |

## Practice Test 36 (Answers on page 249)

Put the following words in alphabetical order according to their first letter. Write your answer in the space provided.

|   | A      | B       | C      |          |          |          |
|---|--------|---------|--------|----------|----------|----------|
| 1 | liquid | rainbow | den    | _____ | _____ | _____ |
| 2 | poem   | child   | story  | _____ | _____ | _____ |
| 3 | enjoy  | whale   | little | _____ | _____ | _____ |
| 4 | ark    | sleep   | night  | _____ | _____ | _____ |
| 5 | soft   | drowsy  | angel  | _____ | _____ | _____ |
| 6 | peace  | gentle  | creep  | _____ | _____ | _____ |

PRACTICE TESTS IN VERBAL REASONING

| | | | | | | |
|---|---|---|---|---|---|---|
| 7 | delight | breath | attend | _____ | _____ | _____ |
| 8 | guardian | daily | leave | _____ | _____ | _____ |
| 9 | teach | grow | goodness | _____ | _____ | _____ |
| 10 | dust | life | friend | _____ | _____ | _____ |
| 11 | poor | hear | ways | _____ | _____ | _____ |
| 12 | eyes | part | feet | _____ | _____ | _____ |
| 13 | mountain | hill | trees | _____ | _____ | _____ |
| 14 | bless | thank | arise | _____ | _____ | _____ |
| 15 | words | accept | divide | _____ | _____ | _____ |
| 16 | match | copy | north | _____ | _____ | _____ |
| 17 | publish | quote | whole | _____ | _____ | _____ |
| 18 | radio | video | television | _____ | _____ | _____ |
| 19 | permit | write | reserve | _____ | _____ | _____ |
| 20 | adapt | draw | cubic | _____ | _____ | _____ |
| 21 | trademark | commerce | purpose | _____ | _____ | _____ |
| 22 | electric | verbal | remember | _____ | _____ | _____ |
| 23 | involve | divulge | union | _____ | _____ | _____ |
| 24 | quest | international | piano | _____ | _____ | _____ |
| 25 | keyboard | string | floor | _____ | _____ | _____ |
| 26 | base | stair | bath | _____ | _____ | _____ |
| 27 | violin | lamp | bag | _____ | _____ | _____ |
| 28 | sack | trunk | abide | _____ | _____ | _____ |
| 29 | log | keep | jacket | _____ | _____ | _____ |
| 30 | hair | tickle | pencil | _____ | _____ | _____ |

| Record Your Progress |||||
|---|---|---|---|---|
| Number of Times You Have Taken the Test | Record ||| Record Your Completion Time |
| | Number of Questions Completed | Your Total Score | Total No. of Questions | |
| 1 | | | | |
| 2 | | | | |
| 3 | | | | |
| 4 | | | | |
| 5 | | | | |

PRACTICE TESTS IN VERBAL REASONING

# SAMPLE TEST 18: ALPHABETICAL POSITION OF WORDS

If the words in the following questions were arranged in alphabetical order, then which one would be

|   | | A | B | C | D | Answer |
|---|---|---|---|---|---|---|
| 1. | first? | bounce | ace | onion | apple | B |
| 2. | third? | cream | crisp | camp | cliff | A |

Write your answer in the space provided as in the example above.

Now attempt the following questions.

## Practice Test 37 (Answers on page 250)

If the words in the following questions were arranged in alphabetical order, then which one would be

| | | A | B | C | D | |
|---|---|---|---|---|---|---|
| 1 | third? | ball | mouse | bell | chimney | _____ |
| 2 | first? | dog | whistle | toy | train | _____ |
| 3 | fourth? | wall | cat | pipe | string | _____ |
| 4 | second? | mat | ribbon | needle | chair | _____ |
| 5 | second? | water | jar | toaster | tap | _____ |
| 6 | fourth? | boat | cord | vehicle | deck | _____ |
| 7 | first? | kettle | mist | oar | bin | _____ |
| 8 | third? | machine | squeeze | push | wash | _____ |
| 9 | second? | octopus | smooth | office | sash | _____ |
| 10 | third? | suit | plane | sail | tough | _____ |
| 11 | second? | tug | whale | sky | salt | _____ |
| 12 | fourth? | cake | ship | hill | smooth | _____ |
| 13 | first? | caress | wine | sea | weigh | _____ |
| 14 | third? | helicopter | lid | single | eat | _____ |
| 15 | second? | shower | pull | color | bird | _____ |
| 16 | third? | balloon | ocean | tank | hair | _____ |
| 17 | third? | fuel | ear | vegetable | bag | _____ |
| 18 | first? | steel | bake | lift | shark | _____ |

113

## PRACTICE TESTS IN VERBAL REASONING

|    |         | A             | B           | C          | D         |      |
|----|---------|---------------|-------------|------------|-----------|------|
| 19 | fourth? | system        | slipstream  | glove      | tie       | _____ |
| 20 | second? | spoon         | pulse       | jet        | scarf     | _____ |
| 21 | second? | coat          | nose        | boiler     | tea       | _____ |
| 22 | third?  | valley        | car         | double     | river     | _____ |
| 23 | first?  | luggage       | thermal     | mouth      | quilt     | _____ |
| 24 | fourth? | plastic       | sugar       | mountain   | air       | _____ |
| 25 | second? | fruit         | soup        | petrol     | hat       | _____ |
| 26 | third?  | fleece        | youth       | steal      | flask     | _____ |
| 27 | second? | glider        | boots       | handle     | sheep     | _____ |
| 28 | fourth? | ceramic       | dry cleaner | silver     | box       | _____ |
| 29 | first?  | jacket        | triple      | airplane   | salon     | _____ |
| 30 | third?  | ruby          | beautician  | crockery   | fish      | _____ |
| 31 | second? | fur           | dingy       | coffee     | feet      | _____ |
| 32 | third?  | jewelry       | property    | frame      | bowl      | _____ |
| 33 | first?  | goat          | land        | skin       | diamond   | _____ |
| 34 | fourth? | milk          | copper      | lipstick   | hen       | _____ |
| 35 | second? | earring       | pool        | strawberry | paint     | _____ |
| 36 | first?  | cosmetic      | mobile      | outdoor    | lost      | _____ |
| 37 | fourth? | raincoat      | gold        | bed        | pear      | _____ |
| 38 | first?  | house         | quill       | dam        | silk      | _____ |
| 39 | second? | black currant | swim        | cotton     | rings     | _____ |
| 40 | third?  | surface       | door        | storage    | lecturer  | _____ |
| 41 | first?  | pearl         | duster      | walk       | energy    | _____ |
| 42 | fourth? | pillow        | ravine      | flat       | fowl      | _____ |
| 43 | second? | eggs          | jog         | sapphire   | idea      | _____ |
| 44 | first?  | apartment     | apple       | power      | wire      | _____ |
| 45 | third?  | telephone     | turquoise   | launderette| dream     | _____ |
| 46 | fourth? | feather       | garden      | white      | dumpling  | _____ |
| 47 | first?  | lace          | teacher     | eye        | knife     | _____ |
| 48 | second? | socks         | trousers    | taste      | hope      | _____ |
| 49 | third?  | entrance      | yogurt      | skeleton   | chocolate | _____ |
| 50 | first?  | fork          | red         | scent      | wish      | _____ |

# PRACTICE TESTS IN VERBAL REASONING

| Number of Times You Have Taken the Test | Record |||| Record Your Completion Time |
|---|---|---|---|---|---|
| | Number of Questions Completed | Your Total Score | Total No. of Questions | | |
| 1 | | | | | |
| 2 | | | | | |
| 3 | | | | | |
| 4 | | | | | |
| 5 | | | | | |

## Practice Test 38 (Answers on page 250)

If the words in the following questions were arranged in alphabetical order, then which one would be

| | | A | B | C | D | |
|---|---|---|---|---|---|---|
| 1 | fourth? | laundry | lavender | chicken | lever | |
| 2 | second? | veil | same | sunset | feel | |
| 3 | first? | art | button | direct | dirt | |
| 4 | fourth? | run | rough | store | black | |
| 5 | second? | flower | shirt | arch | shed | |
| 6 | first? | ditch | sun | boss | view | |
| 7 | third? | money | sportswear | amend | pupil | |
| 8 | fourth? | client | star | horse | head | |
| 9 | first? | pants | purple | administrator | uncle | |
| 10 | second? | moon | team | blouse | amber | |
| 11 | third? | rose | spine | supervisor | mansion | |
| 12 | first? | mud | son | lawyer | donor | |
| 13 | fourth? | channel | trainers | trench | mother | |
| 14 | second? | associate | country | skirt | police | |
| 15 | first? | linen | pig | daughter | vest | |
| 16 | third? | chief | accountant | animal | estate | |
| 17 | second? | peach | grandmother | grocer | partner | |
| 18 | third? | touch | T-shirt | business | manuscript | |

## PRACTICE TESTS IN VERBAL REASONING

|    |         | A         | B          | C          | D          |
|----|---------|-----------|------------|------------|------------|
| 19 | first?  | aunt      | officer    | deputy     | waterway   |
| 20 | fourth? | butcher   | smell      | den        | manner     |
| 21 | second? | executive | tongue     | polite     | cover      |
| 22 | first?  | donkey    | military   | lantern    | spectator  |
| 23 | fourth? | father    | fields     | utensil    | Vatican    |
| 24 | first?  | respect   | cash       | drain      | baker      |
| 25 | second? | tomato    | velvet     | vapor      | bicycle    |
| 26 | third?  | tricycle  | judge      | motorcycle | raspberry  |
| 27 | first?  | van       | cousin     | costume    | patrol     |
| 28 | fourth? | artist    | project    | rat        | patient    |
| 29 | second? | authority | cranberry  | atmosphere | nephew     |
| 30 | first?  | constable | butter     | lorry      | peal       |
| 31 | third?  | party     | painter    | gas        | broom      |
| 32 | fourth? | trough    | soldier    | solicitor  | pebble     |
| 33 | first?  | pet       | student    | pouch      | truck      |
| 34 | second? | hospital  | credit     | assignment | butler     |
| 35 | third?  | manor     | professor  | granite    | publication|
| 36 | second? | trolley   | stone      | government | sauce      |
| 37 | third?  | manager   | kennel     | economy    | pub        |
| 38 | second? | swimsuit  | marble     | shovel     | analyst    |
| 39 | fourth? | niece     | electricity| rock       | palace     |
| 40 | first?  | astronaut | gully      | puzzle     | pyramid    |
| 41 | third?  | market    | town       | purse      | bank       |
| 42 | second? | dustpan   | grandfather| spend      | evening    |
| 43 | third?  | peel      | laugh      | earth      | garage     |
| 44 | first?  | survey    | pajamas    | parrot     | restaurant |
| 45 | fourth? | shopping  | sand       | circus     | wind       |
| 46 | second? | slate     | table      | beach      | cage       |
| 47 | second? | public    | save       | salt       | galaxy     |
| 48 | third?  | bike      | hamster    | holiday    | country    |
| 49 | first?  | wallet    | morning    | planet     | artisan    |
| 50 | fourth? | resource  | crockery   | puddle     | glimmer    |

| Record Your Progress |||||
|---|---|---|---|---|
| Number of Times You Have Taken the Test | Record ||| Record Your Completion Time |
| | Number of Questions Completed | Your Total Score | Total No. of Questions | |
| 1 | | | | |
| 2 | | | | |
| 3 | | | | |
| 4 | | | | |
| 5 | | | | |

# PRACTICE TESTS IN VERBAL REASONING

## SAMPLE TEST 19: WORD PYRAMID

Word pyramids are also not common. The test focuses on your speed of comprehension and deduction. All these elements are essential and should be worked upon. You will be provided with the a six-letter word and its definition, and you are required to find the other five-, four-, three-, two-, and one-letter words that will complete the pyramid. Write your answer in the pyramid. Here is an example.

| i | the middle part of something | c e n t e r |
| ii | to go in or come in | e n t e r |
| iii | money you pay to someone for staying in their house | r e n t |
| iv | another word for the Internet | n e t |
| v | an alien in a Steven Spielberg film | e t |
| vi | the letter after S in the alphabet | t |

Now attempt the following questions.

### Practice Test 39 (Answers on page 251)

**CLUE**

1
| i | someone who manages a group of people | l e a d e r |
| ii | an older person | _ _ _ _ _ |
| iii | a kind of grass that grows in wet places | _ _ _ _ |
| iv | the color of blood | _ _ _ |
| v | the abbreviation for a medical professional | _ _ |
| vi | the letter after Q in the alphabet | _ |

**CLUE**

2
| i | when the police takes someone prisoner | a r r e s t |
| ii | to look at someone for a long time | _ _ _ _ _ |
| iii | a place where you sit, such as a chair | _ _ _ _ |
| iv | a very big area of water with land around most of it | _ _ _ |
| v | used when comparing things | _ _ |
| vi | the letter before T in the alphabet | _ |

PRACTICE TESTS IN VERBAL REASONING

**CLUE**

| 3 | i | a part of a pattern with different colored lines | s t r i p e |
|---|---|---|---|
|   | ii | to take off ones clothes | _ _ _ _ _ |
|   | iii | to eject saliva from the mouth | _ _ _ _ |
|   | iv | to rest your buttocks on an object | _ _ _ |
|   | v | used to describe an object | _ _ |
|   | vi | the letter after *H* in the alphabet | _ |

**CLUE**

| 4 | i | not fully | p a r t l y |
|---|---|---|---|
|   | ii | a celebration | _ _ _ _ _ |
|   | iii | a piece of something | _ _ _ _ |
|   | iv | substance formed by burning tobacco | _ _ _ |
|   | v | to express one's position in a place or time of day | _ _ |
|   | vi | the letter six before *Z* in the alphabet | _ |

**CLUE**

| 5 | i | a long open trough in a stable for horses to eat from | m a n g e r |
|---|---|---|---|
|   | ii | a line or tier of a series of things | _ _ _ _ _ |
|   | iii | by or close to | _ _ _ _ |
|   | iv | an organ of hearing in man or some animals | _ _ _ |
|   | v | abbreviation for regarding | _ _ |
|   | vi | the letter after *D* in the alphabet | _ |

| Record Your Progress ||||
|---|---|---|---|---|
| Number of Times You Have Taken the Test | Record ||| Record Your Completion Time |
| | Number of Questions Completed | Your Total Score | Total No. of Questions | |
| 1 | | | | |
| 2 | | | | |
| 3 | | | | |
| 4 | | | | |
| 5 | | | | |

# Practice Test 40 (Answers on page 251)

**CLUE**

1. 
   i. any of the bodies moving around the sun — <u>p</u> <u>l</u> <u>a</u> <u>n</u> <u>e</u> <u>t</u>
   ii. a way to get from place to place by air — _ _ _ _ _
   iii. a narrow road or track — _ _ _ _
   iv. beer — _ _ _
   v. the last two letters of the fourth answer — _ _
   vi. the twelfth letter of the alphabet — _

**CLUE**

2. 
   i. a mythical monster — <u>d</u> <u>r</u> <u>a</u> <u>g</u> <u>o</u> <u>n</u>
   ii. a creaking noise expressing pain or grief — _ _ _ _ _
   iii. a female name — _ _ _ _
   iv. a pole with a flat blade to propel a boat — _ _ _
   v. a conjunction meaning "as an alternative" — _ _
   vi. letter after Q in the alphabet — _

**CLUE**

3. 
   i. formal, not smiling or cheerful — <u>s</u> <u>o</u> <u>l</u> <u>e</u> <u>m</u> <u>n</u>
   ii. an oval fruit with sour juice — _ _ _ _ _
   iii. a man's name, "Christmas" in French — _ _ _ _
   iv. sign of the zodiac — _ _ _
   v. last two letters of the word *one* — _ _
   vi. fifth letter of the alphabet — _

**CLUE**

4. 
   i. plural of *grain* — <u>g</u> <u>r</u> <u>a</u> <u>i</u> <u>n</u> <u>s</u>
   ii. small hard seed of rice or wheat — _ _ _ _ _
   iii. past tense of *ring* — _ _ _ _
   iv. to make scolding remarks — _ _ _
   v. used before vowel sounds instead of *a* — _ _
   vi. letter after M in the alphabet — _

PRACTICE TESTS IN VERBAL REASONING

**CLUE**

5  i   a style of West Indian music    r e g g a e
   ii  enthusiastic, full of strong desire    _ _ _ _ _
   iii violent anger    _ _ _ _
   iv  the length of time a person has lived    _ _ _ _
   v   first two letters of second answer    _ _
   vi  fifth letter in the alphabet    _

| Record Your Progress |||||
|---|---|---|---|---|
| Number of Times You Have Taken the Test | Record ||| Record Your Completion Time |
|  | Number of Questions Completed | Your Total Score | Total No. of Questions |  |
| 1 |  |  |  |  |
| 2 |  |  |  |  |
| 3 |  |  |  |  |
| 4 |  |  |  |  |
| 5 |  |  |  |  |

## Practice Test 41 (Answers on page 251)

**CLUE**

1  i   to become free from confinement    e s c a p e
   ii  cloak    _ _ _ _ _
   iii green vegetables with seeds in a pod    _ _ _ _
   iv  very large expanse of water that surrounds continents    _ _ _
   v   a slang for *father*    _ _
   vi  first letter in the alphabet    _

**CLUE**

2  i   an piece of land surrounded by water    i s l a n d
   ii  the participal form of *slay*    _ _ _ _ _
   iii a claw or talon    _ _ _ _
   iv  nothing    _ _ _
   v   to be    _ _
   vi  the ninth letter in the alphabet    _

# PRACTICE TESTS IN VERBAL REASONING

**CLUE**

3
- i   physically powerful — s t r o n g
- ii  sound made to express disgust — _ _ _ _ _
- iii past tense of *tear* — _ _ _ _
- iv  conjunction for *and not* — _ _ _
- v   a word used as a refusal of something — _ _
- vi  the last letter in the word *yo-yo* — _

**CLUE**

4
- i   movable, not fixed — m o b i l e
- ii  a kind of West Indian dance — _ _ _ _ _
- iii abbreviation of *limousine* — _ _ _ _
- iv  a slippery liquid, petroleum — _ _ _
- v   the first two letters of the word *low* — _ _
- vi  the sixth letter in the word *petroleum* — _

**CLUE**

5
- i   to feel sorry for something — r e g r e t
- ii  an address to welcome someone on arrival — _ _ _ _ _
- iii a perennial plant with a single stem — _ _ _ _
- iv  a small peg in golf where the ball is placed — _ _ _
- v   the vowels in the word *teen* — _ _
- vi  fourth letter in the word *calendar* — _

| Record Your Progress |||||
|---|---|---|---|---|
| Number of Times You Have Taken the Test | Record ||| Record Your Completion Time |
| | Number of Questions Completed | Your Total Score | Total No. of Questions | |
| 1 | | | | |
| 2 | | | | |
| 3 | | | | |
| 4 | | | | |
| 5 | | | | |

# Practice Test 42 (Answers on page 252)

**CLUE**

1. 
   i. to be in insufficient supply — <u>s</u> <u>c</u> <u>a</u> <u>r</u> <u>c</u> <u>e</u>
   ii. to frighten — _ _ _ _ _
   iii. a feel affection or liking — _ _ _ _
   iv. an automobile — _ _ _
   v. the musical note after do and before mi — _ _
   vi. the letter before *S* in the alphabet — _

**CLUE**

2. 
   i. a system of government — <u>r</u> <u>e</u> <u>g</u> <u>i</u> <u>m</u> <u>e</u>
   ii. dust, dirt, or soot ingrained in a surface — _ _ _ _ _
   iii. stern in appearance — _ _ _ _
   iv. the outer edge of something circular — _ _ _
   v. abbreviation of *mister* — _ _
   vi. thirteenth letter in the alphabet — _

**CLUE**

3. 
   i. a response to a question — <u>a</u> <u>n</u> <u>s</u> <u>w</u> <u>e</u> <u>r</u>
   ii. to state an oath — _ _ _ _ _
   iii. to put clothes on — _ _ _ _
   iv. uncooked — _ _ _
   v. fourth and last letters of third answer — _ _
   vi. the letter before *X* in the alphabet — _

**CLUE**

4. 
   i. a human being — <u>p</u> <u>e</u> <u>r</u> <u>s</u> <u>o</u> <u>n</u>
   ii. spoken language not in verse form — _ _ _ _ _
   iii. tiny opening on an animal's skin — _ _ _ _
   iv. synonym for *apiece* — _ _ _
   v. first and last letters of the word *rip* — _ _
   vi. sixteenth letter of the alphabet — _

PRACTICE TESTS IN VERBAL REASONING

**CLUE**

**5**  i   a fourteen-lined rhyming poem     <u>s</u>   <u>o</u>   <u>n</u>   <u>n</u>   <u>e</u>   <u>t</u>
   ii  short comments or a passage in a book    _ _ _ _ _
   iii a musical or vocal sound    _ _ _ _
   iv the first positive whole number after zero    _ _ _
   v  the opposite of *yes*    _ _
   vi the letter after *M* in the alphabet    _

| Record Your Progress ||||
|---|---|---|---|---|
| Number of Times You Have Taken the Test | Record ||| Record Your Completion Time |
| | Number of Questions Completed | Your Total Score | Total No. of Questions | |
| 1 | | | | |
| 2 | | | | |
| 3 | | | | |
| 4 | | | | |
| 5 | | | | |

PRACTICE TESTS IN VERBAL REASONING

# SAMPLE TEST 20: LETTER SEQUENCE

ABCDEFGHIJKLMN
OPQRSTUVWXYZ

You have been provided with the letters of the alphabet above to assist you with this question. You are required to find the next pair of letters in the series and write it in the brackets provided.

AZ BY DW (?)

The answer is *EV*. Write *EV* in the space provided.

Now attempt this test.

## Practice Test 43 (Answers on page 252)

ABCDEFGHIJKLMN
OPQRSTUVWXYZ

The alphabet has been written above to help you answer the following questions. Find the next pair of letters to complete the sequence.

| | | | | |
|---|---|---|---|---|
| 1 | LM | PQ | TU | _____ |
| 2 | OM | KI | GE | _____ |
| 3 | DE | KL | RS | _____ |
| 4 | EA | JF | OK | _____ |
| 5 | AZ | BY | CX | _____ |
| 6 | FH | IK | LN | _____ |
| 7 | CA | ZX | FD | _____ |
| 8 | DE | IJ | NO | _____ |
| 9 | FA | KF | PK | _____ |
| 10 | AC | CF | FJ | _____ |
| 11 | XW | UT | PQ | _____ |
| 12 | BA | ED | HG | _____ |
| 13 | BY | CX | DW | _____ |
| 14 | ZA | YB | XC | _____ |
| 15 | KL | NO | QR | _____ |
| 16 | FA | GB | HC | _____ |

## PRACTICE TESTS IN VERBAL REASONING

| 17 | OA | NB | MC | _____ |
|---|---|---|---|---|
| 18 | LQ | MR | NS | _____ |
| 19 | TH | UI | VJ | _____ |
| 20 | BA | DC | FE | _____ |

| Number of Times You Have Taken the Test | Record Your Progress ||| Record Your Completion Time |
|---|---|---|---|---|
| | Number of Questions Completed | Your Total Score | Total No. of Questions | |
| 1 | | | | |
| 2 | | | | |
| 3 | | | | |
| 4 | | | | |
| 5 | | | | |

PRACTICE TESTS IN VERBAL REASONING

## SAMPLE TEST 21: NUMBER SEQUENCE

Find the two missing numbers in the following sequence.

1  3  5  7  ?  ?

The answer is 9 and 11 because the numbers increase each time by 2.

Now answer the following questions.

## Practice Test 44 (Answers on page 252)

Find the two missing numbers in the following sequence. Write your answer in the space provided.

| | | | | | | | |
|---|---|---|---|---|---|---|---|
| 1 | 2 | 4 | 6 | 8 | ____ | ____ | |
| 2 | 5 | ____ | ____ | 20 | 25 | 30 | |
| 3 | 40 | 47 | ____ | ____ | 68 | 75 | |
| 4 | ____ | 12 | 24 | ____ | 96 | 192 | |
| 5 | 8 | 16 | ____ | 32 | ____ | 48 | |
| 6 | 13 | 21 | 29 | ____ | 45 | ____ | |
| 7 | 72 | ____ | 64 | ____ | 56 | 52 | |
| 8 | 14 | 15 | ____ | 20 | 24 | ____ | |
| 9 | 99 | 91 | ____ | 75 | ____ | 60 | |
| 10 | 51 | 56 | 62 | ____ | ____ | 86 | |
| 11 | 17 | ____ | 36 | 47 | 59 | ____ | |
| 12 | 44 | ____ | 51 | 56 | ____ | 69 | |
| 13 | 23 | 21 | ____ | 14 | ____ | 3 | |
| 14 | 8 | ____ | 22 | ____ | 36 | 45 | |
| 15 | 87 | ____ | 79 | 75 | ____ | 67 | |
| 16 | 46 | 37 | ____ | 19 | 10 | ____ | |
| 17 | 0 | 2 | 5 | ____ | ____ | 20 | |
| 18 | 71 | 73 | ____ | 80 | ____ | 91 | |
| 19 | 12 | 19 | ____ | ____ | 46 | 57 | |
| 20 | 46 | 42 | 38 | ____ | 30 | ____ | |

PRACTICE TESTS IN VERBAL REASONING

| Number of Times You Have Taken the Test | Record ||| Record Your Completion Time |
|---|---|---|---|---|
| | Number of Questions Completed | Your Total Score | Total No. of Questions | |
| 1 | | | | |
| 2 | | | | |
| 3 | | | | |
| 4 | | | | |
| 5 | | | | |

PRACTICE TESTS IN VERBAL REASONING

## SAMPLE TEST 22: CHECKING

Some verbal reasoning tests measure speed, accuracy, and how you deal with information.

The aim of this test is to measure speed and accuracy. You are required to find the two codes that are the same in each line. Mark the letters of the two words in the space provided.

| A | B | C | D | E | | |
|---|---|---|---|---|---|---|
| SMDOQ | SDQMO | SODMQ | SMDOQ | SMQOD | A | D |

The answer is *A* and *D*.

## Practice Test 45 (Answers on page 253)
Find two codes which are the same in each line, and write the letters of the two codes in the boxes provided.

|   | A | B | C | D | E | | |
|---|---|---|---|---|---|---|---|
| 1 | ABJMLQ | AJBMMLQ | BMLQAJ | ABJMLQ | AJBMQL | | |
| 2 | HRFYIG | HFRGYI | HIGFRY | FHIFRY | HFRGYI | | |
| 3 | CQKEX | CKEXQ | CQKEX | CKKXOE | CKMQY | | |
| 4 | 8563401 | 8764013 | 8564031 | 8561034 | 8563401 | | |
| 5 | 651042 | 615042 | 604215 | 615042 | 642150 | | |
| 6 | QCEWAP | CEWAPQ | QCEWAP | ECWAPQ | CAWPQE | | |
| 7 | ZQDJEP | ZDQJPE | JPZQPE | ZDPJQE | ZDQJPE | | |
| 8 | 7630123 | 7360123 | 7630123 | 7363201 | 7336012 | | |
| 9 | ZXSGAH | XZSHAG | ZXGSHA | XZSHAG | SHAZXG | | |

PRACTICE TESTS IN VERBAL REASONING

|    | A | B | C | D | E |   |   |
|----|---|---|---|---|---|---|---|
| 10 | 4503291 | 4532091 | 4051329 | 4520913 | 4051329 | | |
| 11 | YUTERWMB | UYERTMWB | YETURMWB | TERYUBMW | YUTERWMB | | |
| 12 | RCQGOAV | RGCQOVA | RGCVQOA | RVCQGOA | RGCVQOA | | |
| 13 | 653476 | 654376 | 654673 | 654376 | 656374 | | |
| 14 | YVXZQOP | YXVZQOP | YVXZQOP | YXVZOQP | YXZVOQP | | |
| 15 | BBKLIAG | BBKLIGA | BBLKIGA | BBKLGIA | BBKLIGA | | |
| 16 | JKKRTLIQ | JKRKTLIQ | JKKRTILQ | JKKQTLIR | JKKRTLIQ | | |
| 17 | 456578 | 455678 | 455687 | 455678 | 458675 | | |
| 18 | 234432 | 234423 | 234432 | 234342 | 243432 | | |
| 19 | 77688645 | 77688465 | 77688456 | 77688465 | 77688546 | | |
| 20 | DEFRQWOP | DFERQWOP | DEFRWQOP | DFEQRWOP | DFERQWOP | | |
| 21 | VGBLOIAP | VBGLOIAP | VBGLOIAP | VBLGOIAP | VBGLIOAP | | |
| 22 | 5690232 | 5690322 | 5960232 | 5690322 | 5692230 | | |
| 23 | WRD543 | WDR543 | WRD354 | WDR543 | WRD345 | | |
| 24 | 24356123 | 23456123 | 24356132 | 24351632 | 23456123 | | |
| 25 | DSERMQO | DSERQMO | DSREMQO | DSRMEQO | DSERQMO | | |
| 26 | DCNEM | DNCEM | DCNME | DNCEM | DNECM | | |
| 27 | RSBTTNZ | RBSTTNZ | RBSTTZN | RBSTTNZ | RSBTTZN | | |

PRACTICE TESTS IN VERBAL REASONING

|    | A | B | C | D | E |   |   |
|----|---|---|---|---|---|---|---|
| 28 | TAHCHEE | THACHEE | TAHHCEE | TAHCHEE | THACEHE | | |
| 29 | QQPTURR | QPTRRUQ | QPTRRQU | QQTPURR | QQPTURR | | |
| 30 | YKISHWI | YIKSHWI | YIKSWHI | YKISHWI | YISKWHI | | |
| 31 | 6938396 | 6398396 | 6938369 | 6393896 | 6398396 | | |
| 32 | 389655 | 398655 | 389565 | 398655 | 396855 | | |
| 33 | AFJYRMJ | AJFYRMJ | AJFYRJM | AFJRYMJ | AFJYRMJ | | |
| 34 | KHDGFT | KGHDTF | KHGDFT | KGHDFT | KHGDFT | | |
| 35 | SFDDFG | SDFDFG | SFDDGF | SDFDFG | SDFDGF | | |
| 36 | MJKFGSIO | MKJFGSIO | MJKFGSIO | MKJFGISO | MJFKGSIO | | |
| 38 | 6867456 | 6687456 | 6864756 | 6687456 | 6846756 | | |
| 39 | 38706 | 37806 | 38706 | 37860 | 38760 | | |
| 40 | INDPN | INDNP | IDNNP | INDNP | IPNND | | |
| 41 | GXMNLO | GMXNLO | GXMNOL | GXNMOL | GMXNLO | | |
| 42 | OPKSK | OKPSK | OPKSK | OKPKS | OPSKK | | |
| 43 | ASKJH | AKSJH | AKSHJ | AKHSJ | ASKJH | | |
| 44 | VHLISJ | VLHISJ | VHLIJS | VLHISJ | VLHIJS | | |
| 45 | XUYIUE | XYUIUE | XUYIUE | XYUIEU | XUYIEU | | |
| 46 | 75689 | 75698 | 76598 | 75896 | 76598 | | |

## PRACTICE TESTS IN VERBAL REASONING

|    | A       | B       | C       | D       | E       |   |   |
|----|---------|---------|---------|---------|---------|---|---|
| 47 | 351494  | 315494  | 351449  | 315449  | 315494  |   |   |
| 48 | 8723604 | 8273604 | 8723604 | 8273640 | 8723640 |   |   |
| 49 | THISOI  | TIHSOI  | THISIO  | TIHSOI  | TIHSIO  |   |   |
| 50 | JSYGD   | JYSGD   | JSYGD   | JYSDG   | JSYDG   |   |   |

| Record Your Progress ||||| 
|---|---|---|---|---|
| Number of Times You Have Taken the Test | Record ||| Record Your Completion Time |
|  | Number of Questions Completed | Your Total Score | Total No. of Questions |  |
| 1 |  |  |  |  |
| 2 |  |  |  |  |
| 3 |  |  |  |  |
| 4 |  |  |  |  |
| 5 |  |  |  |  |

PRACTICE TESTS IN VERBAL REASONING

## SAMPLE TEST 23: CODE

If the code for *Candy* is £$%!+, what is the code for Andy? _____

Write your answer in the space provided.

The answer is $%!+.

**Practice Test 46 (Answers on page 254)**

You are required to work out the different code for each question. Choose the correct answer and mark it on the answer sheet.

If the code for *multidimensional* is

\   #   &   $   @   %   @   \   ?   £   ]   @   ^   £   !   &

write the code for the following words in the space provided.

| | | |
|---|---|---|
| 1 | dental | _____ |
| 2 | taunt | _____ |
| 3 | mental | _____ |
| 4 | timid | _____ |
| 5 | men | _____ |
| 6 | emotion | _____ |
| 7 | tidal | _____ |
| 8 | dime | _____ |
| 9 | limit | _____ |
| 10 | tide | _____ |
| 11 | medal | _____ |
| 12 | ultimate | _____ |
| 13 | monument | _____ |
| 14 | dame | _____ |
| 15 | mention | _____ |
| 16 | moat | _____ |
| 17 | out | _____ |
| 18 | limitation | _____ |

PRACTICE TESTS IN VERBAL REASONING

19 mule  _____
20 mental _____
21 date _____
22 imminent _____
23 ale _____
24 dimension _____
25 mansion _____
26 allude _____
27 motion _____
28 dominate _____
29 stem _____
30 stile _____

| Record Your Progress |||||
|---|---|---|---|---|
| Number of Times You Have Taken the Test | Record ||| Record Your Completion Time |
|  | Number of Questions Completed | Your Total Score | Total No. of Questions |  |
| 1 |  |  |  |  |
| 2 |  |  |  |  |
| 3 |  |  |  |  |
| 4 |  |  |  |  |
| 5 |  |  |  |  |

# SAMPLE TEST 24: ALGEBRA

The alphabet is here to help you with the questions.

    1   A = 33, B = 150, C = 111, D = 3, E = 28       [(E + A) × D] − B

The answer is *A*, so write *A* in the space provided.

Now answer the following questions.

## Practice Test 47 (Answers on page 254)

1. If A = 45, B = 2, C = 146, D = 7, E = 21,    what is    E + A + D × B    ___
2. If A = 200, B = 100, C = 25, D = 125, E = 75,    what is    B + D − C    ___
3. If A = 10, B = 4, C = 2, D = 15, E = 52,    what is    (A − C + E) ÷ B    ___
4. If A = 15, B = 702, C = 68, D = 7, E = 61,    what is    A + C − D − E    ___
5. If A = 5, B = 10, C = 85, D = 3, E = 45,    what is    (C − B) ÷ A × D    ___
6. If A = 2, B = 55, C = 11, D = 10, E = 3,    what is    D ÷ A × C    ___
7. If A = 39, B = 99, C = 12, D = 3, E = 6,    what is    (B + E + C) ÷ D    ___
8. If A = 36, B = 12, C = 30, D = 18, E = 29,    what is    (A + B) − C    ___
9. If A = 5, B = 3, C = 9, D = 19, E = 8,    what is    D + E ÷ B    ___
10. If A = 26, B = 9, C = 4, D = 60, E = 8,    what is    (A ÷ E × C) − B    ___
11. If A = 12, B = 144, C = 5, D = 2, E = 50,    what is    (B ÷ A − D) × C    ___
12. If A = 178, B = 2, C = 44, D = 20, E = 67,    what is    (C + E) × B − A    ___
13. If A = 35, B = 19, C = 68, D = 15, E = 48,    what is    C − A + D    ___
14. If A = 13, B = 79, C = 86, D = 14, E = 90,    what is    (D × A) − E − B    ___
15. If A = 47, B = 10, C = 78, D = 6, E = 53,    what is    (C ÷ D + A) ÷ B    ___
16. If A = 180, B = 57, C = 3, D = 94, E = 22,    what is    (B + A ÷ C) − E    ___
17. If A = 11, B = 26, C = 13, D = 53, E = 29,    what is    E − C + B + A    ___
18. If A = 7, B = 34, C = 22, D = 8, E = 19,    what is    C + B ÷ A    ___
19. If A = 12, B = 30, C = 7, D = 68, E = 114,    what is    A × C + B    ___
20. If A = 23, B = 56, C = 14, D = 16, E = 9,    what is    B − A + E + C    ___
21. If A = 41, B = 15, C = 2, D = 87, E = 185,    what is    D − B × C + A    ___
22. If A = 5, B = 23, C = 45, D = 31, E = 65,    what is    C + E ÷ A + B    ___
23. If A = 8, B = 32, C = 2, D = 10, E = 19,    what is    B − A ÷ C − D    ___
24. If A = 71, B = 12, C = 5, D = 57, E = 3,    what is    D + B − E + C    ___
25. If A = 54, B = 20, C = 6, D = 88, E = 84,    what is    E ÷ C + B + A    ___
26. If A = 9, B = 7, C = 78, D = 11, E = 28,    what is    A × D − E + B    ___

# PRACTICE TESTS IN VERBAL REASONING

27  If  A = 8, B = 6, C = 3, D = 32, E = 2,   what is   (B × A ÷ C) × E   ___
28  If  A = 9, B = 10, C = 8, D = 12, E = 14,  what is   D + B − C        ___
29  If  A = 13, B = 6, C = 34, D = 44, E = 27, what is   C + D ÷ B        ___
30  If  A = 42, B = 6, C = 4, D = 2, E = 48,   what is   (E − B) + C + D  ___

### Record Your Progress

| Number of Times You Have Taken the Test | Record | | | Record Your Completion Time |
|---|---|---|---|---|
| | Number of Questions Completed | Your Total Score | Total No. of Questions | |
| 1 | | | | |
| 2 | | | | |
| 3 | | | | |
| 4 | | | | |
| 5 | | | | |

## Practice Test 48 (Answers on page 254)

1   If  A = 6, B = 71, C = 5, D = 14, E = 58,    what is   B − C + A − E     ___
2   If  A = 61, B = 65, C = 18, D = 20, E = 16,  what is   A + D − E         ___
3   If  A = 15, B = 43, C = 7, D = 4, E = 3,     what is   (D × C) + A       ___
4   If  A = 87, B = 2, C = 46, D = 13, E = 30,   what is   (E + C + D) − B   ___
5   If  A = 2, B = 55, C = 36, D = 49, E = 72,   what is   (E ÷ A + B) − C   ___
6   If  A = 86, B = 7, C = 10, D = 16, E = 49,   what is   C × B + D         ___
7   If  A = 62, B = 41, C = 20, D = 61, E = 78,  what is   (C + A + B) − D   ___
8   If  A = 12, B = 50, C = 76, D = 37, E = 51,  what is   (D + E) − A       ___
9   If  A = 46, B = 25, C = 89, D = 79, E = 68,  what is   A + E − B         ___
10  If  A = 6, B = 7, C = 3, D = 12, E = 34,     what is   B × D ÷ C + A     ___
11  If  A = 4, B = 95, C = 100, D = 5, E = 76,   what is   (C ÷ D) ÷ A + B   ___
12  If  A = 45, B = 7, C = 8, D = 6, E = 11,     what is   (E − C + B) × D   ___
13  If  A = 6, B = 5, C = 4, D = 24, E = 36,     what is   (A × C) + B − D   ___
14  If  A = 2, B = 42, C = 4, D = 76, E = 38,    what is   (B − C) × A       ___
15  If  A = 9, B = 4, C = 16, D = 26, E = 13,    what is   (C ÷ B) + E + A   ___
16  If  A = 3, B = 8, C = 41, D = 77, E = 2,     what is   (D − A + B) ÷ E   ___
17  If  A = 18, B = 48, C = 65, D = 30, E = 73,  what is   E + D + A − B     ___

136

| | | | | | |
|---|---|---|---|---|---|
| 18 | If | A = 66, B = 11, C = 1, D = 67, E = 12, | what is | (A − B × C) + E | ___ |
| 19 | If | A = 8, B = 16, C = 5, D = 10, E = 17, | what is | (B × C ÷ D) + A | ___ |
| 20 | If | A = 9, B = 2, C = 118, D = 44, E = 6, | what is | (D + E + A) × B | ___ |
| 21 | If | A = 7, B = 14, C = 1, D = 6, E = 56, | what is | (E − B) ÷ D + A | ___ |
| 22 | If | A = 31, B = 61, C = 38, D = 23, E = 47, | what is | C + D + A − B | ___ |
| 23 | If | A = 108, B = 9, C = 2, D = 50, E = 4, | what is | (A ÷ B) × E + C | ___ |
| 24 | If | A = 54, B = 61, C = 86, D = 19, E = 48, | what is | (B − E + D) + A | ___ |
| 25 | If | A = 26, B = 2, C = 50, D = 13, E = 37, | what is | (E + A − C) × B | ___ |
| 26 | If | A = 3, B = 85, C = 5, D = 34, E = 69, | what is | (B ÷ C) × A + D | ___ |
| 27 | If | A = 2, B = 27, C = 51, D = 7, E = 8, | what is | (D × E) + A − C | ___ |
| 28 | If | A = 10, B = 11, C = 19, D = 80, E = 17, | what is | (E + B) − C + A | ___ |
| 29 | If | A = 41, B = 71, C = 30, D = 6, E = 5, | what is | (A − C) × D + E | ___ |
| 30 | If | A = 40, B = 5, C = 4, D = 1, E = 8, | what is | (B − D) + (C × E) | ___ |

### Record Your Progress

| Number of Times You Have Taken the Test | Record || | Record Your Completion Time |
|---|---|---|---|---|
| | Number of Questions Completed | Your Total Score | Total No. of Questions | |
| 1 | | | | |
| 2 | | | | |
| 3 | | | | |
| 4 | | | | |
| 5 | | | | |

# PRACTICE TESTS IN VERBAL REASONING

## SAMPLE TEST 25: CROSSWORDS

Fill in this crossword so that all the words written below each grid are used. You have been provided with a letter from one of the words to give you a clue in each crossword.

Question

Answer

| | | | | | t | r | u | s | t |
| --- | --- | --- | --- | --- | --- | --- | --- | --- | --- |
| | | | | | a | | | | h |
| | | | | | c | | | | i |
| | | | | | i | | | | g |
| | e | | | | t | e | a | c | h |

tacit   thigh   trust   teach

## Practice Test 49 (Answers on page 255)

Fill in the crosswords so that all the words written below each grid are used. You have been provided with a letter from one of the words to give you a clue in each crossword.

**Questions**

1.

noble   colon   create   trade

7.

sweet   trail   small   Scots

2.

treat   track   trunk   knock

8.

tread   dread   great   greed

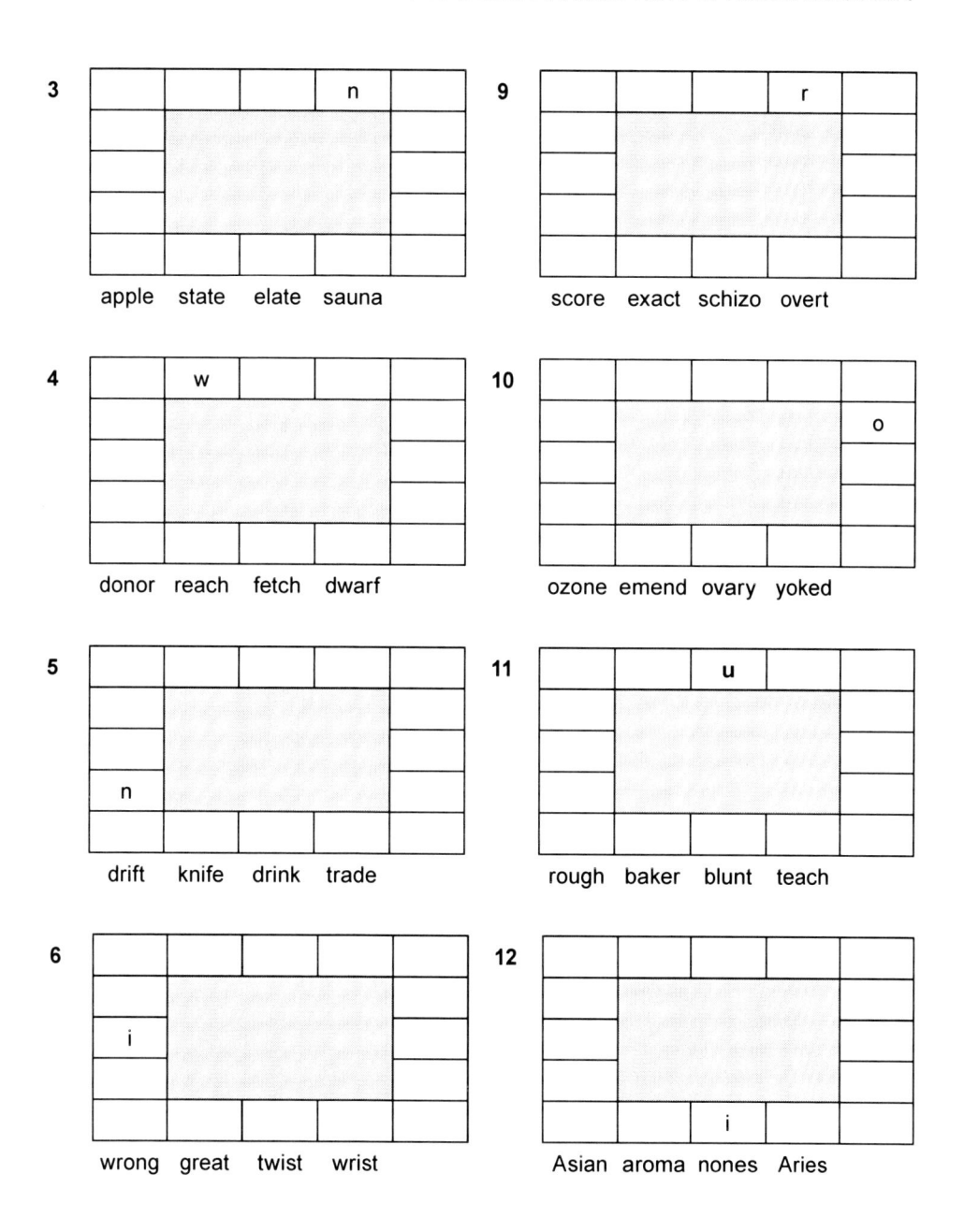

PRACTICE TESTS IN VERBAL REASONING

**3** n
apple state elate sauna

**9** r
score exact schizo overt

**4** w
donor reach fetch dwarf

**10** o
ozone emend ovary yoked

**5** n
drift knife drink trade

**11** u
rough baker blunt teach

**6** i
wrong great twist wrist

**12** i
Asian aroma nones Aries

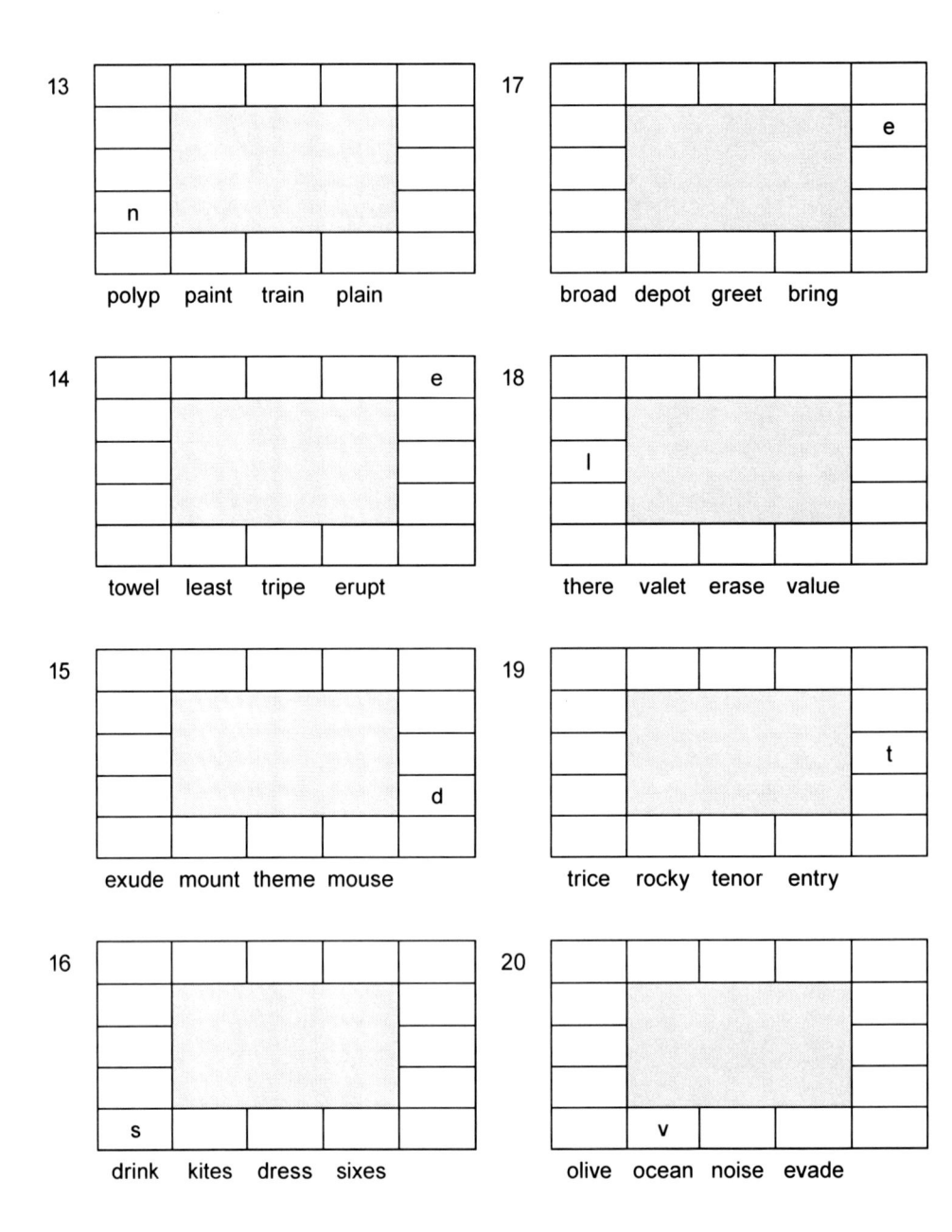

PRACTICE TESTS IN VERBAL REASONING

13. n
polyp  paint  train  plain

14. e
towel  least  tripe  erupt

15. d
exude  mount  theme  mouse

16. s
drink  kites  dress  sixes

17. e
broad  depot  greet  bring

18. l
there  valet  erase  value

19. t
trice  rocky  tenor  entry

20. v
olive  ocean  noise  evade

PRACTICE TESTS IN VERBAL REASONING

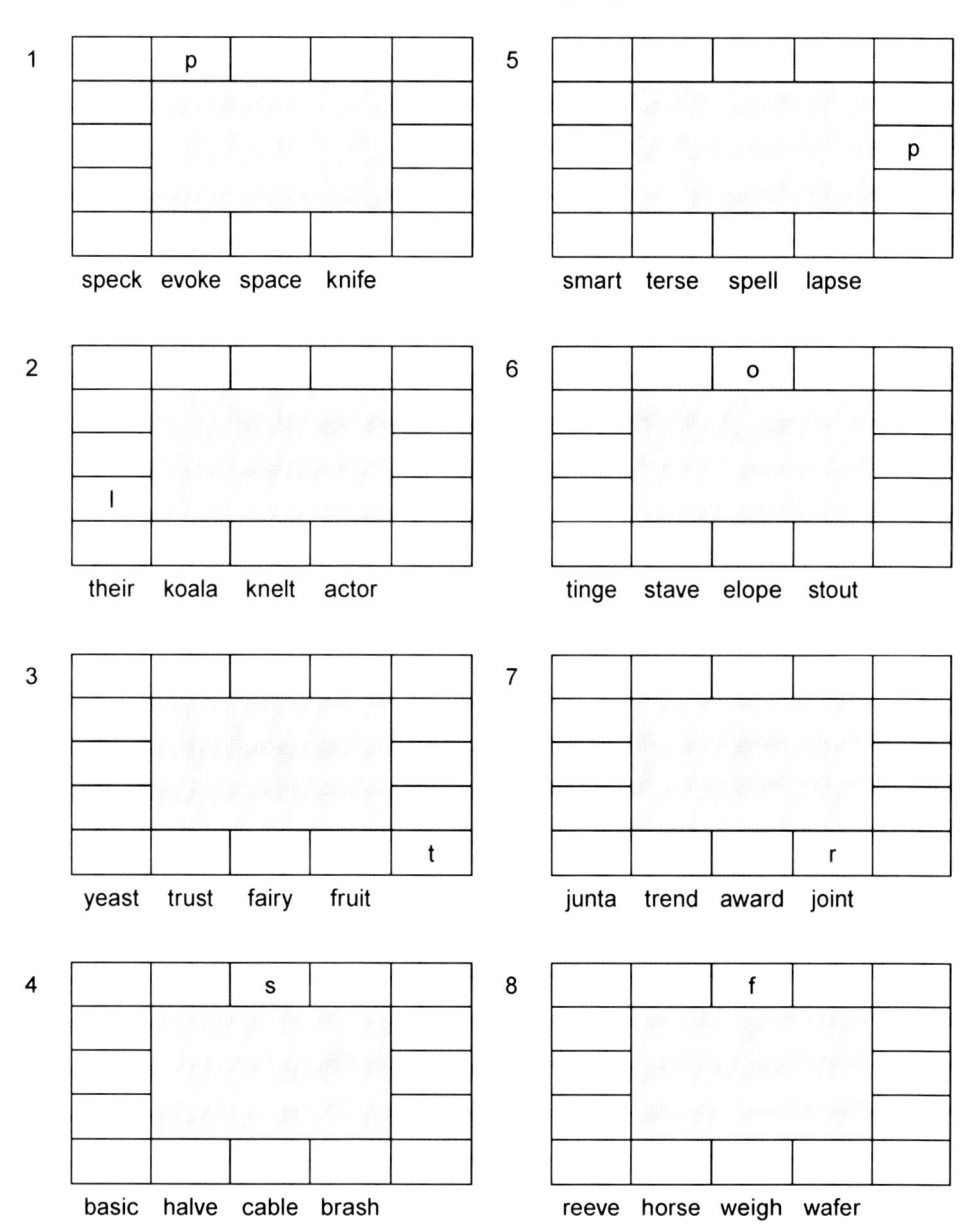

**Practice Test 50 (Answers on page 256)**

Fill in the crosswords so that all the words written below each grid are used. You have been provided with a letter from one of the words to give you a clue in each crossword.

1.  speck  evoke  space  knife

2.  their  koala  knelt  actor

3.  yeast  trust  fairy  fruit

4.  basic  halve  cable  brash

5.  smart  terse  spell  lapse

6.  tinge  stave  elope  stout

7.  junta  trend  award  joint

8.  reeve  horse  weigh  wafer

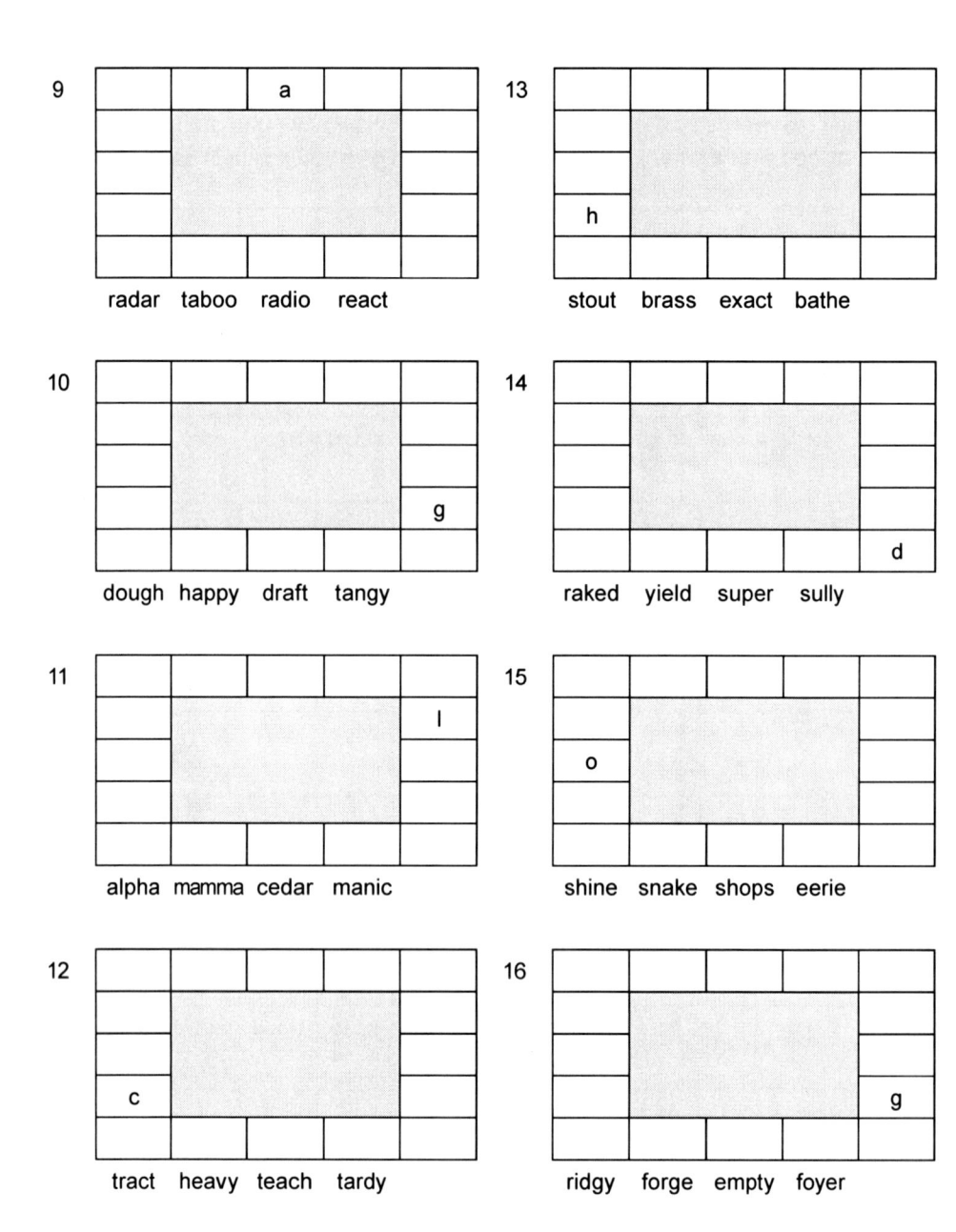

PRACTICE TESTS IN VERBAL REASONING

9   a

radar  taboo  radio  react

13   h

stout  brass  exact  bathe

10   g

dough  happy  draft  tangy

14   d

raked  yield  super  sully

11   l

alpha  mamma  cedar  manic

15   o

shine  snake  shops  eerie

12   c

tract  heavy  teach  tardy

16   g

ridgy  forge  empty  foyer

142

PRACTICE TESTS IN VERBAL REASONING

**17**

worry   tough   throw   hussy
(clue letter: o)

**19**

heart   bravo   ought   bench
(clue letter: a)

**18**

humpy   hydro   hunch   ovary
(clue letter: h)

**20**

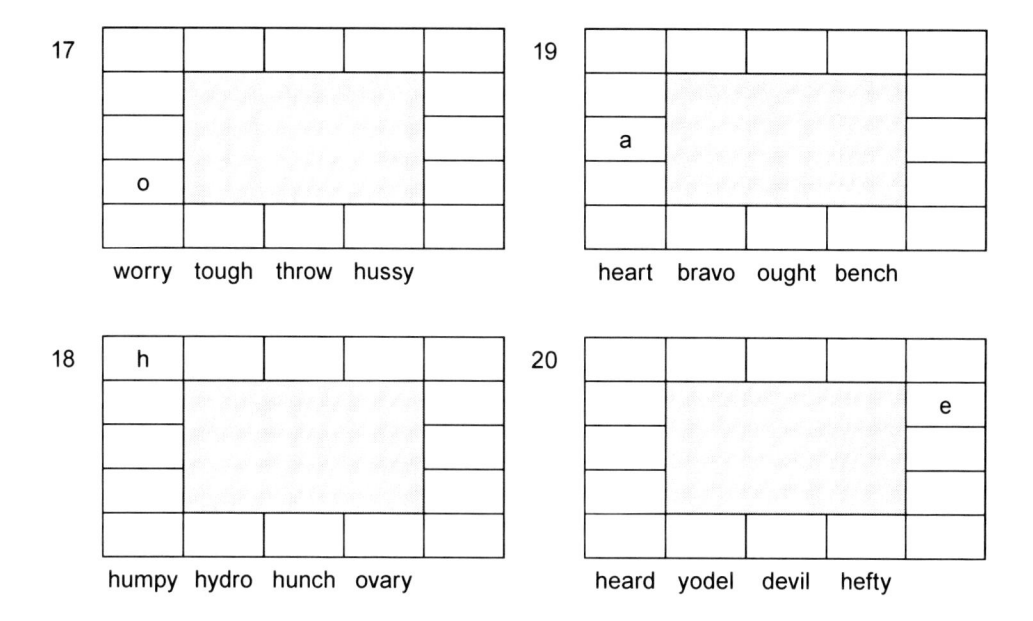

heard   yodel   devil   hefty
(clue letter: e)

## Practice Test 51 (Answers on page 257)

Fill in the crosswords so that all the words written below each grid are used. You have been provided with a letter from one of the words to give you a clue in each crossword.

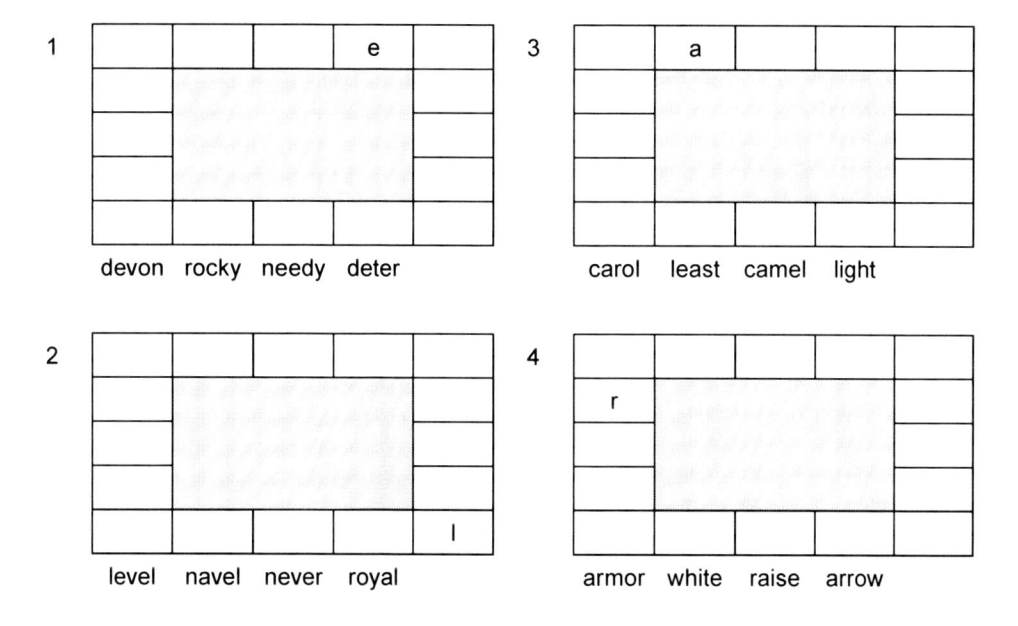

**1**

devon   rocky   needy   deter
(clue letter: e)

**3**

carol   least   camel   light
(clue letter: a)

**2**

level   navel   never   royal
(clue letter: l)

**4**

armor   white   raise   arrow
(clue letter: r)

143

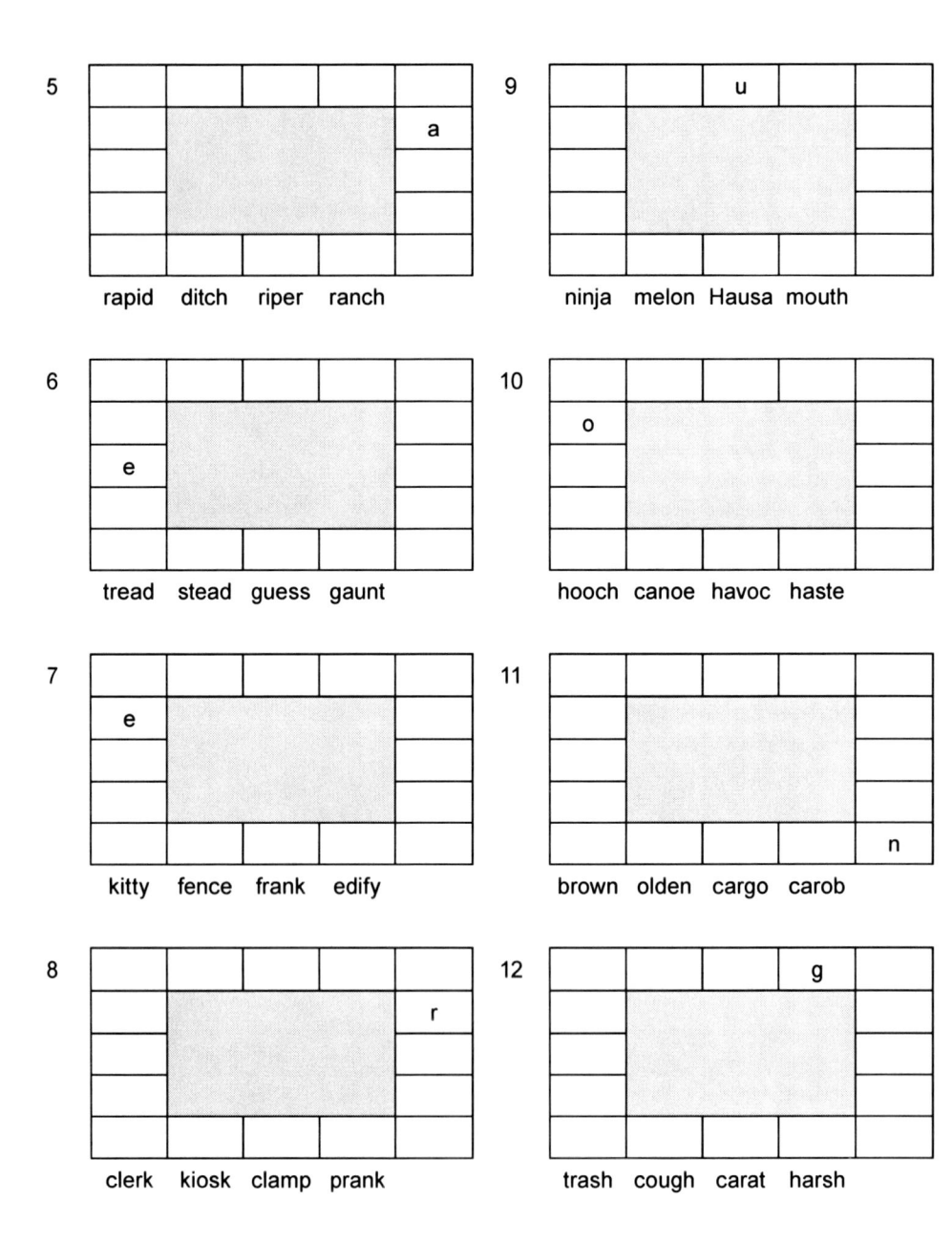

PRACTICE TESTS IN VERBAL REASONING

5  [grid with 'a']  rapid  ditch  riper  ranch

9  [grid with 'u']  ninja  melon  Hausa  mouth

6  [grid with 'e']  tread  stead  guess  gaunt

10  [grid with 'o']  hooch  canoe  havoc  haste

7  [grid with 'e']  kitty  fence  frank  edify

11  [grid with 'n']  brown  olden  cargo  carob

8  [grid with 'r']  clerk  kiosk  clamp  prank

12  [grid with 'g']  trash  cough  carat  harsh

144

**13**

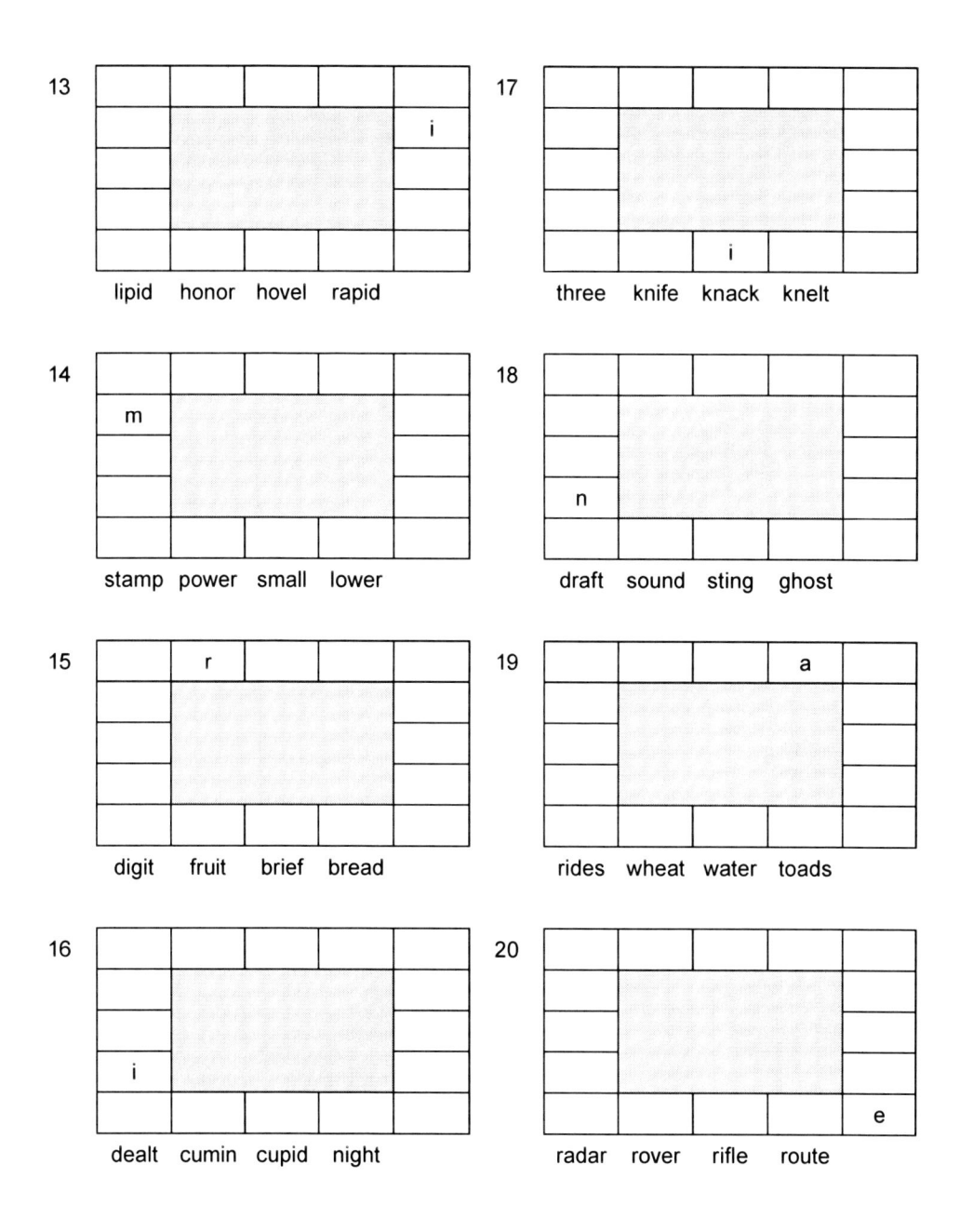

|  |  |  |  |  |
|---|---|---|---|---|
|  |   |   |   | i |
|  |   |   |   |  |
|  |   |   |   |  |
|  |  |  |  |  |

lipid   honor   hovel   rapid

**17**

|  |  |  |  |  |
|---|---|---|---|---|
|  |   |   |   |  |
|  |   |   |   |  |
|  |   |   |   |  |
|  |  | i |  |  |

three   knife   knack   knelt

**14**

|  |  |  |  |  |
|---|---|---|---|---|
| m |   |   |   |  |
|  |   |   |   |  |
|  |   |   |   |  |
|  |  |  |  |  |

stamp   power   small   lower

**18**

|  |  |  |  |  |
|---|---|---|---|---|
|  |   |   |   |  |
|  |   |   |   |  |
| n |   |   |   |  |
|  |  |  |  |  |

draft   sound   sting   ghost

**15**

|  | r |  |  |  |
|---|---|---|---|---|
|  |   |   |   |  |
|  |   |   |   |  |
|  |   |   |   |  |
|  |  |  |  |  |

digit   fruit   brief   bread

**19**

|  |  |  | a |  |
|---|---|---|---|---|
|  |   |   |   |  |
|  |   |   |   |  |
|  |   |   |   |  |
|  |  |  |  |  |

rides   wheat   water   toads

**16**

|  |  |  |  |  |
|---|---|---|---|---|
|  |   |   |   |  |
| i |   |   |   |  |
|  |   |   |   |  |
|  |  |  |  |  |

dealt   cumin   cupid   night

**20**

|  |  |  |  |  |
|---|---|---|---|---|
|  |   |   |   |  |
|  |   |   |   |  |
|  |   |   |   |  |
|  |  |  |  | e |

radar   rover   rifle   route

# PRACTICE TESTS IN VERBAL REASONING

## SAMPLE TEST 26: ADDITION AND SUBTRACTION

Some verbal reasoning tests do include elements of numerical reasoning. This sample question and the following practice tests are some of the types you may be presented with. These questions simply assess your ability to solve arithmetic exercises. You are required to complete the sums. Here is an example.

```
   Problem     ?  2  0        Answer      1  2  0
            +  2  3  ?                 +  2  3  4
               ―――――――                    ―――――――
               3  5  4                    3  5  4
```

Now do the following sums.

## Practice Test 52 (Answers on page 258)

In the following sums, an ? has taken the place of some missing numbers. Write the missing numbers above the line provided.

```
1      ?  3  6        2      1  ?  0        3      3  4  ?
    +  2  3  ?            +  6  ?  0            +  ?  2  3
       ―――――――               ―――――――               ―――――――
       3  7  1               8  1  0               4  6  3

4      4  ?  0        5      ?  3  ?        6      ?  8  7
    +  1  7  ?            +  4  2  1            +  0  ?  2
       ―――――――               ―――――――               ―――――――
       6  2  7               9  5  3               9  9  9

7      8  7  ?        8      6  4  ?        9      3  2  ?
    +  1  ?  1            +  ?  1  3            +  ?  3  4
       ―――――――               ―――――――               ―――――――
       9  9  7               8  6  0               6  5  7
```

PRACTICE TESTS IN VERBAL REASONING

10.  ? 3 1
    + 1 ? 1
    ─────────
      6 0 2

11.  1 8 ?
    + ? 9 0
    ─────────
      2 7 1

12.  2 7 ?
    + 1 ? 7
    ─────────
      4 4 8

13.  1 ? 1
    + 2 3 1
    ─────────
      3 5 2

14.  6 ? 3
    + ? 1 1
    ─────────
      7 5 4

15.  ? 2 2
    + 3 ? 3
    ─────────
      5 6 5

16.  1 ? 9
    + 5 ? 1
    ─────────
      7 0 0

17.  4 4 ?
    + ? 2 1
    ─────────
      6 6 5

18.  3 ? 2
    + 1 ? 4
    ─────────
      4 7 6

19.  ? 6 1
    + 2 ? 1
    ─────────
      3 9 2

20.  ? 4 1
    + 3 ? 1
    ─────────
      4 6 2

21.  4 3 ?
    + ? 1 1
    ─────────
      6 4 3

22.  ? 2 3
    + 1 0 ?
    ─────────
      5 2 4

23.  3 ? 6
    + 1 6 ?
    ─────────
      5 2 5

24.  2 5 ?
    + ? 3 7
    ─────────
      4 9 5

147

PRACTICE TESTS IN VERBAL REASONING

**Practice Test 53 (Answers on page 258)**

In the following sums, a ? has taken the place of some missing numbers. Write the missing numbers above the line provided.

| 1 | 9 ? 7<br>− 2 ?<br>9 2 7 | 2 | 3 ? 2<br>−   4<br>2 9 8 | 3 | 7 8 ?<br>−   4<br>7 5 4 |

| 4 | 5 ? 3<br>− 1 4 ?<br>4 0 3 | 5 | 7 ? 7<br>− ? 2 7<br>4 5 0 | 6 | ? 4 9<br>− 1 ? 9<br>4 3 0 |

| 7 | 7 6 ?<br>− ? 7<br>7 0 6 | 8 | 8 9 ?<br>− ? 7<br>8 3 2 | 9 | 2 9 ?<br>− ? 2 ?<br>− 1 2 6 |

| 10 | 3 ? 7<br>− 5 ? 3<br>−1 2 6 | 11 | 7 ? 9<br>− ? 5 4<br>4 8 5 | 12 | 6 5 ?<br>− 3 ? 7<br>2 7 9 |

| 13 | 4 5 ?<br>− ? 3<br>4 3 7 | 14 | 3 8 ?<br>− 2 ? 9<br>1 4 1 | 15 | ? 8 4<br>− 6 7 ?<br>3 1 0 |

148

PRACTICE TESTS IN VERBAL REASONING

**16**   3  ?  0
     −   1  ?
     ─────────
         3  0  7

**17**   2  8  ?
     −   3  ?  1
     ─────────
            −3  2

**18**   ?  0  2
     −   1  ?
     ─────────
         5  8  5

**19**   2  7  ?
     −   ?  6  0
     ─────────
         1  1  0

**20**   8  ?  1
     −   1  3  ?
     ─────────
         7  5  5

**21**   6  7  ?
     −   5  ?  9
     ─────────
            8  2

**22**   ?  4  9
     −   8  8  ?
     ─────────
        −1  3  2

**23**   ?  7  9
     −   3  ?  5
     ─────────
         3  3  4

**24**   4  5  ?
     −   ?  2  3
     ─────────
         3  3  6

# 4. Verbal Analysis

Verbal analysis tests are used to assess your ability to reason with written information and make deductions. These types of tests are used in the selection of graduates and managers for various roles in various sectors of industry. The format of the questions can vary, but you are generally provided with some information and required to provide the answer. Here are two sample questions, followed by the practice tests.

## SAMPLE TEST 27: PROBLEM SOLVING

Read the following questions, and write your answer in the space provided.

Example 1

| 1 | In a horse race Hill Royal came in ahead of Trigger. Hill Royal finished after Black Beauty. Copenhagen beat Black Beauty but finished after Bucephalus. Where did Copenhagen finish? Second<br>Bucephalus, Copenhagen, Black Beauty, Hill Royal, Trigger |
|---|---|

The answer is *second*, so write *second* in the space provided.

Example 2

| 2 | 4th | Where did Hill Royal finish? Fourth |
|---|---|---|

The answer is *fourth*, so write *fourth* in the space provided.

Now attempt the following questions.

## Practice Test 54 (Answers on page 259)

1. Debbie, Kimi, and Michael have Ferraris. Michael also has a Reliant Robin. Jensen has a Mercedes and a Model T. Rubens also has a Mercedes. Debbie also has a Bugatti Veyron. Rubens has just bought a Toyota Prius. Who has the least cars?
   _____

PRACTICE TESTS IN VERBAL REASONING

2. If ⅓ of a number is 4 times 11, what is half of that number?

　————————————

3. Jensen, Lewis, and Mika need to be able to run 100 meters in under 12.5 seconds to qualify for a championship. Lewis and Mika run faster than Jensen. Jensen's best time for the 100 meters is 13.1 seconds. Which of the following *must* be true?

　————————————

4. Wayne is double the age of Fernando and ⅓ as old as Didier, who will be 48 years old in 6 years. How old is Fernando?

　————————————

5. Hanif, Horace, Hilary, and Hannah are polyglots. Hanif and Horace speak Chinese, whereas the others speak Arabic. Horace and Hannah speak Albanian. Everyone except Hanif speaks Esperanto. 5. Who only speaks Arabic and Esperanto?

　————————————

6. Who speaks more than one language but not Arabic?

　————————————

7. Josh, the postman, has 11 red rubber bands. He gives Sunita 3 bands. Sunita now has twice the amount of bands Josh has left. How many bands did Sunita have at the beginning?

　————————————

8. Simon, Cheryl, and Dannii are all going by train to London to watch a singing competition. Cheryl gets the 2:15 p.m. train. Simon's train journey takes 50 percent longer than Dannii's. Simon catches the 3:00 train. Dannii leaves 20 minutes after Cheryl and arrives at 3:25 pm. When will Simon arrive?

　————————————

9. If 5 bricklayers can lay a total of 50 bricks in 30 minutes, how many bricklayers are required to lay a total of 60 bricks in 20 minutes?

　————————————

10. An old treasure map has the following instructions: "Stand next to the black rock, and face west. Walk 20 yards and then turn 90 degrees clockwise. Walk another 10 yards and then turn 45 degrees anticlockwise. Walk another 15 yards, reverse your direction, and walk 5 yards back. Turn 135 degrees clockwise, and walk another 10 yards." In which direction are you now facing?

　————————————

PRACTICE TESTS IN VERBAL REASONING

11. You work in purchasing for a company and must buy the following 9 cars for the company pool in the next 3 months. The company is bureaucratic and has a rule that exactly £60,000 must be spent in each of the 3 months, and you are only allowed to buy 3 cars each month. In the first month, you buy the Fiat Uno. Which other 2 cars must you buy that month?

------------------

- BMW Series 3—£40,000
- Lexus—£36,000
- Volvo Estate—£32,000
- Skoda Octavia—£12,000
- Fiat Uno—£8,000
- Ford Focus—£14,000
- Ford Focus—£14,000
- Ford Focus—£14,000
- Ford Ka—£10,000

12. Athos, Portos, and Aramis live in three adjoining houses. Aramis has a black cat called d'Artagnan, Portos has a white dog, whereas Athos has a red herring. Portos has a neighbor with a red door. The owner of a four-legged animal has a blue door. Either a feline or fish owner has a green door. Aramis and Portos are not neighbors. Whose door is red?

------------------

13. Mrs. Krashem, a driving instructor, has to arrange bookings for some of her pupils. She has 8 new pupils who wish to book either a morning or afternoon of a particular day. These are two-hour introductory lessons, so she only sees one pupil each morning or afternoon.

Ms. Banger is only available Tuesday mornings, but Mr. Bumpem can make any time on a Wednesday. Mrs. Exhaust is free on Tuesdays all day, but Mr. Hilstart is only free Wednesday afternoons. Ms. Boot is only available Friday mornings, whereas Miss Bonnet can only make Saturday afternoons. Mrs. Speed is available all day Fridays, whereas Mr. Parker can make any time on a Saturday.

Which two of the people mentioned above must have *morning* appointments?

------------------

14. Which two of the people mentioned above must have *afternoon* appointments?

------------------

PRACTICE TESTS IN VERBAL REASONING

15. How many degrees are there between the two hands of a clock at 6:30 am?

    _____

16. You are holding a children's party for 7 children and have asked the children what activities they would like at the party. Because of time constraints, you will only have time for two activities but want to make sure that everyone gets either their first or second choice. The children and activity preferences, in order, are as follows. Which two activities should you choose?

    _____

    | **Rachel** | face painting | magician | bouncy castle | ball games | disco |
    | **Debbie** | bouncy castle | ball games | face painting | magician | disco |
    | **Sunita** | magician | face painting | magician | disco | ball games |
    | **Ben** | ball games | face painting | disco | magician | bouncy castle |
    | **Mia** | disco | magician | face painting | bouncy castle | ball games |
    | **Jo** | magician | bouncy castle | disco | face painting | ball games |
    | **Amel** | face painting | ball games | bouncy castle | magician | disco |

17. You spend 56 pounds in total on a cactus, a stuffed porcupine, and a pack of bandages. The cactus costs twice as much as the bandages, and the stuffed porcupine double the price of the cactus. How much pounds did the cactus cost?

    _____

18. You take seven children to a toy shop to buy each a soft toy. The toy shop only has one of each type, so you ask the children their preferences. You decide to give each child one of their preferred toys. Which animal will you give Jezebel?

    _____

    | **James** | wombat | panda | gorilla | kitten | rat |
    | **Josh** | panda | donkey | dog | | |
    | **Jezebel** | panda | donkey | kitten | dog | |
    | **Jamelia** | panda | donkey | dog | | |
    | **Janine** | wombat | gorilla | donkey | kitten | rat |
    | **Jasbeet** | panda | dog | | | |
    | **Jason** | wombat | gorilla | dog | rat | kitten |

19. A crofter has to get to his herd of sheep quickly as he has been told they are being attacked by a dog. His sheep are on the other side of a steep hill. He can run over the hill (3 miles) at 4 miles an hour or take his tractor via an old dirt track that is 5 miles at an average of 6 miles an hour, or he can drive his car along a very

153

narrow, winding road, but this is 14 miles, and he can only go at 18 miles an hour on average. Which method should he choose?

_____

20. If 42 is 7 times a particular number, what is 11 times that number?

_____

| Record Your Progress |||||
|---|---|---|---|---|
| Number of Times You Have Taken the Test | Record ||| Record Your Completion Time |
| | Number of Questions Completed | Your Total Score | Total No. of Questions | |
| 1 | | | | |
| 2 | | | | |
| 3 | | | | |
| 4 | | | | |
| 5 | | | | |

# 5. Verbal Analogy

An *analogy* is two words with a direct relationship. Verbal analogies test your knowledge of the relationship between words. The most common relationships are synonyms and antonyms. *Synonyms* are words that are the same or similar in meaning, and *antonyms* are words that are opposite in meaning. The tests in this section will require you to identify such relationship between words. There are other types of relationships between words, and some of these can be listed below.

- Order/sequence          e.g., *spring'* is to *summer*

- Cause and effect        e.g., *diet* is to *slimmer*

- "Is a place where"      e.g., *school* is to *teacher*

- "Is used to"            e.g., *oven* is to *bake*

- Groups                  e.g., *red* is to *green*

- Part to whole           e.g., *room* is to *house*

This list is not exhaustive. You can refer to a thesaurus of synonyms and antonyms for more examples.

## SAMPLE TEST 28: RELATIONSHIP BETWEEN WORDS

You are provided with a pair of words, and you are required to identify the relationship between the words. You are to choose from the following three options: A = same, B = opposite, C = different, and write your answer in the space provided.

                nice                    pleasant

The answer is *A* because the words are the same in meaning.

Now attempt the following questions.

# PRACTICE TESTS IN VERBAL REASONING

## Practice Test 55 (Answers on page 264)

Here are fifty pairs of words. Some pairs are synonyms, some are antonyms, and some have no relationship. You are to identify which pairs are the same, opposite, or different.

A = same, B = opposite, C = different

Write your answer in the box provided.

| 1  | handicap      | incapacitate |
|----|---------------|--------------|
| 2  | rebel         | dissident    |
| 3  | condemnatory  | damning      |
| 4  | alert         | inattentive  |
| 5  | trustworthy   | deceptive    |
| 6  | interdict     | correspond   |
| 7  | perversion    | distortion   |
| 8  | controller    | director     |
| 9  | smart         | daft         |
| 10 | deliberately  | haphazardly  |
| 11 | contented     | satisfied    |
| 12 | perky         | dull         |
| 13 | opponent      | ally         |
| 14 | unclear       | obvious      |
| 15 | distinguished | eminent      |
| 16 | conflict      | dispute      |
| 17 | appendix      | addendum     |
| 18 | dismayed      | daunted      |
| 19 | implement     | accolade     |
| 20 | anxiety       | confidence   |
| 21 | decorum       | propriety    |
| 22 | assessment    | appraisal    |
| 23 | authentic     | fake         |
| 24 | allow         | permit       |
| 25 | genuine       | diamond      |
| 26 | ignore        | disregard    |
| 27 | draftsman     | architect    |
| 28 | writer        | author       |

# PRACTICE TESTS IN VERBAL REASONING

| 29 | concert | equipment | |
| 30 | factual | real | |
| 31 | disgruntled | dissatisfied | |
| 32 | monitor | mechanical | |
| 33 | dart | arrow | |
| 34 | canoe | indulge | |
| 35 | keen | eager | |
| 36 | avoidable | inevitable | |
| 37 | penetrate | inferior | |
| 38 | fragment | excerpt | |
| 39 | surpass | exceed | |
| 40 | individual | direction | |
| 41 | courage | scare | |
| 42 | aberrant | deviant | |
| 43 | congenial | unfriendly | |
| 44 | true | incorrect | |
| 45 | ethics | standards | |
| 46 | shipment | freight | |
| 47 | family | fame | |
| 48 | idiosyncratic | ordinary | |
| 49 | obscurity | prominence | |
| 50 | celestial | divine | |

| Record Your Progress ||||| 
|---|---|---|---|---|
| Number of Times You Have Taken the Test | Record ||| Record Your Completion Time |
| | Number of Questions Completed | Your Total Score | Total No. of Questions | |
| 1 | | | | |
| 2 | | | | |
| 3 | | | | |
| 4 | | | | |
| 5 | | | | |

# PRACTICE TESTS IN VERBAL REASONING

## Practice Test 56 (Answers on page 265)

Here are fifty pairs of words. Some pairs are synonyms, some are antonyms, and some have no relationship. You are to identify which pairs are the same, opposite, or different.

A = same, B = opposite, C = different

Write your answer in the box provided.

| 1  | auspicious    | frantic        | _____ |
|----|---------------|----------------|----------------|
| 2  | numerous      | countless      | _____ |
| 3  | naught        | zero           | _____ |
| 4  | entire        | incomplete     | _____ |
| 5  | short         | long           | _____ |
| 6  | chirpy        | gloomy         | _____ |
| 7  | proliferation | multiplication | _____ |
| 8  | capable       | incompetent    | _____ |
| 9  | essential     | dispensable    | _____ |
| 10 | timeless      | deathless      | _____ |
| 11 | hub           | edge           | _____ |
| 12 | charitable    | unkind         | _____ |
| 13 | copyright     | patent         | _____ |
| 14 | civil         | rude           | _____ |
| 15 | collect       | disperse       | _____ |
| 16 | comprise      | constitute     | _____ |
| 17 | influential   | unimportant    | _____ |
| 18 | wholesome     | deleterious    | _____ |
| 19 | compulsory    | voluntary      | _____ |
| 20 | crisp         | crunchy        | _____ |
| 21 | autumn        | avenge         | _____ |
| 22 | litter        | automotive     | _____ |
| 23 | isolate       | separate       | _____ |
| 24 | herald        | presage        | _____ |
| 25 | casual        | formal         | _____ |
| 26 | isle          | island         | _____ |
| 27 | crop          | yield          | _____ |
| 28 | retail        | forces         | _____ |

| 29 | vital | crucial | _____ |
| --- | --- | --- | --- |
| 30 | gateway | ancestry | _____ |
| 31 | lavatory | latrine | _____ |
| 32 | terse | digressive | _____ |
| 33 | dopey | bright | _____ |
| 34 | impoverish | enrichment | _____ |
| 35 | crèche | nursery | _____ |
| 36 | valuable | worthless | _____ |
| 37 | uneasy | calm | _____ |
| 38 | nuisance | irritation | _____ |
| 39 | arid | wet | _____ |
| 40 | diffusion | dispersion | _____ |
| 41 | elite | aristocracy | _____ |
| 42 | hypothetical | factual | _____ |
| 43 | bare | full | _____ |
| 44 | encourage | dissuade | _____ |
| 45 | rustic | peasant | _____ |
| 46 | features | clinical | _____ |
| 47 | crescent | succeed | _____ |
| 48 | equinox | amphibians | _____ |
| 49 | embarrass | discountenance | _____ |
| 50 | forbearance | patience | _____ |

| Record Your Progress |||||
| --- | --- | --- | --- | --- |
| Number of Times You Have Taken the Test | Record ||| Record Your Completion Time |
| | Number of Questions Completed | Your Total Score | Total No. of Questions | |
| 1 | | | | |
| 2 | | | | |
| 3 | | | | |
| 4 | | | | |
| 5 | | | | |

## SAMPLE TEST 29: PAIRS OF WORDS

You have been provided with two words in capital letters that are related in some way. You have also been given six words on the lower line, three in each half. Your task is to identify two words, one from each half, that form a verbal analogy when paired with the words in the upper line. Record your answer in the boxes provided.

| ROOM | | | HOUSE | | |
|---|---|---|---|---|---|
| slice | loan | tragedy | vote | bread | cry |

The answer is *slice* and *bread*, so write 'your answer in the boxes provided beside the question.

Now do the following questions.

## Practice Test 57 (Answers on page 265)

You have been provided with two words in capital letters that are related in some way. You have also been given six words on the lower line, three in each half. Your task is to identify two words, one from each half, that form a verbal analogy when paired with the words in the upper line. Record your answer in the boxes provided.

1. 
| MYSTERY | | | UNRIDDLE | | |
|---|---|---|---|---|---|
| salt | cipher | stockist | crack | wedge | beam |

2. 
| MEDICINE | | | ILLNESS | | |
|---|---|---|---|---|---|
| law | gelatin | galaxy | barley | anarchy | poach |

3. 
| LENS | | | TELESCOPE | | |
|---|---|---|---|---|---|
| supply | nib | gateway | laborer | grass | pen |

4. 
| LEVEE | | | FLOOD | | |
|---|---|---|---|---|---|
| helmet | earth | journal | stool | wheat | injury |

160

PRACTICE TESTS IN VERBAL REASONING

| 5 | ACTIVE | | | DORMANT | | | | |
|---|---|---|---|---|---|---|---|---|
| | cover | employed | raw | plate | bridge | unemployed | | |

| 6 | SQUARE | | | CUBE | | | | |
|---|---|---|---|---|---|---|---|---|
| | solar | plant | circle | cave | sphere | plough | | |

| 7 | GREEN | | | RED | | | | |
|---|---|---|---|---|---|---|---|---|
| | injury | spinach | demand | tomato | power | tree | | |

| 8 | JUDGE | | | BENCH | | | | |
|---|---|---|---|---|---|---|---|---|
| | season | king | plasma | radar | throne | ravine | | |

| 9 | WAVES | | | SOUND | | | | |
|---|---|---|---|---|---|---|---|---|
| | plank | color | dust | spectrum | radiator | sew | | |

| 10 | SETTLEMENT | | | INJURY | | | | |
|---|---|---|---|---|---|---|---|---|
| | railway | pension | seaside | retirement | stock | bowl | | |

| 11 | MONROVIA | | | VIENNA | | | | |
|---|---|---|---|---|---|---|---|---|
| | rap | Liberia | knife | confess | Austria | pencil | | |

| 12 | CUP | | | DRINK | | | | |
|---|---|---|---|---|---|---|---|---|
| | tool | tonsil | bed | shade | sleep | rake | | |

| 13 | TEACHER | | | LECTURER | | | | |
|---|---|---|---|---|---|---|---|---|
| | college | temple | saucer | university | tempo | therapy | | |

## PRACTICE TESTS IN VERBAL REASONING

| 14 | STEAL | | | BORROW | | |
|---|---|---|---|---|---|---|
| | read | extort | tendon | toast | obtain | term |

| 15 | DANCER | | | FLOOR | | |
|---|---|---|---|---|---|---|
| | shaft | thermal | footballer | toga | traffic | pitch |

| 16 | PEDESTRIAN | | | FOOTPATH | | |
|---|---|---|---|---|---|---|
| | bear | value | train | pedestrian | tourism | track |

| 17 | HEEL | | | FOOT | | |
|---|---|---|---|---|---|---|
| | dispatch | stern | trigger | thermos | well-being | boat |

| 18 | BEGINNING | | | END | | |
|---|---|---|---|---|---|---|
| | rain | wrinkle | start | squeal | train | finish |

| 19 | DIVIDE | | | NUMBER | | |
|---|---|---|---|---|---|---|
| | slice | alarm | trail | transfer | bread | welfare |

| 20 | HAMMER | | | ANVIL | | |
|---|---|---|---|---|---|---|
| | pestle | trap | fire | mortar | pamper | march |

| 21 | NOSE | | | SMELL | | |
|---|---|---|---|---|---|---|
| | tongue | marrow | fingers | taste | tropical | supply |

| 22 | LONDON | | | PARIS | | |
|---|---|---|---|---|---|---|
| | placid | England | stock market | France | radio | perfume |

PRACTICE TESTS IN VERBAL REASONING

| 23 | BARBER ||| HAIR |||  ||
|---|---|---|---|---|---|---|---|---|
|  | post | tread | draper | shoe | boat | cloth |  |  |

| 24 | MINUTE ||| SECONDS |||  ||
|---|---|---|---|---|---|---|---|---|
|  | monopoly | thatch | week | triple | unique | days |  |  |

| 25 | FLORIST ||| FLOWER |||  ||
|---|---|---|---|---|---|---|---|---|
|  | troop | milliner | stamp | hat | trapeze | farmer |  |  |

| 26 | FISH ||| FISHBONE |||  ||
|---|---|---|---|---|---|---|---|---|
|  | special | bone | thimble | bell | horse | mature |  |  |

| 27 | THROW ||| CATCH |||  ||
|---|---|---|---|---|---|---|---|---|
|  | possession | push | spill | pull | placate | trial |  |  |

| 28 | LEGS ||| MOTION |||  ||
|---|---|---|---|---|---|---|---|---|
|  | eyes | hoist | prompt | deliver | leak | vision |  |  |

| 29 | ALPS ||| EUROPE |||  ||
|---|---|---|---|---|---|---|---|---|
|  | Rockies | chrome | garden | city | America | planet |  |  |

| 30 | FRUIT ||| VEGETABLES |||  ||
|---|---|---|---|---|---|---|---|---|
|  | apple | wood | reunion | cabbage | melon | fisherman |  |  |

| 31 | SHARD ||| POTTERY |||  ||
|---|---|---|---|---|---|---|---|---|
|  | net | reject | fragment | seatbelt | bone | revenge |  |  |

# PRACTICE TESTS IN VERBAL REASONING

| 32 | TABLE TENNIS ||| BAT |||
|---|---|---|---|---|---|---|
| | lawn tennis | golf | swim | massage | whimper | racket |

| 33 | DEBIT ||| CREDIT |||
|---|---|---|---|---|---|---|
| | income | generate | scare | expenditure | hire | hotel |

| 34 | MASTER ||| SERVANT |||
|---|---|---|---|---|---|---|
| | herd | groom | monarch | retain | fishmonger | subject |

| 35 | PILOT ||| PLANE |||
|---|---|---|---|---|---|---|
| | driver | scatter | unpack | ship | island | car |

| 36 | WOOL ||| WINTER |||
|---|---|---|---|---|---|---|
| | mattress | linen | special | pattern | summer | calendar |

| 37 | HAND ||| PALM |||
|---|---|---|---|---|---|---|
| | greet | feet | select | lotion | sole | eye |

| 38 | POEM ||| POET |||
|---|---|---|---|---|---|---|
| | sermon | grain | whistle | mask | book | priest |

| 39 | HEART ||| PUMP |||
|---|---|---|---|---|---|---|
| | goldfish | herd | teeth | breeze | growl | chew |

| 40 | HOT ||| COLD |||
|---|---|---|---|---|---|---|
| | summer | seam | revel | iceberg | reservoir | winter |

PRACTICE TESTS IN VERBAL REASONING

| Record Your Progress |||||  |
|---|---|---|---|---|---|
| Number of Times You Have Taken the Test | Record |||| Record Your Completion Time |
|  | Number of Questions Completed | Your Total Score || Total No. of Questions |  |
| 1 |  |  ||  |  |
| 2 |  |  ||  |  |
| 3 |  |  ||  |  |
| 4 |  |  ||  |  |
| 5 |  |  ||  |  |

## Practice Test 58 (Answers on page 266)

You have been provided with two words in capital letters that are related in some way. You have also been given six words on the lower line, three in each half. Your task is to identify two words, one from each half, that form a verbal analogy when paired with the words in the upper line. Record your answer in the boxes provided.

1

| MORTGAGEE ||| MORTGAGER |||  |  |
|---|---|---|---|---|---|---|---|
| landlord | town | clothes | segment | transport | tenant |  |  |

2

| BOOKS ||| LIBRARY |||  |  |
|---|---|---|---|---|---|---|---|
| tradition | utensils | retain | kitchen | seal | shelves |  |  |

3

| KINGSTON ||| JAMAICA |||  |  |
|---|---|---|---|---|---|---|---|
| Brussels | group | seaport | Belgium | heat | moisture |  |  |

4

| BANGLE ||| WRIST |||  |  |
|---|---|---|---|---|---|---|---|
| costume | hose | ring | event | finger | retract |  |  |

5

| WRITE ||| PAINT |||  |  |
|---|---|---|---|---|---|---|---|
| thin | grind | pen | hook | house | paintbrush |  |  |

PRACTICE TESTS IN VERBAL REASONING

| 6 | TROUSERS ||| LEGS |||  ||
|---|---|---|---|---|---|---|---|---|
|  | stone | press | belt | street | waist | sign |  |  |

| 7 | CITY ||| VILLAGE |||  ||
|---|---|---|---|---|---|---|---|---|
|  | dry-clean | urban | umbrella | rural | order | football |  |  |

| 8 | PAINT ||| BRUSH |||  ||
|---|---|---|---|---|---|---|---|---|
|  | stitch | scan | ink | plywood | pen | rough |  |  |

| 9 | CHRISTIANITY ||| ISLAM |||  ||
|---|---|---|---|---|---|---|---|---|
|  | mixed | covenant | church | retrieve | muster | mosque |  |  |

| 10 | GRAPE ||| WINE |||  ||
|---|---|---|---|---|---|---|---|---|
|  | marzipan | cake | orange | candle | cheese | juice |  |  |

| 11 | RARE ||| MANY |||  ||
|---|---|---|---|---|---|---|---|---|
|  | historian | corrode | few | hatch | cosmopolitan | common |  |  |

| 12 | MILK ||| COW |||  ||
|---|---|---|---|---|---|---|---|---|
|  | wheat | breakfast | egg | gravy | chicken | butter |  |  |

| 13 | NIGHT ||| DAY |||  ||
|---|---|---|---|---|---|---|---|---|
|  | famine | heavy | dark | eyelid | thin | light |  |  |

| 14 | PUPPY ||| DOG |||  ||
|---|---|---|---|---|---|---|---|---|
|  | vessel | kitten | vitamin | cat | mule | system |  |  |

| 15 | TENNIS PLAYER ||| COURT |||  ||
|---|---|---|---|---|---|---|---|---|
|  | exhaust | victim | actor | haven | villa | stage |  |  |

| 16 | WORDS ||| DICTIONARY |||  ||
|---|---|---|---|---|---|---|---|---|
|  | lyrics | harmony | small | stork | songs | memoir |  |  |

PRACTICE TESTS IN VERBAL REASONING

| 17 | POEM | | | RECITE | | |  |  |
|---|---|---|---|---|---|---|---|---|
|  | story | music | mud | harvest | heartbeat | tell |  |  |

| 18 | PENNINES | | | ENGLAND | | |  |  |
|---|---|---|---|---|---|---|---|---|
|  | emerald | meadow | Kilimanjaro | mound | gulf | Tanzania |  |  |

| 19 | SHIP | | | SEA | | |  |  |
|---|---|---|---|---|---|---|---|---|
|  | grease | empire | plane | lake | spin | air |  |  |

| 20 | PESTLE | | | MORTAR | | |  |  |
|---|---|---|---|---|---|---|---|---|
|  | screen | coat | hammer | workplace | hay | anvil |  |  |

| 21 | UNIVERSITY | | | STUDENTS | | |  |  |
|---|---|---|---|---|---|---|---|---|
|  | globe | geography | school | save | expense | pupils |  |  |

| 22 | LASS | | | FEMININE | | |  |  |
|---|---|---|---|---|---|---|---|---|
|  | litter | hoard | lad | dress | language | masculine |  |  |

| 23 | MATCH | | | CROWD | | |  |  |
|---|---|---|---|---|---|---|---|---|
|  | chase | lintel | cinema | guest | hive | audience |  |  |

| 24 | OVEN | | | BAKE | | |  |  |
|---|---|---|---|---|---|---|---|---|
|  | lens | ginger | kettle | gravy | earthquake | boil |  |  |

| 25 | BONE | | | FRAGMENT | | |  |  |
|---|---|---|---|---|---|---|---|---|
|  | giant | meteor | pottery | mast | straw | shard |  |  |

| 26 | GIRL | | | MOTHER | | |  |  |
|---|---|---|---|---|---|---|---|---|
|  | boy | jasmine | knot | king | father | lane |  |  |

| 27 | COME | | | ARRIVE | | |  |  |
|---|---|---|---|---|---|---|---|---|
|  | jump | map | go | leisure | key | depart |  |  |

## PRACTICE TESTS IN VERBAL REASONING

| 28 | PRINCE | | | KING | | | | |
|---|---|---|---|---|---|---|---|---|
| | guardian | marine | princess | luxury | gold | queen | | |

| 29 | SHOE | | | FOOT | | | | |
|---|---|---|---|---|---|---|---|---|
| | budget | tap | hat | gum | lock | head | | |

| 30 | HUNGER | | | FOOD | | | | |
|---|---|---|---|---|---|---|---|---|
| | loaf | lobster | thirst | lettuce | vinegar | drink | | |

| 31 | WALK | | | LEG | | | | |
|---|---|---|---|---|---|---|---|---|
| | guide | march | clap | volt | muscle | hand | | |

| 32 | EARLY | | | LATE | | | | |
|---|---|---|---|---|---|---|---|---|
| | sunrise | medal | lining | muggy | liquor | sunset | | |

| 33 | ANTARCTIC | | | ARCTIC | | | | |
|---|---|---|---|---|---|---|---|---|
| | thin | sapphire | South Pole | volcano | lizard | North Pole | | |

| 34 | JOIN | | | DETACH | | | | |
|---|---|---|---|---|---|---|---|---|
| | attach | groan | flood | voucher | jury | separate | | |

| 35 | MOON | | | NIGHT | | | | |
|---|---|---|---|---|---|---|---|---|
| | sun | medal | silver | lamp | menace | day | | |

| 36 | HIGH | | | LOW | | | | |
|---|---|---|---|---|---|---|---|---|
| | volt | glide | mountain | lift | lounge | valley | | |

| 37 | MOBILE | | | STATIONARY | | | | |
|---|---|---|---|---|---|---|---|---|
| | metal | lapel | motion | ladder | landscape | still | | |

| 38 | LAND | | | SHIP | | | | |
|---|---|---|---|---|---|---|---|---|
| | grounding | mayor | car | violin | jungle | sea | | |

168

| 39 | CHILL ||| FRIDGE ||| | |
|---|---|---|---|---|---|---|---|---|
| | sink | jumper | oven | jelly | glass | bake | | |

| 40 | COMEDY ||| LAUGH ||| | |
|---|---|---|---|---|---|---|---|---|
| | jacket | loan | tragedy | vote | knock | cry | | |

| Record Your Progress ||||| 
|---|---|---|---|---|
| Number of Times You Have Taken the Test | Record |||  Record Your Completion Time |
| | Number of Questions Completed | Your Total Score | Total No. of Questions | |
| 1 | | | | |
| 2 | | | | |
| 3 | | | | |
| 4 | | | | |
| 5 | | | | |

PRACTICE TESTS IN VERBAL REASONING

## SAMPLE TEST 30: SYNONYMS AND ANTONYMS

Which of the following words are closest in meaning to the words in capitals? Write the letter in the box.

1  HUGE
   a  transform
   b  baseless
   c  colossal
   d  emblem

The answer is C, so write this letter in the box.

Now do the following questions.

**Practice Test 59 (Answers on page 266)**

Which of the following words are closest in meaning to the words in capitals? Write the letter in the box.

1  LACKADAISICAL
   a  Antilles
   b  orderly
   c  enjoy
   d  apathetic

2  IGNOMINIOUS
   a  disgraceful
   b  beautiful
   c  delightful
   d  pleasing

3  CIRCUITOUS
   a  wholesome
   b  moody
   c  ambiguous
   d  detain

4  BOISTEROUS
   a  shallow
   b  tranquil
   c  bogus
   d  noisy

5  DURESS
   a  deaden
   b  pressure
   c  essential
   d  clouding

6  EVADE
   a  rebel
   b  culture
   c  blister
   d  avoid

PRACTICE TESTS IN VERBAL REASONING

7  **INSUPPORTABLE**
   a  sympathetic
   b  unbearable
   c  devout
   d  unlively

8  **ACCENTUATE**
   a  disturb
   b  expel
   c  emphasize
   d  devise

9  **IMPEL**
   a  urge
   b  imply
   c  excuse
   d  release

10  **FAMOUS**
    a  contracted
    b  disorganized
    c  haphazard
    d  important

11  **INEXORABLE**
    a  ethic
    b  expiry
    c  relentless
    d  infant

12  **COMMANDANT**
    a  officer
    b  destruction
    c  implosion
    d  restructure

13  **PERPENDICULAR**
    a  upright
    b  circular
    c  repetitive
    d  reflective

14  **UNWIELDY**
    a  unwise
    b  awkward
    c  upbeat
    d  suspicious

15  **NOBLEMAN**
    a  lounge
    b  press
    c  overflow
    d  lord

16  **DISCONSOLATE**
    a  discarded
    b  discrete
    c  disappointed
    d  irrational

## 17 INAUGURATE
a investigate
b introduce
c separate
d inaudible

## 18 DELICIOUS
a tasty
b undecided
c rebellion
d devious

## 19 RECTITUDE
a ingratitude
b honesty
c falsely
d resourceful

## 20 GLORIOUS
a heavy
b mirthful
c challenged
d magnificent

## 21 PERILOUS
a muddled
b sensible
c Persia
d dangerous

## 22 TUMBLE
a solid
b unclear
c fall
d blockade

## 23 SAFEGUARD
a protect
b practice
c teach
d survey

## 24 BIGOT
a intolerant
b remorse
c distinguished
d Severn

## 25 CONQUER
a bare
b loose
c defeat
d excuse

## 26 DILAPIDATED
a force
b collide
c ruined
d coincidence

27 **SAGACIOUS**
   a sensible
   b toneless
   c crafty
   d vex

28 **INDELICATE**
   a peach
   b indigo
   c sure
   d tactless

29 **DALLY**
   a deceive
   b dawdle
   c dance
   d trouble

30 **PROPITIATE**
   a display
   b indefinite
   c placate
   d protein

31 **HABITUATE**
   a familiarize
   b dismantle
   c fill
   d renew

32 **FETID**
   a churlish
   b ferret
   c stinking
   d fresh

33 **SELFISH**
   a forward
   b friendly
   c approachable
   d mean

34 **CUMBERSOME**
   a variable
   b steady
   c heavy
   d smoker

35 **ECHO**
   a command
   b reverberate
   c regard
   d prose

36 **SANGUINE**
   a repose
   b optimistic
   c grove
   d relieved

PRACTICE TESTS IN VERBAL REASONING

37  PLEASANT
    a   meekness
    b   offensive
    c   rotate
    d   enjoyable

38  PERHAPS
    a   fussy
    b   cruel
    c   possibly
    d   decaying

39  LUNACY
    a   rigid
    b   feeble
    c   weakness
    d   insanity

40  MOREOVER
    a   season
    b   molten
    c   besides
    d   mortar

| Record Your Progress |||||
|---|---|---|---|---|
| Number of Times You Have Taken the Test | Record ||| Record Your Completion Time |
| | Number of Questions Completed | Your Total Score | Total No. of Questions | |
| 1 | | | | |
| 2 | | | | |
| 3 | | | | |
| 4 | | | | |
| 5 | | | | |

## Practice Test 60 (Answers on page 266)

Which of the following words are closest in meaning to the words in capitals? Write the letter in the box.

1   SEVER
    a   separate
    b   collect
    c   remember
    d   train

2   COGNATE
    a   related
    b   desire
    c   covet
    d   promise

## PRACTICE TESTS IN VERBAL REASONING

**3 INSALUBRIOUS**
a healthy
b youthful
c unhygienic
d innuendo

**4 TUMULTUOUS**
a Tunisia
b confusion
c compassion
d mermaid

**5 COMMENCE**
a kind
b relax
c begin
d amateur

**6 PRICKLE**
a artisan
b statue
c puncture
d thorn

**7 VALUABLE**
a dark
b sumptuous
c metallic
d precious

**8 VIGILANT**
a stubborn
b vibrant
c permit
d watchful

**9 PALPABLE**
a obvious
b acknowledge
c prepare
d heighten

**10 DOGMATIC**
a reserved
b opinionated
c endure
d invalid

**11 COMPULSORY**
a optional
b unavoidable
c palmist
d insufferable

**12 VIVACIOUS**
a volt
b aorta
c lively
d encourage

PRACTICE TESTS IN VERBAL REASONING

13 PURCHASE
a buy
b floral
c uniform
d flashy

14 APPELLATION
a title
b vision
c outfit
d tame

15 FOLIAGE
a buoyancy
b term
c dress
d leaves

16 PRECARIOUS
a dumbfounded
b barrier
c enforced
d unsafe

17 ACADEMY
a unsettle
b denounce
c school
d rebuke

18 POSSESS
a bare
b satellite
c own
d postscript

19 RETURN
a overcast
b designation
c back
d harmful

20 CONGENIAL
a kindred
b confuse
c enforced
d loss

21 CORRIDOR
a immaterial
b passage
c unimportant
d tawdry

22 LITTER
a investigate
b rubbish
c discover
d shed

PRACTICE TESTS IN VERBAL REASONING

23 SMUDGE
a material
b narrate
c escape
d smear

24 CONFUTE
a porter
b porous
c prove
d portion

25 CONCOURSE
a depend
b crowd
c concrete
d conversation

26 CHARACTERISTIC
a trait
b underscore
c strikethrough
d assent

27 REPREHEND
a poser
b rebuke
c unsteady
d innocent

28 ACCORD
a guilty
b offensive
c consent
d illegal

29 FRIGHTEN
a impress
b surprise
c introduce
d scare

30 ELEVATE
a inflate
b presume
c tripe
d propose

31 JOCUND
a speak
b despondent
c abuse
d merry

32 OSTENTATION
a slander
b discuss
c showy
d teach

# PRACTICE TESTS IN VERBAL REASONING

**33 RESULT**
- a external
- b score
- c orchard
- d property

**34 RIDDLE**
- a delusional
- b puzzle
- c amorous
- d prosaic

**35 INSUBORDINATE**
- a rebellion
- b pressure
- c continue
- d deprivation

**36 MENTOR**
- a palpable
- b fetid
- c undulate
- d adviser

**37 COPIOUS**
- a small
- b impractical
- c plentiful
- d idealistic

**38 SQUABBLE**
- a quarrel
- b whimsical
- c dictator
- d astounded

**39 CONCEIVABLE**
- a eject
- b evade
- c disperse
- d imaginable

**40 WARBLE**
- a target
- b casualty
- c sing
- d quarry

PRACTICE TESTS IN VERBAL REASONING

| Record Your Progress |||||
|---|---|---|---|---|
| Number of Times You Have Taken the Test | Record ||| Record Your Completion Time |
|  | Number of Questions Completed | Your Total Score | Total No. of Questions |  |
| 1 |  |  |  |  |
| 2 |  |  |  |  |
| 3 |  |  |  |  |
| 4 |  |  |  |  |
| 5 |  |  |  |  |

## Practice Test 61 (Answers on page 267)

Which of the following words are closest in meaning to the words in capitals? Write the letter in the box.

1  **DISTORT**

| A | B | C | D | E |
|---|---|---|---|---|
| proximity | deflate | twist | gather | expel |

2  **BUDDY**

| A | B | C | D | E |
|---|---|---|---|---|
| friend | swordsman | writer | agent | actor |

3  **MAGNIFICENT**

| A | B | C | D | E |
|---|---|---|---|---|
| buffet | rule | daydream | ponder | splendid |

4  **BEGUILE**

| A | B | C | D | E |
|---|---|---|---|---|
| deceive | govern | dictate | impress | marriage |

5  **ANOINT**

| A | B | C | D | E |
|---|---|---|---|---|
| impress | spill | consecrate | rate | congregate |

PRACTICE TESTS IN VERBAL REASONING

**6 STUBBORN**

| A | B | C | D | E |
|---|---|---|---|---|
| unwilling | deliberate | exercise | speak | tolerate |

**7 ETHICAL**

| A | B | C | D | E |
|---|---|---|---|---|
| essential | irresolute | complete | upright | blame |

**8 LASS**

| A | B | C | D | E |
|---|---|---|---|---|
| dogmatic | girl | meticulous | vivacious | garish |

**9 SUFFICIENT**

| A | B | C | D | E |
|---|---|---|---|---|
| sprout | impale | grow | honor | enough |

**10 ASTUTE**

| A | B | C | D | E |
|---|---|---|---|---|
| shrewd | appraise | agree | partner | astound |

**11 OSTENSIBLE**

| A | B | C | D | E |
|---|---|---|---|---|
| avoidable | outcry | apparent | pretentious | oust |

**12 KERFUFFLE**

| A | B | C | D | E |
|---|---|---|---|---|
| declaration | communicate | drain | commotion | authorize |

**13 PEACEFUL**

| A | B | C | D | E |
|---|---|---|---|---|
| calm | decorate | visionary | temporal | lighthearted |

**14 VIRTUOUS**

| A | B | C | D | E |
|---|---|---|---|---|
| cumbersome | immoral | somber | faithless | ethical |

## 15 APPLAUD

| A | B | C | D | E |
|---|---|---|---|---|
| turn | praise | convert | empty | plea |

## 16 PROXIMITY

| A | B | C | D | E |
|---|---|---|---|---|
| city | decrease | town | neighborhood | distance |

## 17 ABHORRENT

| A | B | C | D | E |
|---|---|---|---|---|
| revealing | attractive | withdrawn | mellowed | distasteful |

## 18 CHAMPION

| A | B | C | D | E |
|---|---|---|---|---|
| denouncing | breach | judicial | winner | explosion |

## 19 APPREHEND

| A | B | C | D | E |
|---|---|---|---|---|
| prudent | discriminating | arrest | sensible | obtuse |

## 20 ANONYMOUS

| A | B | C | D | E |
|---|---|---|---|---|
| unsigned | detail | suited | accord | consent |

## 21 MOROSE

| A | B | C | D | E |
|---|---|---|---|---|
| elated | racket | unsociable | confident | delighted |

## 22 INTERLOPER

| A | B | C | D | E |
|---|---|---|---|---|
| measured | abhorrent | nauseous | appropriate | intruder |

## 23 FOWL

| A | B | C | D | E |
|---|---|---|---|---|
| chicken | scream | number | compete | outsmart |

## PRACTICE TESTS IN VERBAL REASONING

**24 APPEND**

| A | B | C | D | E |
|---|---|---|---|---|
| attach | pattern | prototype | level | mechanism |

**25 OBSTRUCT**

| A | B | C | D | E |
|---|---|---|---|---|
| thwart | enthused | occlude | opaque | suppressed |

**26 MINISCULE**

| A | B | C | D | E |
|---|---|---|---|---|
| enlightened | omen | thoughtful | stressed | minute |

**27 PROTECT**

| A | B | C | D | E |
|---|---|---|---|---|
| embracing | resistance | fierceness | defend | cruelty |

**28 ABSTRUSE**

| A | B | C | D | E |
|---|---|---|---|---|
| boldness | profound | breach | decorate | gulf |

**29 DISCONTENTED**

| A | B | C | D | E |
|---|---|---|---|---|
| liberty | dark | unhappy | myth | wonder |

**30 EXIGENCY**

| A | B | C | D | E |
|---|---|---|---|---|
| emergency | chaotic | schedule | disheveled | organized |

**31 DOZEN**

| A | B | C | D | E |
|---|---|---|---|---|
| assertive | prolific | excessive | crafty | twelve |

**32 IRRESOLUTE**

| A | B | C | D | E |
|---|---|---|---|---|
| attentive | distasteful | restraining | hesitating | immovable |

PRACTICE TESTS IN VERBAL REASONING

**33 IRKSOME**

| A | B | C | D | E |
|---|---|---|---|---|
| tiresome | expressive | sullen | liberated | open |

**34 MYRIAD**

| A | B | C | D | E |
|---|---|---|---|---|
| circle | mirage | method | round | innumerable |

**35 BABOON**

| A | B | C | D | E |
|---|---|---|---|---|
| permit | monkey | awaken | retaliate | bestow |

**36 ERECT**

| A | B | C | D | E |
|---|---|---|---|---|
| irregular | willful | disturbed | build | daunting |

**37 RELIABLE**

| A | B | C | D | E |
|---|---|---|---|---|
| agricultural | trusting | notability | simple | celebrity |

**38 DISCIPLINE**

| A | B | C | D | E |
|---|---|---|---|---|
| antiquated | difficult | secure | punish | embellished |

**39 FAMISHED**

| A | B | C | D | E |
|---|---|---|---|---|
| changeable | downcast | hungry | productive | undecided |

**40 DESCENDANTS**

| A | B | C | D | E |
|---|---|---|---|---|
| offspring | decrease | indent | standpoint | foundation |

PRACTICE TESTS IN VERBAL REASONING

| Record Your Progress |||||
| Number of Times You Have Taken the Test | Record ||| Record Your Completion Time |
| | Number of Questions Completed | Your Total Score | Total No. of Questions | |
| 1 | | | | |
| 2 | | | | |
| 3 | | | | |
| 4 | | | | |
| 5 | | | | |

## Practice Test 62 (Answers on page 267)

Which of the following words are closest in meaning to the words in capitals? Write the letter in the box.

1 **IRASCIBLE**

| A | B | C | D | E |
|---|---|---|---|---|
| nauseous | irritable | wavering | modest | timid |

2 **FEEBLE**

| A | B | C | D | E |
|---|---|---|---|---|
| puzzled | unchangeable | confused | nonexistence | weak |

3 **MISTAKE**

| A | B | C | D | E |
|---|---|---|---|---|
| foreboding | cranky | blind | fault | cringing |

4 **FIERCE**

| A | B | C | D | E |
|---|---|---|---|---|
| amenities | cruel | irritable | opinion | method |

5 **MINIMAL**

| A | B | C | D | E |
|---|---|---|---|---|
| encircle | horde | ground | nominal | symmetry |

184

PRACTICE TESTS IN VERBAL REASONING

6  **FILTHY**

| A | B | C | D | E |
|---|---|---|---|---|
| amend | irascible | dirty | resistance | cryptic |

7  **CHAPLAIN**

| A | B | C | D | E |
|---|---|---|---|---|
| clergyman | impatient | comment | prognosis | token |

8  **OBLITERATE**

| A | B | C | D | E |
|---|---|---|---|---|
| broil | manifest | pretentious | glower | destroy |

9  **IOTA**

| A | B | C | D | E |
|---|---|---|---|---|
| trifle | theory | sport | expand | view |

10  **ADORNMENT**

| A | B | C | D | E |
|---|---|---|---|---|
| warrior | thorough | marmalade | ornament | facsimile |

11  **MISTY**

| A | B | C | D | E |
|---|---|---|---|---|
| cranky | foggy | choleric | probe | faltering |

12  **INHIBIT**

| A | B | C | D | E |
|---|---|---|---|---|
| moral | guilty | restrain | shadow | glimmer |

13  **GAMMON**

| A | B | C | D | E |
|---|---|---|---|---|
| vilify | teach | trace | austere | ham |

14  **CONTRABAND**

| A | B | C | D | E |
|---|---|---|---|---|
| game | galore | forbidden | belt | undecided |

## PRACTICE TESTS IN VERBAL REASONING

**15 LIBERTY**

| A | B | C | D | E |
|---|---|---|---|---|
| occupied | condition | cramp | freedom | resign |

**16 NOXIOUS**

| A | B | C | D | E |
|---|---|---|---|---|
| create | educate | harmful | teach | unacceptable |

**17 CUMBERSOME**

| A | B | C | D | E |
|---|---|---|---|---|
| clumsy | cushion | detrimental | custody | crate |

**18 INSINUATE**

| A | B | C | D | E |
|---|---|---|---|---|
| faithful | incomplete | mischievous | compulsive | hint |

**19 PARDON**

| A | B | C | D | E |
|---|---|---|---|---|
| impulsive | forgive | destructive | disloyal | wakefulness |

**20 ILLEGAL**

| A | B | C | D | E |
|---|---|---|---|---|
| wicked | teacher | unfair | unlawful | mighty |

**21 INSUFFERABLE**

| A | B | C | D | E |
|---|---|---|---|---|
| production | unbearable | license | govern | reign |

**22 CAPACIOUS**

| A | B | C | D | E |
|---|---|---|---|---|
| charge | narrow | conceited | witty | broad |

**23 RAGE**

| A | B | C | D | E |
|---|---|---|---|---|
| whimsical | jubilant | fury | ample | humorist |

## PRACTICE TESTS IN VERBAL REASONING

**24 ENAMORED**

| A | B | C | D | E |
|---|---|---|---|---|
| fond | dogged | comprehensive | pleasantry | jest |

**25 ENCOUNTER**

| A | B | C | D | E |
|---|---|---|---|---|
| enfold | endurance | bashful | elegance | meet |

**26 SPARKLE**

| A | B | C | D | E |
|---|---|---|---|---|
| glitter | quirk | villainous | exhibited | offspring |

**27 MISERABLE**

| A | B | C | D | E |
|---|---|---|---|---|
| repair | profess | act | gloomy | express |

**28 EMINENT**

| A | B | C | D | E |
|---|---|---|---|---|
| lawful | famous | marching | jovial | self-controlled |

**29 ESTRANGE**

| A | B | C | D | E |
|---|---|---|---|---|
| fatigue | fright | alienate | inflate | unjust |

**30 SUBDUE**

| A | B | C | D | E |
|---|---|---|---|---|
| overcome | distress | shade | illness | illuminate |

**31 PENURY**

| A | B | C | D | E |
|---|---|---|---|---|
| hold | brighten | poverty | accumulate | collect |

**32 DWARF**

| A | B | C | D | E |
|---|---|---|---|---|
| deflate | demand | test | gnome | utilize |

# PRACTICE TESTS IN VERBAL REASONING

**33 TARGET**

| A | B | C | D | E |
|---|---|---|---|---|
| goal | inflate | desire | recall | dictate |

**34 OBSCENE**

| A | B | C | D | E |
|---|---|---|---|---|
| conform | reshape | rethink | weaken | indecent |

**35 UMPIRE**

| A | B | C | D | E |
|---|---|---|---|---|
| dislodge | injury | referee | yield | experience |

**36 ADDER**

| A | B | C | D | E |
|---|---|---|---|---|
| viper | clothe | uncover | conceal | alert |

**37 TUSSLE**

| A | B | C | D | E |
|---|---|---|---|---|
| guard | cloud | puff | conflict | obscure |

**38 TETCHY**

| A | B | C | D | E |
|---|---|---|---|---|
| distant | peevish | lewd | offensive | dim |

**39 NONSENSE**

| A | B | C | D | E |
|---|---|---|---|---|
| debase | straits | twaddle | comprehensive | plump |

**40 GUARDIANSHIP**

| A | B | C | D | E |
|---|---|---|---|---|
| tutelage | holiday | sabbatical | injection | immunity |

PRACTICE TESTS IN VERBAL REASONING

| Record Your Progress |||||
|---|---|---|---|---|
| Number of Times You Have Taken the Test | Record ||| Record Your Completion Time |
| | Number of Questions Completed | Your Total Score | Total No. of Questions | |
| 1 | | | | |
| 2 | | | | |
| 3 | | | | |
| 4 | | | | |
| 5 | | | | |

## Practice Test 63 (Answers on page 267)

Which of the following words are opposite in meaning to the words in capitals? Write the letter in the box.

1  CREATE

| A | B | C | D | E |
|---|---|---|---|---|
| rebuild | deliver | reduce | destroy | link |

2  ANTIQUATED

| A | B | C | D | E |
|---|---|---|---|---|
| equate | modern | denounce | gift | dire |

3  PAUCITY

| A | B | C | D | E |
|---|---|---|---|---|
| clumsy | awful | devious | awkward | surplus |

4  IMPERTINENT

| A | B | C | D | E |
|---|---|---|---|---|
| courteous | imply | cheeky | import | possible |

5  HYPOTHETICAL

| A | B | C | D | E |
|---|---|---|---|---|
| encourage | short | concrete | temporal | message |

## 6 OPTIONAL

| A | B | C | D | E |
|---|---|---|---|---|
| quarry | distort | target | required | casualty |

## 7 CONDENSE

| A | B | C | D | E |
|---|---|---|---|---|
| protract | elevate | continue | deprivation | pressure |

## 8 REJECT

| A | B | C | D | E |
|---|---|---|---|---|
| inactive | trifle | approve | loud | gaunt |

## 9 DANGEROUS

| A | B | C | D | E |
|---|---|---|---|---|
| safe | handful | tendency | stretch | leaning |

## 10 EXPENSIVE

| A | B | C | D | E |
|---|---|---|---|---|
| inspire | fondness | shorten | silenced | cheap |

## 11 APPROACH

| A | B | C | D | E |
|---|---|---|---|---|
| depart | aristocratic | liking | platform | associate |

## 12 CLANDESTINE

| A | B | C | D | E |
|---|---|---|---|---|
| covert | partiality | overt | noble | stage |

## 13 PROMINENT

| A | B | C | D | E |
|---|---|---|---|---|
| inconspicuous | covert | penchant | podium | distinction |

## 14 ALLOW

| A | B | C | D | E |
|---|---|---|---|---|
| temporary | seasonable | prehistoric | hinder | outdated |

## 15 DESTRUCTIVE

| A | B | C | D | E |
|---|---|---|---|---|
| perform | constructive | taste | posh | stand |

## 16 FOLLOW

| A | B | C | D | E |
|---|---|---|---|---|
| present | weakness | phase | titled | precede |

## 17 ARTIFICIAL

| A | B | C | D | E |
|---|---|---|---|---|
| natural | upper-class | tendency | period | finicky |

## 18 MINIMUM

| A | B | C | D | E |
|---|---|---|---|---|
| particular | step | maximum | juncture | leg |

## 19 INTERNAL

| A | B | C | D | E |
|---|---|---|---|---|
| demanding | point | external | theater | refined |

## 20 FAILURE

| A | B | C | D | E |
|---|---|---|---|---|
| success | difficult | arena | dainty | elope |

## 21 PERFIDIOUS

| A | B | C | D | E |
|---|---|---|---|---|
| honor | choosy | delicate | playhouse | faithful |

## 22 ABUNDANT

| A | B | C | D | E |
|---|---|---|---|---|
| scarce | boards | careful | honesty | respectability |

## 23 COMPLEX

| A | B | C | D | E |
|---|---|---|---|---|
| attentive | morality | simple | rostrum | disrespect |

# PRACTICE TESTS IN VERBAL REASONING

**24 ENABLE**

| A | B | C | D | E |
|---|---|---|---|---|
| disable | renown | exacting | painstaking | honorableness |

**25 WIDE**

| A | B | C | D | E |
|---|---|---|---|---|
| precise | worthiness | scaffold | narrow | importance |

**26 ATTRACTIVE**

| A | B | C | D | E |
|---|---|---|---|---|
| podium | harsh | honor | underground | repulsive |

**27 INTENTIONAL**

| A | B | C | D | E |
|---|---|---|---|---|
| meticulous | strident | stealthy | accidental | distinction |

**28 NOURISH**

| A | B | C | D | E |
|---|---|---|---|---|
| careless | prominence | starve | furtive | hoarse |

**29 SEQUENTIAL**

| A | B | C | D | E |
|---|---|---|---|---|
| disordered | grating | secret | undercover | dissonant |

**30 DISCORD**

| A | B | C | D | E |
|---|---|---|---|---|
| cumbersome | heavy | bare | loose | harmony |

**31 TERRIFY**

| A | B | C | D | E |
|---|---|---|---|---|
| embolden | surreptitious | guttural | jarring | pomade |

**32 EXACT**

| A | B | C | D | E |
|---|---|---|---|---|
| rasping | unmusical | approximate | illegal | furtive |

## 33 AUTHENTIC

| A | B | C | D | E |
|---|---|---|---|---|
| imitation | secret | gruff | sneaky | amenable |

## 34 CONVEX

| A | B | C | D | E |
|---|---|---|---|---|
| soft | clandestine | wild | concave | sly |

## 35 LIBERATE

| A | B | C | D | E |
|---|---|---|---|---|
| distinguished | determined | remorseful | intolerant | capture |

## 36 MILITARY

| A | B | C | D | E |
|---|---|---|---|---|
| stealthy | boisterous | friendly | civilian | guarded |

## 37 CANTANKEROUS

| A | B | C | D | E |
|---|---|---|---|---|
| underhanded | exposed | docile | disorderly | direct |

## 38 FIGURATIVE

| A | B | C | D | E |
|---|---|---|---|---|
| straight | receptive | unruly | uncluttered | literal |

## 39 SQUALOR

| A | B | C | D | E |
|---|---|---|---|---|
| abscond | riotous | amicable | luxury | frank |

## 40 FRESH

| A | B | C | D | E |
|---|---|---|---|---|
| churlish | fetid | rank | cheerless | honesty |

PRACTICE TESTS IN VERBAL REASONING

| Record Your Progress ||||
| --- | --- | --- | --- |
| Number of Times You Have Taken the Test | Record ||| Record Your Completion Time |
|  | Number of Questions Completed | Your Total Score | Total No. of Questions |  |
| 1 |  |  |  |  |
| 2 |  |  |  |  |
| 3 |  |  |  |  |
| 4 |  |  |  |  |
| 5 |  |  |  |  |

## Practice Test 64 (Answers on page 268)

Which of the following words are opposite in meaning to the words in capitals? Write the letter in the box.

1 IGNITE

| A | B | C | D | E |
| --- | --- | --- | --- | --- |
| undeveloped | sincere | extinguish | rowdy | sweeping |

2 COMMENCE

| A | B | C | D | E |
| --- | --- | --- | --- | --- |
| finish | unguarded | response | noisy | orderly |

3 IGNORANCE

| A | B | C | D | E |
| --- | --- | --- | --- | --- |
| candid | initiate | unlocked | abandon | knowledge |

4 DISSATISFIED

| A | B | C | D | E |
| --- | --- | --- | --- | --- |
| launch | gaping | diversion | content | activity |

5 SANGUINE

| A | B | C | D | E |
| --- | --- | --- | --- | --- |
| discouraged | relieved | optimistic | gross | sad |

PRACTICE TESTS IN VERBAL REASONING

6  CLOSE

| A | B | C | D | E |
|---|---|---|---|---|
| distraction | unbolt | elude | obstacle | open |

7  JUDICIOUS

| A | B | C | D | E |
|---|---|---|---|---|
| undo | imprudent | pastime | obstruction | overcoat |

8  INDUSTRIOUS

| A | B | C | D | E |
|---|---|---|---|---|
| unfasten | leisure | avoid | lazy | barrier |

9  SURREPTITIOUS

| A | B | C | D | E |
|---|---|---|---|---|
| hurdle | overt | teenage | untie | evade |

10  ETERNAL

| A | B | C | D | E |
|---|---|---|---|---|
| appease | approachable | lively | mortal | empathetic |

11  SENSIBLE

| A | B | C | D | E |
|---|---|---|---|---|
| unwrap | unhygienic | unwise | reprehensible | escapism |

12  HAUGHTY

| A | B | C | D | E |
|---|---|---|---|---|
| humble | baffling | dull | unlock | close |

13  TENTATIVE

| A | B | C | D | E |
|---|---|---|---|---|
| colorless | sure | dodge | hindrance | seep |

14  RELUCTANT

| A | B | C | D | E |
|---|---|---|---|---|
| avoidance | impede | leak | glitch | enthusiastic |

## PRACTICE TESTS IN VERBAL REASONING

**15 ESSENTIAL**

| A | B | C | D | E |
|---|---|---|---|---|
| ruthless | delicate | unavoidable | optional | insufferable |

**16 PROFIT**

| A | B | C | D | E |
|---|---|---|---|---|
| delay | loss | flow | detain | haste |

**17 VAGUE**

| A | B | C | D | E |
|---|---|---|---|---|
| drain | mystifying | hitch | certain | support |

**18 SUAVE**

| A | B | C | D | E |
|---|---|---|---|---|
| discourteous | discharge | snag | sustain | buttress |

**19 ENCUMBER**

| A | B | C | D | E |
|---|---|---|---|---|
| stoppage | outflow | access | assault | reinforcement |

**20 BLAMEWORTHY**

| A | B | C | D | E |
|---|---|---|---|---|
| innocent | somber | unsteady | sullen | puzzling |

**21 SUFFIX**

| A | B | C | D | E |
|---|---|---|---|---|
| burgle | difficulty | prefix | structure | underpin |

**22 DEBONAIR**

| A | B | C | D | E |
|---|---|---|---|---|
| graceless | bewildering | bottleneck | emphasize | quixotic |

**23 IMPULSIVE**

| A | B | C | D | E |
|---|---|---|---|---|
| bolster | partition | underline | deliberate | mountainous |

PRACTICE TESTS IN VERBAL REASONING

### 24 RETICENT

| A | B | C | D | E |
|---|---|---|---|---|
| highlight | confusing | fence | restriction | arrogant |

### 25 MUNDANE

| A | B | C | D | E |
|---|---|---|---|---|
| amorous | delusional | perplexing | inspiring | ordinary |

### 26 SWIFTLY

| A | B | C | D | E |
|---|---|---|---|---|
| dull | fortify | slowly | mass | enclose |

### 27 CIRCUMSPECT

| A | B | C | D | E |
|---|---|---|---|---|
| bamboozling | pile | commonplace | boost | imprudent |

### 28 EXEMPT

| A | B | C | D | E |
|---|---|---|---|---|
| access | edge | hidden | subject | actuality |

### 29 PERMANENT

| A | B | C | D | E |
|---|---|---|---|---|
| boarder | temporary | pedestrian | guttural | enlightening |

### 30 DIFFIDENT

| A | B | C | D | E |
|---|---|---|---|---|
| obstacle | banal | unresolved | blind | suppressed |

### 31 IMAGINARY

| A | B | C | D | E |
|---|---|---|---|---|
| real | concealed | exact | assistance | layer |

### 32 SOPHISTICATED

| A | B | C | D | E |
|---|---|---|---|---|
| masked | defend | declare | beneficial | primitive |

## 33 SUBSEQUENT

| A | B | C | D | E |
|---|---|---|---|---|
| contributory | private | swathe | prior | head |

## 34 MONK

| A | B | C | D | E |
|---|---|---|---|---|
| nun | undiscovered | involve | favorable | shelter |

## 35 SPONTANEOUSLY

| A | B | C | D | E |
|---|---|---|---|---|
| shield | encase | relentless | abyss | scripted |

## 36 INFREQUENT

| A | B | C | D | E |
|---|---|---|---|---|
| useful | often | comprise | esteem | intimation |

## 37 PRIMORDIAL

| A | B | C | D | E |
|---|---|---|---|---|
| embrace | proposition | aura | modern | decay |

## 38 JERKY

| A | B | C | D | E |
|---|---|---|---|---|
| camouflage | smooth | contain | submission | indication |

## 39 POLISHED

| A | B | C | D | E |
|---|---|---|---|---|
| proposal | scheme | implication | coarse | communicate |

## 40 INDETERMINATE

| A | B | C | D | E |
|---|---|---|---|---|
| talkative | offer | clear | propose | rope |

PRACTICE TESTS IN VERBAL REASONING

| Number of Times You Have Taken the Test | Record | | | Record Your Completion Time |
|---|---|---|---|---|
| | Number of Questions Completed | Your Total Score | Total No. of Questions | |
| 1 | | | | |
| 2 | | | | |
| 3 | | | | |
| 4 | | | | |
| 5 | | | | |

## Practice Test 65 (Answers on page 268)

Which of the following words are opposite in meaning to the words in capitals? Write the letter in the box.

1   NARROW
   a   wide
   b   withdrawn
   c   adjacent
   d   fine

2   CIRCUMVENT
   a   overreach
   b   miser
   c   cheat
   d   praiseworthy

3   ELONGATE
   a   surprised
   b   scared
   c   horrible
   d   shortened

4   WONDERFUL
   a   graceless
   b   proud
   c   awful
   d   forward

5   SEA
   a   mammal
   b   humble
   c   heavens
   d   land

6   EXHIBIT
   a   apprentice
   b   prideful
   c   conceal
   d   shameful

## PRACTICE TESTS IN VERBAL REASONING

7  AGITATED
   a  initiate
   b  learning
   c  noise
   d  calm

8  TUMULT
   a  gross
   b  uproar
   c  peace
   d  contrary

9  CENSURE
   a  doubt
   b  insecure
   c  openness
   d  difficulty

10 SOBER
   a  drunk
   b  earth
   c  pet
   d  man

11 CLUSTER
   a  odd
   b  inappropriate
   c  scatter
   d  darken

12 PLAUSIBLE
   a  swindle
   b  unlikely
   c  succumb
   d  ample

13 FASTIDIOUS
   a  demanding
   b  clumsy
   c  plenty
   d  relaxed

14 DWARF
   a  giant
   b  scrupulous
   c  trivial
   d  fussy

15 WEALTHY
   a  flush
   b  poor
   c  finicky
   d  agreeable

16 MODERN
   a  formless
   b  prosperous
   c  painstaking
   d  antique

17 MOUNTED
   a  opening
   b  assiduous
   c  afoot
   d  inept

18 VOLUMINOUS
   a  awkward
   b  small
   c  careful
   d  full

| | | | | |
|---|---|---|---|---|
| 19 | **TYRANNIZE** | | 20 | **SHALLOW** |
| a | liberate | | a | thorough |
| b | shapeless | | b | deep |
| c | particular | | c | commemorate |
| d | overwhelm | | d | pillar |

| | | | | |
|---|---|---|---|---|
| 21 | **ARROGANCE** | | 22 | **AVARICIOUS** |
| a | wealth | | a | covetous |
| b | meticulous | | b | maladroit |
| c | polite | | c | conscientious |
| d | ungainly | | d | generous |

| | | | | |
|---|---|---|---|---|
| 23 | **MISERABLE** | | 24 | **SUMPTUOUS** |
| a | envoy | | a | luxurious |
| b | nebulous | | b | vague |
| c | gauche | | c | lumbering |
| d | happy | | d | meager |

| | | | | |
|---|---|---|---|---|
| 25 | **PROSPERITY** | | 26 | **LEAST** |
| a | wellbeing | | a | impoverished |
| b | inelegant | | b | most |
| c | destitute | | c | gawky |
| d | unstructured | | d | stingy |

| | | | | |
|---|---|---|---|---|
| 27 | **PARSIMONIOUS** | | 28 | **ADMIT** |
| a | capacious | | a | deny |
| b | generous | | b | huge |
| c | amend | | c | desecrate |
| d | fluid | | d | monument |

| | | | | |
|---|---|---|---|---|
| 29 | **BEAUTIFUL** | | 30 | **TIGHT** |
| a | tribute | | a | team |
| b | benevolence | | b | accomplice |
| c | disagreeable | | c | loose |
| d | ugly | | d | courteous |

PRACTICE TESTS IN VERBAL REASONING

31 INDUCE
a lose
b polite
c bulky
d obtain

32 USELESS
a correct
b memorial
c ancient
d necessary

33 TRAGEDY
a punctilious
b exuberant
c comedy
d proper

34 CREDIT
a great
b debit
c commemoration
d resounding

35 TRIUMPH
a fail
b extravagant
c celebrate
d surround

36 PROBLEM
a remembrance
b costly
c solution
d deafening

37 HORIZONTAL
a lavish
b vertical
c materialistic
d rebellious

38 INSOLENT
a opulent
b dedicate
c respectful
d impertinent

39 CORRECT
a characterless
b plush
c error
d blame

40 PANDEMONIUM
a depraved
b uproar
c outcry
d tranquil

## Record Your Progress

| Number of Times You Have Taken the Test | Record | | | Record Your Completion Time |
|---|---|---|---|---|
| | Number of Questions Completed | Your Total Score | Total No. of Questions | |
| 1 | | | | |
| 2 | | | | |
| 3 | | | | |
| 4 | | | | |
| 5 | | | | |

## Practice Test 66 (Answers on page 268)

Which of the following words are opposite in meaning to the words in capitals? Write the letter in the box.

1  REWARD
   a  defamation
   b  spectacular
   c  fitness
   d  penalty

2  OPTIMISM
   a  pessimistic
   b  healthiness
   c  characteristic
   d  superb

3  MAJUSCULE
   a  magnificent
   b  miniscule
   c  strength
   d  unconverted

4  BORROW
   a  corpulent
   b  vigor
   c  lend
   d  illusory

5  AFFILIATE
   a  disassociate
   b  shape
   c  sturdiness
   d  link

6  AUGMENT
   a  flaw
   b  robustness
   c  increase
   d  nondescript

# PRACTICE TESTS IN VERBAL REASONING

7  **STINGY**
   a generous
   b stoutness
   c indescribable
   d jovial

8  **COGNITION**
   a success
   b toughness
   c liberal
   d unaware

9  **CONVICT**
   a accommodating
   b charity
   c correlate
   d exonerate

10 **DETACH**
   a overcome
   b ordinary
   c fix
   d dimension

11 **PROCURE**
   a entrust
   b demolish
   c discard
   d prevail

12 **GRANT**
   a dispose
   b withhold
   c appoint
   d deaden

13 **PATRIMONY**
   a divest
   b allocate
   c indigent
   d legacy

14 **NONCHALANT**
   a common
   b concerned
   c penniless
   d indifferent

15 **DECIMATE**
   a organize
   b poor
   c peculiar
   d dull

16 **EREMITE**
   a arrange
   b rapacious
   c approachable
   d deranged

17 **ILLUSTRIOUS**
   a avid
   b depute
   c celebrity
   d forgettable

18 **COGNIZANCE**
   a assign
   b oblivious
   c lonesome
   d grasping

19  CHEERFUL
    a  invent
    b  designate
    c  acquisitive
    d  dismal

20  DIFFICULT
    a  disperse
    b  easy
    c  obsess
    d  odd

21  PATIENT
    a  diplomat
    b  elect
    c  doctor
    d  administrator

22  STRONG
    a  feeble
    b  detail
    c  commissioner
    d  attentive

23  ECONOMIZE
    a  waste
    b  choose
    c  spokesperson
    d  mature

24  SELDOM
    a  grudging
    b  frequent
    c  contributions
    d  cruel

25  DEVOUR
    a  conserve
    b  mausoleum
    c  unclassifiable
    d  engulf

26  STALE
    a  depriving
    b  representative
    c  fresh
    d  sensible

27  LUCRATIVE
    a  evocative
    b  unproductive
    c  remote
    d  agent

28  PALATABLE
    a  expressive
    b  conscientious
    c  acceptable
    d  insipid

29  LOST
    a  deputized
    b  found
    c  accomplished
    d  altruistic

30  VALLEY
    a  emissary
    b  hill
    c  serious
    d  mindful

## PRACTICE TESTS IN VERBAL REASONING

31 **ALLEGIANCE**
 a disloyal
 b typical
 c attribute
 d gratify

32 **OSTENTATIOUS**
 a demonstrative
 b modest
 c quality
 d profitable

33 **DAWN**
 a openhanded
 b donations
 c reward
 d dusk

34 **CAPTIVITY**
 a hassle
 b offerings
 c altruism
 d freedom

35 **EMPLOYER**
 a distinguishing
 b normal
 c employee
 d hindrance

36 **GUARDIAN**
 a ward
 b kindness
 c scrap
 d handout

37 **IMMENSE**
 a tiny
 b socialize
 c whit
 d tolerance

38 **SUPERIOR**
 a inferior
 b frequent
 c glaring
 d humanity

39 **COMATOSE**
 a disband
 b compassion
 c energize
 d confident

40 **PRESUME**
 a actuality
 b combine
 c hinder
 d generosity

PRACTICE TESTS IN VERBAL REASONING

| Number of Times You Have Taken the Test | Record ||| Record Your Completion Time |
|---|---|---|---|---|
| | Number of Questions Completed | Your Total Score | Total No. of Questions | |
| 1 | | | | |
| 2 | | | | |
| 3 | | | | |
| 4 | | | | |
| 5 | | | | |

# PRACTICE TESTS IN VERBAL REASONING

## SAMPLE TEST 31: ODD ONE OUT

Which word does not belong with the other three? Here is an example.

1. a bedroom
   b kitchen
   c voyage
   d pantry

The answer is c because all the other words are rooms in a house.

## Practice Test 67 (Answers on page 268)

Which word does not belong with the other three? Write the letter corresponding to the correct answer in the box.

1. a car
   b van
   c lorry
   d ship

2. a oil
   b apple
   c pear
   d pink

3. a unusual
   b irregular
   c abnormal
   d weight

4. a spontaneous
   b improvised
   c rebellious
   d unpremeditated

5. a polyester
   b viscose
   c cotton
   d lime

6. a curator
   b strange
   c peculiar
   d weird

7. a fashionable
   b stylist
   c trendy
   d knight

8. a sugar
   b honey
   c syrup
   d acid

| | | | | | | | |
|---|---|---|---|---|---|---|---|
| 9 | a | miserable | | 10 | a | solicitor | |
| | b | glum | | | b | accountant | |
| | c | cheerful | | | c | engineer | |
| | d | downcast | | | d | quartet | |
| 11 | a | slate | | 12 | a | unremarkable | |
| | b | marble | | | b | astounding | |
| | c | granite | | | c | marvelous | |
| | d | fluid | | | d | startling | |
| 13 | a | violin | | 14 | a | river | |
| | b | earthenware | | | b | canal | |
| | c | clarinet | | | c | stream | |
| | d | cello | | | d | Sahara | |
| 15 | a | apple | | 16 | a | crimson | |
| | b | red | | | b | boring | |
| | c | blue | | | c | tedious | |
| | d | purple | | | d | tiresome | |
| 17 | a | monk | | 18 | a | head | |
| | b | hermit | | | b | pinnacle | |
| | c | mishap | | | c | unreceptive | |
| | d | recluse | | | d | summit | |
| 19 | a | assistance | | 20 | a | pirate | |
| | b | aid | | | b | encase | |
| | c | misbehavior | | | c | cloaked | |
| | d | support | | | d | concealed | |
| 21 | a | deterrent | | 22 | a | honor | |
| | b | hindrance | | | b | misconduct | |
| | c | blockage | | | c | exalt | |
| | d | novel | | | d | glorify | |

| | | | | | | | |
|---|---|---|---|---|---|---|---|
| 23 | a | insinuation | | 24 | a | headstrong | |
| | b | hint | | | b | cantankerous | |
| | c | clashing | | | c | stubborn | |
| | d | suggestion | | | d | collection | |
| | | | | | | | |
| 25 | a | dire | | 26 | a | honesty | |
| | b | replenish | | | b | bulky | |
| | c | ominous | | | c | cumbersome | |
| | d | awful | | | d | heavy | |
| | | | | | | | |
| 27 | a | chair | | 28 | a | pertinacious | |
| | b | table | | | b | persistent | |
| | c | cabinet | | | c | material | |
| | d | vehicle | | | d | determined | |
| | | | | | | | |
| 29 | a | raw | | 30 | a | denigrate | |
| | b | fresh | | | b | inaugurate | |
| | c | bare | | | c | install | |
| | d | joke | | | d | introduce | |
| | | | | | | | |
| 31 | a | basil | | 32 | a | untiring | |
| | b | poultry | | | b | unfaltering | |
| | c | mint | | | c | excoriate | |
| | d | parsley | | | d | indefatigable | |
| | | | | | | | |
| 33 | a | mismatched | | 34 | a | praise | |
| | b | banter | | | b | acclaim | |
| | c | repartee | | | c | squalid | |
| | d | teasing | | | d | extol | |
| | | | | | | | |
| 35 | a | sensible | | 36 | a | petrol | |
| | b | reasonable | | | b | flour | |
| | c | judicious | | | c | eggs | |
| | d | taxidermist | | | d | butter | |

PRACTICE TESTS IN VERBAL REASONING

| 37 | a | reprimand | | 38 | a | eyes |
| | b | delight | | | b | nose |
| | c | scold | | | c | mouth |
| | d | berate | | | d | telephone |

| 39 | a | improper | | 40 | a | blouse |
| | b | educate | | | b | skirt |
| | c | indelicate | | | c | bin liner |
| | d | unseemly | | | d | dress |

| 41 | a | unmovable | | 42 | a | intimidate |
| | b | adamant | | | b | docile |
| | c | steadfast | | | c | aggressive |
| | d | beautiful | | | d | antagonistic |

| 43 | a | charitable | | 44 | a | sunshine |
| | b | generous | | | b | printer |
| | c | openhanded | | | c | scanner |
| | d | contradictory | | | d | fax |

| 45 | a | clumsy | | 46 | a | harsh |
| | b | knowledgeable | | | b | unpleasant |
| | c | ungainly | | | c | discordant |
| | d | awkward | | | d | collection |

| 47 | a | kind | | 48 | a | variable |
| | b | conflicting | | | b | unstable |
| | c | friendly | | | c | vein |
| | d | amiable | | | d | changeable |

| 49 | a | ancillary | | 50 | a | shrewd |
| | b | agreeable | | | b | garment |
| | c | enjoyable | | | c | intelligent |
| | d | pleasing | | | d | astute |

| Record Your Progress |||||
|---|---|---|---|---|
| Number of Times You Have Taken the Test | Record ||| Record Your Completion Time |
| | Number of Questions Completed | Your Total Score | Total No. of Questions | |
| 1 | | | | |
| 2 | | | | |
| 3 | | | | |
| 4 | | | | |
| 5 | | | | |

## Practice Test 68 (Answers on page 268)

Which word does not belong with the other three? Write the letter corresponding to the correct answer in the box.

1. 
   a. pleasurable
   b. nice
   c. seedy
   d. lovely

2. 
   a. hotel
   b. hostel
   c. motel
   d. nursery

3. 
   a. indecisive
   b. gift
   c. irresolute
   d. hesitant

4. 
   a. picky
   b. choosy
   c. fussy
   d. office

5. 
   a. reliable
   b. dependable
   c. trustworthy
   d. barrier

6. 
   a. habitual
   b. contribute
   c. expected
   d. accustomed

7. 
   a. teacher
   b. pupil
   c. headmaster
   d. mountain

8. 
   a. impolite
   b. lender
   c. ill-mannered
   d. unsteady

| | | | | | | | |
|---|---|---|---|---|---|---|---|
| 9 | a | explanation | | 10 | a | pillow | |
| | b | dictionary | | | b | duvet | |
| | c | diary | | | c | blanket | |
| | d | words | | | d | staple | |
| 11 | a | communicate | | 12 | a | unreceptive | |
| | b | translucent | | | b | argumentative | |
| | c | crystalline | | | c | machine | |
| | d | transparent | | | d | unsympathetic | |
| 13 | a | remorseless | | 14 | a | aware | |
| | b | cruel | | | b | perceptive | |
| | c | merciless | | | c | insightful | |
| | d | prudent | | | d | remedy | |
| 15 | a | fork | | 16 | a | merge | |
| | b | fetlock | | | b | join | |
| | c | spoon | | | c | alight | |
| | d | knife | | | d | reunite | |
| 17 | a | alert | | 18 | a | fresh | |
| | b | conformist | | | b | new | |
| | c | conservative | | | c | rail | |
| | d | unadventurous | | | d | latest | |
| 19 | a | humorous | | 20 | a | mars | |
| | b | infiltrate | | | b | saturn | |
| | c | breakthrough | | | c | drum | |
| | d | penetrate | | | d | venus | |
| 21 | a | resistant | | 22 | a | hoe | |
| | b | diplomat | | | b | cutlass | |
| | c | impermeable | | | c | spade | |
| | d | solid | | | d | oven | |

## PRACTICE TESTS IN VERBAL REASONING

| 23 | a | manager | | 24 | a | vacillating | |
| --- | --- | --- | --- | --- | --- | --- | --- |
| | b | canteen | | | b | erratic | |
| | c | boss | | | c | appoint | |
| | d | supervisor | | | d | indecisive | |

| 25 | a | damask | | 26 | a | militant | |
| --- | --- | --- | --- | --- | --- | --- | --- |
| | b | conventional | | | b | advocate | |
| | c | common | | | c | confrontational | |
| | d | customary | | | d | tailor | |

| 27 | a | marker | | 28 | a | standard | |
| --- | --- | --- | --- | --- | --- | --- | --- |
| | b | pointer | | | b | usual | |
| | c | signpost | | | c | envious | |
| | d | harlequin | | | d | normal | |

| 29 | a | security | | 30 | a | disparage | |
| --- | --- | --- | --- | --- | --- | --- | --- |
| | b | tactless | | | b | degrade | |
| | c | insensitive | | | c | compose | |
| | d | inappropriate | | | d | belittle | |

| 31 | a | fidelity | | 32 | a | good-humored | |
| --- | --- | --- | --- | --- | --- | --- | --- |
| | b | malign | | | b | cheery | |
| | c | defame | | | c | irritable | |
| | d | smear | | | d | welcoming | |

| 33 | a | unfathomable | | 34 | a | defendant | |
| --- | --- | --- | --- | --- | --- | --- | --- |
| | b | unintelligible | | | b | judge | |
| | c | impenetrable | | | c | jury | |
| | d | shareholder | | | d | galaxy | |

| 35 | a | plant | | 36 | a | historic | |
| --- | --- | --- | --- | --- | --- | --- | --- |
| | b | compute | | | b | groundbreaking | |
| | c | trees | | | c | commodity | |
| | d | shrub | | | d | significant | |

PRACTICE TESTS IN VERBAL REASONING

| 37 | a | considerate   |  | 38 | a | genial        |  |
|----|---|---------------|--|----|---|---------------|--|
|    | b | unsuited      |  |    | b | nauseous      |  |
|    | c | incompatible  |  |    | c | nice          |  |
|    | d | irreconcilable|  |    | d | affable       |  |

| 39 | a | crambo        |  | 40 | a | inexplicable  |  |
|----|---|---------------|--|----|---|---------------|--|
|    | b | uncouth       |  |    | b | abundant      |  |
|    | c | boorish       |  |    | c | inconceivable |  |
|    | d | ill-bred      |  |    | d | perplexing    |  |

| 41 | a | pioneering    |  | 42 | a | combative     |  |
|----|---|---------------|--|----|---|---------------|--|
|    | b | inventive     |  |    | b | adornment     |  |
|    | c | innovative    |  |    | c | rebellious    |  |
|    | d | visa          |  |    | d | belligerent   |  |

| 43 | a | tomatoes      |  | 44 | a | needle        |  |
|----|---|---------------|--|----|---|---------------|--|
|    | b | peppers       |  |    | b | thread        |  |
|    | c | bicycle       |  |    | c | editor        |  |
|    | d | onions        |  |    | d | thimble       |  |

| 45 | a | vicar         |  | 46 | a | unswerving    |  |
|----|---|---------------|--|----|---|---------------|--|
|    | b | marriage      |  |    | b | unfailing     |  |
|    | c | church        |  |    | c | disagreeable  |  |
|    | d | zinc          |  |    | d | steady        |  |

| 47 | a | ancestor      |  | 48 | a | tennis        |  |
|    | b | unpredictable |  |    | b | squash        |  |
|    | c | changeable    |  |    | c | mouse         |  |
|    | d | capricious    |  |    | d | badminton     |  |

| 49 | a | winter        |  | 50 | a | run           |  |
|    | b | summer        |  |    | b | scar          |  |
|    | c | spring        |  |    | c | walk          |  |
|    | d | lawn          |  |    | d | crawl         |  |

PRACTICE TESTS IN VERBAL REASONING

| Record Your Progress ||||| 
|---|---|---|---|---|
| Number of Times You Have Taken the Test | Record ||| Record Your Completion Time |
|  | Number of Questions Completed | Your Total Score | Total No. of Questions |  |
| 1 |  |  |  |  |
| 2 |  |  |  |  |
| 3 |  |  |  |  |
| 4 |  |  |  |  |
| 5 |  |  |  |  |

PRACTICE TESTS IN VERBAL REASONING

# SAMPLE TEST 32: ANAGRAMS

*Anagrams* are words made from the letters of another word. They do not have to use all the letters of the word. You are required to find which words in the list provided form another word in the list and write the corresponding words in the space provided

| A | B | C | D | E |
|---|---|---|---|---|
| god | book | take | dog | roof |

_____  _____

The answers are *a* and *d*. Now answer the following questions.

## Practice Test 69 (Answers on page 268)

Find which words in the list that form another word in the list, and write the corresponding letters in the space provided.

|    | A        | B        | C       | D       | E       |         |         |
|----|----------|----------|---------|---------|---------|---------|---------|
| 1  | swim     | never    | pool    | scoop   | loop    | _____  | _____  |
| 2  | move     | tiger    | wolf    | flow    | zebra   | _____  | _____  |
| 3  | yaw      | year     | way     | tree    | seed    | _____  | _____  |
| 4  | door     | window   | rude    | rood    | low     | _____  | _____  |
| 5  | pan      | rest     | sleep   | pot     | nap     | _____  | _____  |
| 6  | pot      | noise    | top     | button  | find    | _____  | _____  |
| 7  | drawer   | prise    | force   | reward  | pull    | _____  | _____  |
| 8  | like     | stressed | tired   | open    | desserts| _____  | _____  |
| 9  | exchange | than     | paws    | foot    | swap    | _____  | _____  |
| 10 | grouse   | taps     | saliva  | spat    | apt     | _____  | _____  |
| 11 | yo-yo    | won      | simple  | scorn   | now     | _____  | _____  |
| 12 | live     | die      | evil    | cunning | good    | _____  | _____  |
| 13 | nappy    | paper    | diaper  | rapid   | repaid  | _____  | _____  |
| 14 | hay      | straw    | warts   | pores   | nose    | _____  | _____  |
| 15 | give     | terrible | take    | deliver | reviled | _____  | _____  |
| 16 | sink     | gulp     | swallow | cry     | plug    | _____  | _____  |
| 17 | ward     | apply    | match   | draw    | paint   | _____  | _____  |
| 18 | quit     | base     | pans    | snap    | open    | _____  | _____  |
| 19 | nuts     | knot     | loft    | stun    | water   | _____  | _____  |
| 20 | rats     | e-mail   | print   | star    | soft    | _____  | _____  |

217

## PRACTICE TESTS IN VERBAL REASONING

| \multicolumn{5}{c|}{**Record Your Progress**} |
|---|---|---|---|---|
| Number of Times You Have Taken the Test | \multicolumn{3}{c|}{Record} | Record Your Completion Time |
| | Number of Questions Completed | Your Total Score | Total No. of Questions | |
| 1 | | | | |
| 2 | | | | |
| 3 | | | | |
| 4 | | | | |
| 5 | | | | |

# SAMPLE TEST 33: LETTER MOVED FROM ONE WORD TO ANOTHER

You are required to move a letter from one word to the second word you will be provided with to form two new words. Here is an example.

                Metal                though    (    )  (    )

The answer is *meal* and *thought*. When you move the letter *t* from *metal*, you get *meal*, and when this letter is added to *though*, it becomes *thought*.

Now answer the following questions.

## Practice Test 70 (Answers on page 269)

In the questions below, you must move one letter from the word on the left to the word on the right to make two new words. You must not rearrange the letters. Write your answer in the space provided.

| | | | | |
|---|---|---|---|---|
| 1. | pink | ill | ( ) | ( ) |
| 2. | horse | tea | ( ) | ( ) |
| 3. | warm | it | ( ) | ( ) |
| 4. | plant | pace | ( ) | ( ) |
| 5. | grime | chap | ( ) | ( ) |
| 6. | brush | tip | ( ) | ( ) |
| 7. | son | hotel | ( ) | ( ) |
| 8. | shop | eat | ( ) | ( ) |
| 9. | hope | ant | ( ) | ( ) |
| 10. | feel | heath | ( ) | ( ) |
| 11. | hat | ash | ( ) | ( ) |
| 12. | blank | ace | ( ) | ( ) |
| 13. | stall | ink | ( ) | ( ) |
| 14. | note | tar | ( ) | ( ) |
| 15. | plan | ice | ( ) | ( ) |
| 16. | off | old | ( ) | ( ) |
| 17. | hear | at | ( ) | ( ) |
| 18. | tall | act | ( ) | ( ) |
| 19. | part | ant | ( ) | ( ) |
| 20. | flip | lame | ( ) | ( ) |

PRACTICE TESTS IN VERBAL REASONING

| 21 | play | ate | ( | ) | ( | ) |
| 22 | when | arm | ( | ) | ( | ) |
| 23 | probe | act | ( | ) | ( | ) |
| 24 | tear | hose | ( | ) | ( | ) |
| 25 | pore | ride | ( | ) | ( | ) |
| 26 | brown | take | ( | ) | ( | ) |
| 27 | globe | lass | ( | ) | ( | ) |
| 28 | coil | harm | ( | ) | ( | ) |
| 29 | baited | pant | ( | ) | ( | ) |
| 30 | bore | ox | ( | ) | ( | ) |
| 31 | pink | ear | ( | ) | ( | ) |
| 32 | blank | pan | ( | ) | ( | ) |
| 33 | player | fight | ( | ) | ( | ) |
| 34 | health | fee | ( | ) | ( | ) |
| 35 | blame | low | ( | ) | ( | ) |
| 36 | brush | cad | ( | ) | ( | ) |
| 37 | place | east | ( | ) | ( | ) |
| 38 | clove | up | ( | ) | ( | ) |
| 39 | pore | inch | ( | ) | ( | ) |
| 40 | place | lot | ( | ) | ( | ) |
| 41 | fright | time | ( | ) | ( | ) |
| 42 | duet | sing | ( | ) | ( | ) |
| 43 | harrow | tank | ( | ) | ( | ) |
| 44 | train | plea | ( | ) | ( | ) |
| 45 | crane | beak | ( | ) | ( | ) |
| 46 | flight | came | ( | ) | ( | ) |
| 47 | tart | able | ( | ) | ( | ) |
| 48 | those | hen | ( | ) | ( | ) |
| 49 | pat | eel | ( | ) | ( | ) |
| 50 | hold | pat | ( | ) | ( | ) |

# PRACTICE TESTS IN VERBAL REASONING

| \multicolumn{5}{|c|}{Record Your Progress} |
|---|---|---|---|---|
| Number of Times You Have Taken the Test | \multicolumn{3}{c|}{Record} | Record Your Completion Time |
| | Number of Questions Completed | Your Total Score | Total No. of Questions | |
| 1 | | | | |
| 2 | | | | |
| 3 | | | | |
| 4 | | | | |
| 5 | | | | |

# CRITICAL VERBAL REASONING TESTS

Your ability to make logical decisions is what is being tested in this section. You will reason with the written information provided. You are only expected to base your response on the questions on the information provided in the passages. Do not make your decisions based on your opinions, beliefs, or other information not in a passage. Keep it simple by only relying on the information contained in each passage as the basis for your judgment. Employers use critical verbal reasoning tests to assess candidates for graduate and managerial positions. These types of verbal tests often contain a degree of ambiguity, unlike mathematical reasoning tests where the answers are more definite. Although they are not intended to be trick questions, there is often room for argument in the interpretation of the answers. These tests are not rigorous and are offered to help you to practice this type of test and gain some familiarity.

Here are some examples.

## SAMPLE TEST 34: DECISION MAKING

> Cardiovascular disease is so prevalent that virtually all businesses are likely to have employees who suffer from, or may develop, this condition. Research shows that between 50–80% of all people who suffer a heart attack are able to return to work. However, this may not be possible if they have previously been involved in heavy physical work. In such cases, it may be possible to move the employee to lighter duties, with appropriate retraining where necessary. Similarly, high-pressure, stressful work, even where it does not involve physical activity, should also be avoided. Human resource managers should be aware of the implications of job roles for employees with a cardiac condition.

1) Physical or stressful work may bring on a heart attack.

   A. The statement is *definitely true* or would be a reasonable conclusion to draw from the passage.

   B. The statement is *definitely untrue* or would not be a reasonable conclusion to draw.

   C. I have *insufficient information* to answer either of the above with any certainty.

The answer is C.

PRACTICE TESTS IN VERBAL REASONING

We have *insufficient information* given in the paragraph to reach a conclusion whether physical or stressful work may bring on a heart attack.

2) The majority of people who have suffered a heart attack can later return to work.

   A. The statement is *definitely true* or would be a reasonable conclusion to draw from the passage.

   B. The statement is *definitely untrue* or would not be a reasonable conclusion to draw.

   C. I have *insufficient information* to answer either of the above with any certainty.

The answer is A.

The text states that over half of heart attack victims can later return to work.

3) Heart disease may affect employees in any type of business.

The answer is A.

This follows logically from the opening statement that virtually all businesses are likely to have employees who suffer from, or may develop, this condition.

4) Heart disease can affect people of any age.

The answer is C.

There is *insufficient information* in the passage to answer. It makes no reference to the age of heart patients and therefore we cannot say if the statement is true.

That was the final example. You are now required to do the following practice tests.

## Practice Test 71 (Answers on page 269)

You are provided with a passage of text followed by two statements. You are required to read each passage carefully and then decide how to classify each of the statements. Each statement can be classified as:

   True: This means that, on the basis of the information in the passage, the statement is true or logically flows from the passage.

# PRACTICE TESTS IN VERBAL REASONING

False: This means that, on the basis of the information in the passage, the statement is false.

Cannot say: This means that, on the basis of the information in the passage, you cannot tell whether the information is true or false.

The test has 34 questions, and you will have 20 minutes to do them.

---

A UN report has warned of the potential problems of global warming. If the production of greenhouse gas continues at the current rate, this will result in the melting of the ice sheets in Greenland and the Antarctic. The consequences of this will be rising sea levels, which will endanger 145 million people. In response to the problem, the report observes the need for an immediate international agreement on reducing emissions.

---

1  Inhabitants of Greenland and Antarctica will be the most severely affected by rising sea levels.

True ☐  False ☐  Cannot say ☐

2  The melting of the ice sheets is the primary consequence of global warming.

True ☐  False ☐  Cannot say ☐

---

Economic research has identified a trend exhibited by one in six Britons of hiding cash in their homes instead of investing it. This is termed the biscuit tin economy. It is estimated that £3.5 billion is currently hidden, sometimes in obscure places such as under mattresses or in fridges, in homes across the country. Reasons for this are varied: for example, 6% are concealing it from their partners, and 4% believe their money to be safer at home than in the bank. Researchers maintain that these actions demonstrate economic folly and that, as a result, Britons are sacrificing up to £174 million in interest every year. This biscuit tin economy is betraying those who trust in it as it renders their hidden money both unproductive and potentially unsafe, whereas it could be profitably invested in a stocks or high-interest savings plan, for example.

---

3  The majority of people who secretly hide cash on their property do so because they do not trust the bank.

True ☐  False ☐  Cannot say ☐

4  Money is safer when invested in a bank than it is when stored at home.

True ☐  False ☐  Cannot say ☐

PRACTICE TESTS IN VERBAL REASONING

A few Safe As Houses alarms have been redesigned in an attempt to reduce the large number of complaints where alarms have sounded by accident. One of the new types of alarms is less sensitive than its predecessors. Studies have shown that these newer alarms are rarely activated for no apparent reason. Safe As Houses still sells a number of the original, sensitive alarm systems because the increase in threshold for motion means that the new style alarms may fail to register break-ins where limited force is being used.

5. All the company alarm systems are now less sensitive.

   True ☐   False ☐   Cannot say ☐

6. The new alarm system should reduce the number of accidental soundings by at least a half.

   True ☐   False ☐   Cannot say ☐

Sagas Stores enjoys an international reputation for quality and style. Nowhere is this more important than in the dress and appearance of its staff. The company sets minimum standards of appearance, which are demanded of all shops' floor staff although some departments have specific additional requirements. Hair must be clean, tidy, and well cut at all times. With very few exceptions, such as Designer Corner, which operates a different staff dress code reflecting their particular style, business dress must be worn. Women should wear tailored suits with a white or cream blouse. Men should wear dark grey trousers with a white shirt and navy blazer.

7. Women in Designer Corner are allowed to wear jewelry.

   True ☐   False ☐   Cannot say ☐

8. Business dress must be worn by staff in all departments.

   True ☐   False ☐   Cannot say ☐

The early chaos of the home computing industry in the United States of America, where it developed, probably has a more detrimental effect in Europe than it did in the States. All the innovators in the field were companies that were too small to cope with or understand foreign sales. As a result, all US companies sold exclusively through European distributors, some of which were only interested in making maximum profits in a minimum amount of time. Home computing in Europe got off to a slow start because greedy distributors worked through incompetent suppliers, none of which had any real interest in the long-term future of the technology.

PRACTICE TESTS IN VERBAL REASONING

9   Incompetent suppliers were one of the reasons for the slow development of home computing in Europe.

    True ☐   False ☐   Cannot say ☐

10  None of the American innovators in the field were able to deal adequately with foreign sales.

    True ☐   False ☐   Cannot say ☐

---

Staff training can have a number of objectives. It can be educational, aiming to develop the knowledge, skills, and abilities of the trainees. It can be a vehicle to promote company policy or values. Or finally, it can raise levels of staff satisfaction by ensuring employees are able to improve their existing skills. Lively debate usually accompanies the allocation of expenditure to the annual training budget. Critics argue that certain costs associated with such programs could be scaled down, and those courses that are unproductive could be axed.

---

11  Knowledge-based training is the most effective form for staff.

    True ☐   False ☐   Cannot say ☐

12  Training sharpens an organization's competitive edge.

    True ☐   False ☐   Cannot say ☐

---

Despite decreases in the miles travelled by the average cyclist in recent years, increase in bicycle sales over the last five years have meant a corresponding increase in cycle accidents. This increase is especially marked among teenagers and young children. Last year, 45% of all cycle casualties were under 14 and another 20% under 20 years. The provisional figures for this year show some improvement, but the fact remains that the number of cyclists of all ages injured each year is unacceptably high.

---

13  The majority of cycle casualties last year involved people under 20 years of age.

    True ☐   False ☐   Cannot say ☐

14  Fewer adults were involved in cycle casualties this year.

    True ☐   False ☐   Cannot say ☐

226

PRACTICE TESTS IN VERBAL REASONING

Hargraves, one of the country's leading specialist electrical engineering companies, announced the rejection of a takeover bid made by the larger, more generalized MLT Group. The board of directors stated that this was the decision of the majority of shareholders, and the announcement kept the price of Hargraves shares where it had stood before the bid had been made. The chairman was known to be very relieved by the decision as he could see no advantage for the shareholders, the company, or its employees in the takeover.

15 Some shareholders were against accepting the proposed takeover.

True ☐   False ☐   Cannot say ☐

16 The employees of Hargraves were against the takeover.

True ☐   False ☐   Cannot say ☐

Although people are buying less sugar to add to their food, the percentage of sugar eaten in manufactured foods is increasing sharply. In that form, it is often referred to on the label as fructose, sucrose, or dextrose. Although there is concern at the growing compulsion to eat oversugared food, there is no proven link between sugar and coronary heart disease, and sugar does not, by itself, make people fat.

17 Overconsumption of sugar sometimes results in heart disease.

True ☐   False ☐   Cannot say ☐

18 The average individual consumption of sugar in all its various forms is increasing.

True ☐   False ☐   Cannot say ☐

A newly developed process of creating artificial skin may be useful for treating burns and wounds. The established method of treating such injuries is by using a skin graft taken from another, usually unseen, part of the body. However, artificial skin, grown in the lab from cells called fibroblasts, has so far shown itself to have better healing properties than "living skin" and a lower tendency toward scarring. The process is currently being refined by researchers who maintain that the wide availability of artificial skin would completely transform the way burns and other skin damage are treated.

19 Fibroblasts are used in the production of artificial skin.

True ☐   False ☐   Cannot say ☐

PRACTICE TESTS IN VERBAL REASONING

20  Lack of scarring is the most important factor when choosing a method of treating burns.

True [ ]  False [ ]  Cannot say [ ]

---

Despite vehicle improvements and campaigns for road safety, many injuries and fatalities are still caused by collisions and other incidents involving vehicles. According to investigations in the United States, some of these accidents could be prevented through the development of a mobile Internet network. All the cars on a stretch of road would be linked to each other, comprising the mobile network. Only one of these vehicles would need to be connected to the Internet to download travel news to the mobile network. The studies highlight the safety advantages of such a system, which would enable drivers to find out about accidents and potential dangers as they happen and in relation to their particular location. Drivers and emergency service teams would have detailed information about problematic areas. There are, however, possible drawbacks to the development of such networks, not least that the availability of data within them could facilitate privacy infringements.

---

21  The advantages of mobile networks outweigh the disadvantages.

True [ ]  False [ ]  Cannot say [ ]

22  All those in the mobile network must be connected to the Internet.

True [ ]  False [ ]  Cannot say [ ]

---

Wi-Fi technology, which allows users to wirelessly connect to the Internet, has an obvious aesthetic benefit in that it can remove some of the unsightly wires that surround computers. However, Wi-Fi technology is also beneficial for businesses as it allows employees to work more flexibly, while it also negates the need for businesses to install expensive cabling, which is particularly useful if their office is a rented building. As a result of the popularity of Wi-Fi, laws have had to be reviewed, and there have been convictions where people have been using someone else's Wi-Fi without paying for the services. These reviews of the laws are crucial in ensuring that Wi-Fi is presented as a secure form of technology as only then will it retain the support of businesses.

---

23  Before the introduction of Wi-Fi, businesses had to install expensive cabling.

True [ ]  False [ ]  Cannot say [ ]

24  Wi-Fi is a new form of technology.

True [ ]  False [ ]  Cannot say [ ]

A report from a prestigious university has urged the world's richest countries to consider the precarious position of bird species from around the world. The study suggests that acting now could ensure the survival of the four hundred to nine hundred species of land bird that are at risk because of the actions of man. The report pays particular attention to the dangers faced by those species that are highly specialized and may not be able to adapt to changes in their environment. Richer countries currently have little awareness of the dangers faced by bird species around the globe and tend to concentrate on the preservation of local species instead.

25  Rich countries show little awareness of the need to preserve bird species.

True ☐  False ☐  Cannot say ☐

26  The report's main focus is on those species of birds that might not be able to change to suit different ecosystems.

True ☐  False ☐  Cannot say ☐

Timed examinations have always played an influential role in assessing the abilities of students; however, with increasing worries that pupils are plagiarizing materials from the Internet for their final year assignments, there is going to be a renewed emphasis on traditional supervised assessment albeit in a revised format. The new form of controlled assessment will still allow students to conduct independent research on the Internet and participate in beneficial practical activities, such as educational trips, but it will also require students to present their final conclusions under supervised conditions within their school. It is hoped that these controlled assessments will maintain the integrity of their school qualifications while also not disadvantaging those students who become stressed by traditional timed examinations.

27  The new form of assessment will not prohibit students from using the Internet to research their work.

True ☐  False ☐  Cannot say ☐

28  Students are going to return to traditional assessment.

True ☐  False ☐  Cannot say ☐

# PRACTICE TESTS IN VERBAL REASONING

Graduates, especially those with backgrounds in chemical engineering, are being welcomed into a thriving industry with some of the finest salaries available to new entrants. Energy production, climate change, alternative energy sources, innovative recycling methods, and the development of sustainable technologies are currently some of the most progressive and sought-after areas for new recruits. Government policies and public concern over the environmental responsibility and sustainability of our current energy sources have had a major role to play. This has led to an increase in the numbers of engineers undertaking work that has a link to sustainable energy. Developments in alternative energy sources are evident, such as in the generation of electrical power by capturing the kinetic energy of wind, waves, and tides. This, in turn, has led to a significant growth rate of 20 percent a year for the alternative-energy industry.

29  Alternative energy sources are one of the key areas attracting engineering graduates.

True ☐   False ☐   Cannot say ☐

30  The energy-generation industry had not utilized naturally occurring energy sources.

True ☐   False ☐   Cannot say ☐

In the future, it may be possible to construct environments in space capable of supporting significant numbers of inhabitants in conditions that resemble those on Earth. New manufacturing technologies are being studied, which will enable work to be done in space by means of a combination of heat and kinetic energy. It has been shown that steel casting and welding is possible, heating the metal using a combination of sunlight and electrical energy. Solar power provides manufacturers with a readily available natural power resource, and this energy can be intensified for use in manufacturing with the utilization of an arrangement of maneuverable mirrors. Theoretically, space manufacturing could require only a very small amount of material being brought from Earth.

31  It is thought that it may be possible in the future to work with only a minimal amount of additional materials from Earth.

True ☐   False ☐   Cannot say ☐

32  A combination of heat and kinetic energy may be used in the manufacture of structures in space.

True ☐   False ☐   Cannot say ☐

The diverse topography of the Peak District is chiefly due to stretching of the earth's crust and thinning of chert and limestone as a result of plate tectonics. Chert is a variety of quartz created where diatoms and microscopic creatures have died and been condensed as a form of liquid silica. The chalk equivalent is flint, which has different properties and was used during the Stone Age for making tools. Limestone is primarily a calcium carbonate and can be created from the integration of shell, algae, or plankton deposits within sediment. Although it would appear that the current topography came about from reexposed earlier features, there is not much that can be uncovered about the geology of the Peak District after the Carboniferous period. It is possible that there were Permo-Triassic deposits as outcrops of this age have been discovered close to the boundaries of the area.

33 Chert has been found to have been used to make Stone Age tools.

True ☐    False ☐    Cannot say ☐

34 Permo-Triassic deposits were left in the Peak District after the Carboniferous period.

True ☐    False ☐    Cannot say ☐

## Practice Test 72 (Answers on Page 270)

Read the passage carefully and then, using only the information given in the passage, for each statement, choose whether it is definitely true, definitely untrue, or you have insufficient information to answer.

The test has 32 questions, and you will have 20 minutes to do them.

So much of the literature of the Western world, including a large part of its greatest literature, was either written for actual speaking or in a mode of speech that we are likely to deform it if we apply our comparatively recent norm of writing for silent reading. It is only that so much of this work is drama or oratory (the latter including the modern forms of sermons, lectures, and addresses, which, as late as the nineteenth century, play a most important part). It is also thought that through classical and medieval times, and in many cases, beyond these, most reading was either aloud or silently articulated as if speaking—a habit we now recognize. Most classical histories were indeed quite close to oratory and public speech rather than silent reading of an artifact, being the central condition of linguistic composition.

## PRACTICE TESTS IN VERBAL REASONING

1. Until the nineteenth century, most people could only read with difficulty.

   True ☐   False ☐   Cannot say ☐

2. In ancient times, literature was intended to be read aloud.

   True ☐   False ☐   Cannot say ☐

3. Classical histories were passed on orally and never written down.

   True ☐   False ☐   Cannot say ☐

4. It is mainly people with literacy problems who now read.

   True ☐   False ☐   Cannot say ☐

---

Millions of lives around the world could be saved and the quality of life of hundreds of millions markedly improved—very inexpensively—by eradicating three vitamin and mineral deficiencies in people's diets. The three vitamins and minerals are vitamin A, iodine, and iron—so-called micronutrients. More than two billion people are at risk from micronutrient deficiencies, and more than one billion people are actually ill or disabled by them, causing mental retardation, learning disabilities, low work capacity, and blindness. It costs little to correct these deficiencies through fortification of food and water supplies. In a country of 50 million people, this would cost about $25 million a year. That $25 million would yield a fortyfold return on investment.

---

5. Most illnesses in developing countries are caused by vitamin and mineral deficiencies.

   True ☐   False ☐   Cannot say ☐

6. Micronutrients provide inadequate nourishment to maintain a healthy life.

   True ☐   False ☐   Cannot say ☐

7. Vitamin A, iodine, and iron are the only micronutrients that people need in their diet.

   True ☐   False ☐   Cannot say ☐

8. Correcting micronutrient deficiencies would cost about $2 per person per year.

   True ☐   False ☐   Cannot say ☐

PRACTICE TESTS IN VERBAL REASONING

> The clinical guidelines in asthma therapy have now moved toward anti-inflammatory therapy—and away from regular bronchiodilator therapy—for all but the mildest asthmatics. This is now being reflected in prescribing patterns. In the United States, combined prescription volumes of the major bronchiodilators peaked in 1991 (having risen slowly in the preceding years) though they still account for around half of the 65 million asthma prescriptions there. During the same period, prescriptions for inhaled steroids have doubled but still account for less than 10 percent of asthma prescriptions in the United States.

9. Only mild cases of asthma can be helped by anti-inflammatory therapy.
   True ☐   False ☐   Cannot say ☐

10. Use of bronchiodilators has been increasing since 1991.
    True ☐   False ☐   Cannot say ☐

11. Doctors are reluctant to treat asthma with inhaled steroids for fear of potential side effects.
    True ☐   False ☐   Cannot say ☐

12. Bronchiodilators are the single most prescribed treatment for asthma.
    True ☐   False ☐   Cannot say ☐

> Relations between Sweden and the European Community had always been restricted in scope by Sweden's traditional neutrality, and for many years, any suggestion of Community membership was out of the question. But the upheavals in Eastern Europe in the early 1990s gradually led to the conclusion that membership of the EC was no longer incompatible with its neutral stance. People came to the conclusion that Sweden has already taken over a large part of the Community rules and began to weigh up the pros and cons of membership along the lines sought by Austria.

13. Political changes in Eastern Europe led to a change in relations between Sweden and the European Community.
    True ☐   False ☐   Cannot say ☐

14. The European Community rejected Sweden's application for membership because of its neutrality.
    True ☐   False ☐   Cannot say ☐

PRACTICE TESTS IN VERBAL REASONING

15  After abandoning its policy of neutrality, Sweden applied to join the European Community.

True ☐   False ☐   Cannot say ☐

16  Sweden applied for membership of the European Community after other neutral countries had joined.

True ☐   False ☐   Cannot say ☐

---

Buddhism was introduced to Japan from India via China and Korea around the middle of the sixth century. After gaining imperial patronage, Buddhism was propagated by the authorities throughout the country. In the early ninth century, Buddhism in Japan entered a new era in which it catered mainly to the court nobility. In the Kamakura period (1192–1338), an age of great political unrest and social confusion, there emerged many new sects of Buddhism, offering hope of salvation to warriors and peasants alike. Buddhism not only flourished as a religion but also did much to enrich the country's arts and learning.

---

17  Buddhism was adopted by the court nobility at the urging of the emperor.

True ☐   False ☐   Cannot say ☐

18  The introduction of Buddhism to Japan led to great political unrest and social confusion.

True ☐   False ☐   Cannot say ☐

19  Buddhism replaced the Shinto religion, which had previously been followed in Japan.

True ☐   False ☐   Cannot say ☐

20  Japanese arts and culture were greatly enriched by the introduction of Buddhism.

True ☐   False ☐   Cannot say ☐

---

In Japan, companies generally expect their employees to put in long hours of overtime. But it is difficult for women, who also have household chores to do and children to take care of, to work at the same pace as men, who are not burdened with such responsibilities. Many women inevitably opt for part-time jobs, which enable them to combine work and domestic duties. At present, 23 percent of all female salaried workers are part-timers, and the ratio has been on the rise in recent years. Part-time work places women at a disadvantage. The wages of part-time workers are considerably lower than those of full-time employees, and part-time work tends to involve menial labor. Moreover, because salary and promotion in Japanese companies are often based on seniority, it is extremely difficult for women either reentering the labor force or switching from part-time to full-time work to climb the ladder.

21 Japanese men do not share household chores and childcare with their wives.
True ☐ False ☐ Cannot say ☐

22 A quarter of all part-time workers in Japan are female.
True ☐ False ☐ Cannot say ☐

23 Part-time workers hold a low status in Japanese companies.
True ☐ False ☐ Cannot say ☐

24 Women in Japan are unwilling to work overtime.
True ☐ False ☐ Cannot say ☐

Abdominal pain in children may be a symptom of emotional disturbance, especially where it appears in conjunction with phobias or sleep disorders such as nightmares or sleepwalking. It may also be linked to eating habits: a study carried out in the United States of America found that children with pain tended to be fussier about what and how much they ate and to have overanxious parents who spent a considerable time trying to persuade them to eat. Although abdominal pain had previously been linked to excessive milk drinking, this research found that children with pain drank rather less milk than those in the control group.

25 There is no clear cause for abdominal pain in children.
True ☐ False ☐ Cannot say ☐

26 Abdominal pain in children may be psychosomatic in nature.
True ☐ False ☐ Cannot say ☐

27 Drinking milk may help to prevent abdominal pain in children.
True ☐ False ☐ Cannot say ☐

28 Children who have problems sleeping are more likely to suffer from abdominal pain.
True ☐ False ☐ Cannot say ☐

# PRACTICE TESTS IN VERBAL REASONING

> When Christianity was first established by law, a corrupt form of Latin had become the common language of all the western parts of Europe. The service of the Church, accordingly, and the translation of the Bible that was read in churches, were both in that corrupted Latin, which was the common language of the country. After the fall of the Roman Empire, Latin gradually ceased to be the language of any part of Europe. However, although Latin was no longer understood anywhere by the great body of the people, Church services still continued to be performed in that language. Two different languages were thus established in Europe: a language of the priests and a language of the people.

**29** After the fall of the Roman Empire, people who had previously spoken Latin returned to their original languages.

True ☐    False ☐    Cannot say ☐

**30** Latin continued to be used in church services because of the continuing influence of the Roman Empire.

True ☐    False ☐    Cannot say ☐

**31** Priests spoke a different language from the common people.

True ☐    False ☐    Cannot say ☐

**32** Prior to the fall of the Roman Empire, Latin had been established by law as the language of the Church in Western Europe.

True ☐    False ☐    Cannot say ☐

# SECTION 3
# ANSWERS AND EXPLANATIONS

Practice Test 1

| | | | | | | | | | | | |
|---|---|---|---|---|---|---|---|---|---|---|---|
| 1 | aberration | A | 14 | parr | C | 27 | amiable | C | 40 | terse | B |
| 2 | duodenary | B | 15 | farinaceous | A | 28 | magnificent | B | 41 | allude | B |
| 3 | amortize | A | 16 | hexagon | B | 29 | acquiesce | D | 42 | nightmare | C |
| 4 | cajole | D | 17 | lunatic | D | 30 | limber | C | 43 | febrile | B |
| 5 | accrue | B | 18 | acquiesce | A | 31 | feign | C | 44 | acrimonious | A |
| 6 | scarce | B | 19 | brutish | A | 32 | rankle | B | 45 | doze | C |
| 7 | enormous | D | 20 | collop | A | 33 | agnostic | C | 46 | auburn | B |
| 8 | caterpillar | A | 21 | perennial | A | 34 | thaw | B | 47 | farrago | D |
| 9 | analgesic | C | 22 | fecund | C | 35 | empoison | A | 48 | attic | D |
| 10 | famished | A | 23 | heroine | C | 36 | viscid | A | 49 | asylum | B |
| 11 | jurisprudent | A | 24 | acumen | B | 37 | adamant | A | 50 | peculiar | A |
| 12 | comical | B | 25 | avarice | A | 38 | makintosh | B | | | |
| 13 | affidavit | D | 26 | dawdle | A | 39 | acuity | A | | | |

Practice Test 2

| | | | | | | | | | | | |
|---|---|---|---|---|---|---|---|---|---|---|---|
| 1 | perpendicular | c | 14 | circumspect | b | 27 | assiduity | a | 40 | conte | B |
| 2 | audacious | b | 15 | jubilant | b | 28 | just | b | 41 | nocuous | A |
| 3 | enjoyable | c | 16 | atelier | d | 29 | epistyle | c | 42 | null | C |
| 4 | liberal | a | 17 | itinerary | c | 30 | skyscraper | d | 43 | skeleton | D |
| 5 | jab | b | 18 | combust | b | 31 | copious | c | 44 | cordate | C |
| 6 | pouch | c | 19 | journal | b | 32 | expressway | b | 45 | indict | A |
| 7 | confine | a | 20 | ledger | a | 33 | fervency | a | 46 | pillage | A |
| 8 | valuable | c | 21 | demure | d | 34 | colossal | b | 47 | opulent | B |
| 9 | convalesce | c | 22 | sincere | c | 35 | anneal | a | 48 | deride | A |

## PRACTICE TESTS IN VERBAL REASONING

| 10 | egocentric | b | 23 | apposite | d | 36 | fiddling | b | 49 | cordwainer | B |
| 11 | enchase | a | 24 | jovial | a | 37 | overwhelm | b | 50 | indocile | C |
| 12 | attest | b | 25 | supplemental | d | 38 | flummox | c | | | |
| 13 | ensign | c | 26 | ascetic | c | 39 | flautist | b | | | |

### Practice Test 3

| 1 | eloquent | a | 14 | annihilate | d | 27 | uncommon | b | 40 | connive | a |
| 2 | smudge | c | 15 | discard | c | 28 | arrogant | d | 41 | doggedness | a |
| 3 | contiguous | c | 16 | renegade | d | 29 | warfare | b | 42 | tenuous | c |
| 4 | plausible | b | 17 | doubting | b | 30 | distorted | c | 43 | doctrine | a |
| 5 | precious | c | 18 | construe | b | 31 | whimsical | b | 44 | abrupt | c |
| 6 | thorn | b | 19 | illustrious | b | 32 | respectable | b | 45 | consternate | a |
| 7 | erudite | a | 20 | python | b | 33 | beneficial | c | 46 | require | b |
| 8 | punctual | a | 21 | automatous | a | 34 | disobedient | c | 47 | sapling | a |
| 9 | predicament | b | 22 | depravity | d | 35 | offensive | c | 48 | sanguine | a |
| 10 | arboreous | b | 23 | consensus | d | 36 | comment | b | 49 | prompt | c |
| 11 | genuine | d | 24 | guardianship | a | 37 | enthusiastic | b | 50 | prohibit | a |
| 12 | reimburse | b | 25 | hypocritical | c | 38 | introverted | d | | | |
| 13 | pullover | c | 26 | consecutive | c | 39 | variety | b | | | |

### Practice Test 4

| 1 | fastidious | d | 14 | dextral | a | 27 | neglect | d | 40 | compelling | b |
| 2 | dehydrated | b | 15 | foundation | a | 28 | suggestion | b | 41 | convey | a |
| 3 | abandoned | c | 16 | antithetical | a | 29 | equipment | c | 42 | feasibility | d |
| 4 | clandestine | b | 17 | overhead | b | 30 | didactic | b | 43 | enlighten | a |
| 5 | handsome | b | 18 | knowingly | c | 31 | vacillate | b | 44 | cargo | b |
| 6 | fealty | a | 19 | inherent | a | 32 | slot | b | 45 | cement | d |
| 7 | unemployed | b | 20 | gloomy | c | 33 | status | c | 46 | mark | b |
| 8 | infinite | d | 21 | devotion | a | 34 | ascend | a | 47 | banquet | d |
| 9 | abroad | c | 22 | appropriate | c | 35 | extract | b | 48 | identification | b |
| 10 | equanimity | b | 23 | standard | d | 36 | curious | c | 49 | base | b |
| 11 | aspiring | c | 24 | unique | b | 37 | ceremony | d | 50 | beneficial | c |
| 12 | permeate | a | 25 | gusto | b | 38 | mediocre | b | | | |
| 13 | crucial | b | 26 | resilience | c | 39 | collapse | d | | | |

### Practice Test 5

| 1 | C | alliteration | 14 | C | balderdash | 27 | A | protagonist | 40 | B | cobbler |
| 2 | A | albatross | 15 | A | moustache | 28 | B | saddlebag | 41 | C | misanthropist |
| 3 | A | budgerigar | 16 | B | hypochondriac | 29 | C | despot | 42 | A | candor |
| 4 | B | ignominious | 17 | A | lumberjack | 30 | D | municipality | 43 | C | salamander |
| 5 | D | pliers | 18 | C | fluoride | 31 | A | neutrality | 44 | D | quadrangle |
| 6 | B | intelligence | 19 | A | insomniac | 32 | c | epigram | 45 | A | askance |
| 7 | C | awkward | 20 | B | Cadillac | 33 | a | parallelogram | 46 | B | Byzantine |

PRACTICE TESTS IN VERBAL REASONING

| 8 | D | contradictory | 21 | C | aphrodisiac | 34 | B | electrocardiogram | 47 | D | Hawaiian |
| 9 | A | diligent | 22 | A | jackal | 35 | A | superficiality | 48 | B | shrapnel |
| 10 | B | crevice | 23 | C | olfactory | 36 | C | diaphragm | 49 | A | tarragon |
| 11 | C | acknowledge | 24 | A | encounter | 37 | A | aerodynamic | 50 | C | peculiarity |
| 12 | A | herbalist | 25 | C | refract | 38 | C | pomegranate | | | |
| 13 | B | syllables | 26 | D | autobiographical | 39 | A | hinterland | | | |

Practice Test 6

| 1 | A | audacity | 14 | A | tarpaulin | 27 | C | annihilate | 40 | A | premonition |
| 2 | C | incapacitate | 15 | C | plaice | 28 | A | rhubarb | 41 | A | quintet |
| 3 | A | sagacity | 16 | A | pliable | 29 | A | narcissus | 42 | D | triplicate |
| 4 | D | enthusiast | 17 | B | parasite | 30 | A | pedestrian | 43 | A | epoch |
| 5 | B | quiver | 18 | B | literacy | 31 | A | stupefy | 44 | B | cagoule |
| 6 | A | panache | 19 | C | iconic | 32 | B | zeppelin | 45 | A | clairvoyant |
| 7 | B | abrade | 20 | A | regulation | 33 | B | spinet | 46 | A | scalpel |
| 8 | C | protuberance | 21 | B | meteor | 34 | B | lenient | 47 | C | amiable |
| 9 | A | rottweiler | 22 | B | villain | 35 | A | cynic | 48 | B | rubella |
| 10 | B | fibula | 23 | B | repertoire | 36 | C | tankard | 49 | B | adjudicator |
| 11 | C | constabulary | 24 | B | escudo | 37 | A | eminent | 50 | B | boisterous |
| 12 | A | desalination | 25 | B | miniature | 38 | A | meager | | | |
| 13 | B | corpulent | 26 | A | decorum | 39 | C | minuet | | | |

Practice Test 7

| 1 | A | notoriety | 14 | C | tomahawk | 27 | B | cauldron | 40 | C | inauspicious |
| 2 | B | magnanimous | 15 | A | kaleidoscope | 28 | B | phenomenal | 41 | A | cyanide |
| 3 | B | vinyl | 16 | D | daffodil | 29 | A | nauseate | 42 | A | asparagus |
| 4 | B | taut | 17 | A | emit | 30 | A | camouflage | 43 | C | avaricious |
| 5 | B | cognac | 18 | A | therapeutic | 31 | D | skiffle | 44 | A | kerosene |
| 6 | C | rancid | 19 | A | septet | 32 | A | scrumpy | 45 | A | inebriated |
| 7 | B | aesthetically | 20 | D | gullible | 33 | A | roulette | 46 | C | arabesque |
| 8 | B | lariat | 21 | A | whippet | 34 | C | amphibious | 47 | A | portmanteau |
| 9 | D | seismology | 22 | A | amnesia | 35 | A | frankfurter | 48 | D | whimsical |
| 10 | A | pyromaniac | 23 | C | terrapin | 36 | D | octogenarian | 49 | A | stalactite |
| 11 | A | beret | 24 | C | diadem | 37 | A | plectrum | 50 | A | excerpt |
| 12 | B | snorkel | 25 | A | blancmange | 38 | B | percolator | | | |
| 13 | B | apathy | 26 | B | catastrophe | 39 | A | flippant | | | |

Practice Test 8

| 1 | D | intransigent | 14 | A | Aphrodite | 27 | D | phlegmatic | 40 | A | hallucination |
| 2 | A | penitentiary | 15 | A | brigadier | 28 | A | lymphatic | 41 | D | brusques |
| 3 | A | purl | 16 | D | pumice | 29 | C | idiosyncratic | 42 | A | delineate |
| 4 | B | thimble | 17 | C | diabolical | 30 | A | seismograph | 43 | B | exonerate |
| 5 | A | milliner | 18 | A | juggernaut | 31 | D | fuselage | 44 | C | proletariat |

PRACTICE TESTS IN VERBAL REASONING

| 6  | A | elated       | 19 | A | kelp         | 32 | A | paraphernalia | 45 | A | variegated     |
|----|---|--------------|----|---|--------------|----|---|---------------|----|---|----------------|
| 7  | C | confidant    | 20 | A | hematology   | 33 | B | balustrade    | 46 | C | innuendo       |
| 8  | C | terrapin     | 21 | D | cajoled      | 34 | B | kamikaze      | 47 | A | lieutenant     |
| 9  | D | intrigue     | 22 | A | gnome        | 35 | C | barricade     | 48 | C | scintillating  |
| 10 | B | unscrupulous | 23 | A | desalination | 36 | D | kleptomaniac  | 49 | A | demisemiquaver |
| 11 | B | epaulet      | 24 | A | oryx         | 37 | A | polyurethane  | 50 | C | exchequer      |
| 12 | B | parlor       | 25 | B | amalgam      | 38 | B | lucent        |    |   |                |
| 13 | C | tadpole      | 26 | C | xenophobia   | 39 | D | stratification|    |   |                |

Practice Test 9

| 1  | B | insurance    | 14 | C | forestation   | 27 | D | arrogance      | 40 | C | gauge          |
|----|---|--------------|----|---|---------------|----|---|----------------|----|---|----------------|
| 2  | C | comfort      | 15 | B | consignment   | 28 | A | choreographer  | 41 | A | insusceptible  |
| 3  | D | reassure     | 16 | A | broccoli      | 29 | B | ephemeral      | 42 | B | juridical      |
| 4  | D | intensive    | 17 | A | eighteen      | 30 | C | fragile        | 43 | B | lacteal        |
| 5  | C | especially   | 18 | A | estrogen      | 31 | C | blithe         | 44 | C | gastronomy     |
| 6  | A | nostalgic    | 19 | A | surveillance  | 32 | D | repertory      | 45 | A | iridescent     |
| 7  | C | penitential  | 20 | B | heterogeneous | 33 | B | asserted       | 46 | B | leaseback      |
| 8  | B | officious    | 21 | C | catarrh       | 34 | C | retrospective  | 47 | B | liturgical     |
| 9  | C | Byzantine    | 22 | A | jollity       | 35 | B | enliven        | 48 | A | malassimilation|
| 10 | A | penultimate  | 23 | A | begrudge      | 36 | B | filaria        | 49 | B | kidney         |
| 11 | A | disrupt      | 24 | B | elsewhere     | 37 | B | Hinduism       | 50 | C | magistrate     |
| 12 | A | borstal      | 25 | C | correctness   | 38 | C | epitome        |    |   |                |
| 13 | C | callous      | 26 | C | suspicious    | 39 | A | intangible     |    |   |                |

Practice Test 10

| 1  | verbose     | 11 | unequivocal | 21 | ululation     |
|----|-------------|----|-------------|----|---------------|
| 2  | epicure     | 12 | otherwise   | 22 | Vogt          |
| 3  | emeritus    | 13 | mural       | 23 | labyrinthine  |
| 4  | fortuitous  | 14 | fulminate   | 24 | mnemonic      |
| 5  | husbandry   | 15 | dilatory    | 25 | dilettante    |
| 6  | messagery   | 16 | mediate     | 26 | ostentatious  |
| 7  | diffident   | 17 | verification| 27 | umbrage       |
| 8  | omnipotent  | 18 | hyssop      | 28 | midday        |
| 9  | zigzag      | 19 | foxtrot     | 29 | lampoon       |
| 10 | megalomania | 20 | emollient   | 30 | lingua franca |

Practice Test 11

| 1 | monetarist  | 11 | unforeseen | 21 | vernacular |
| 2 | vagary      | 12 | definition | 22 | mercenary  |
| 3 | discommode  | 13 | oscillate  | 23 | skeptic    |
| 4 | vow         | 14 | funereal   | 24 | moratorium |
| 5 | odontology  | 15 | enunciate  | 25 | drugget    |

| | | | | | | | |
|---|---|---|---|---|---|---|---|
| 6 | iridescence | 16 | momus | 26 | zealot | | |
| 7 | intrinsic | 17 | opprobrium | 27 | stodge | | |
| 8 | iota | 18 | hyparterial | 28 | miscegenation | | |
| 9 | lather | 19 | dudgeon | 29 | furor | | |
| 10 | liaise | 20 | untoward | 30 | doctrinal | | |

## Practice Test 12

| | | | | | |
|---|---|---|---|---|---|
| 1 | soporific | 11 | dribley | 21 | statute |
| 2 | multifarious | 12 | velocity | 22 | ostrich |
| 3 | epizoon | 13 | value | 23 | python |
| 4 | flippant | 14 | turbulent | 24 | squalid |
| 5 | mettle | 15 | redeploy | 25 | primitive |
| 6 | minchiate | 16 | subutaneous | 26 | ombudsman |
| 7 | duodenum | 17 | property | 27 | nominate |
| 8 | moiety | 18 | thivel | 28 | naira |
| 9 | mezzanine | 19 | preferable | 29 | recuperate |
| 10 | futility | 20 | overcome | 30 | omelete |

## Practice Test 13

| | | | | | | | | | | | |
|---|---|---|---|---|---|---|---|---|---|---|---|
| 1 | C | lifetime | 11 | C | meantime | 21 | B | bypass | 31 | C | spearhead |
| 2 | B | grandmother | 12 | D | backward | 22 | C | spearmint | 32 | D | northeast |
| 3 | C | passport | 13 | D | footprints | 23 | D | throwback | 33 | D | silversmith |
| 4 | C | carpetbagger | 14 | D | backbone | 24 | D | skateboard | 34 | B | watchmaker |
| 5 | B | sunflower | 15 | D | peppermint | 25 | C | crosswalk | 35 | B | bootstrap |
| 6 | B | basketball | 16 | C | airport | 26 | C | supermarket | 36 | B | dishwasher |
| 7 | C | moonlight | 17 | C | butterflies | 27 | C | weatherman | 37 | C | popcorn |
| 8 | B | football | 18 | C | schoolhouse | 28 | D | rattlesnake | 38 | C | spokesperson |
| 9 | C | earthquake | 19 | B | upstream | 29 | D | therefore | 39 | C | honeydew |
| 10 | A | everything | 20 | B | anybody | 30 | C | superhuman | 40 | D | pacemaker |

## Practice Test 14

| | | | | | | | | | | | |
|---|---|---|---|---|---|---|---|---|---|---|---|
| 1 | D | hometown | 11 | C | underground | 21 | C | bookkeeper | 31 | D | bookworm |
| 2 | D | bluefish | 12 | C | sandstone | 22 | C | forklift | 32 | B | lowland |
| 3 | C | thunderstorm | 13 | D | toothpaste | 23 | B | underage | 33 | B | backhand |
| 4 | C | hamburger | 14 | D | housekeeper | 24 | B | noisemaker | 34 | B | superscript |
| 5 | D | household | 15 | D | commonplace | 25 | B | backlog | 35 | B | undercharge |
| 6 | D | riverbank | 16 | C | seashore | 26 | C | waterfall | 36 | A | sunshine |
| 7 | C | touchdown | 17 | C | keyboard | 27 | C | anywhere | 37 | A | bookshelf |
| 8 | C | limestone | 18 | C | babysitter | 28 | C | watchdog | 38 | B | forefinger |
| 9 | D | headquarters | 19 | D | toothpick | 29 | D | somehow | 39 | C | windmill |
| 10 | C | Shadyside | 20 | C | anymore | 30 | D | underbelly | 40 | D | seaside |

## PRACTICE TESTS IN VERBAL REASONING

### Practice Test 15

| | | | | | | | | | | | |
|---|---|---|---|---|---|---|---|---|---|---|---|
| 1 | C | supersonic | 11 | C | foreleg | 21 | B | whitewash | 31 | B | pinstripe |
| 2 | D | backbreaker | 12 | C | softball | 22 | B | blackjack | 32 | B | underachieve |
| 3 | D | crossover | 13 | D | background | 23 | C | pancake | 33 | C | wallpaper |
| 4 | C | sidekick | 14 | D | uptight | 24 | B | brainchild | 34 | C | eyesore |
| 5 | C | airfield | 15 | B | sunbathe | 25 | C | deadline | 35 | D | fishpond |
| 6 | D | backdrop | 16 | B | keystroke | 26 | C | rainbow | 36 | C | taxpayer |
| 7 | B | textbook | 17 | B | blackberries | 27 | B | watermelon | 37 | C | teamwork |
| 8 | C | backbite | 18 | C | loophole | 28 | B | daydream | 38 | B | grandparent |
| 9 | D | underarm | 19 | D | friendship | 29 | A | piglet | 39 | B | upshot |
| 10 | C | milestone | 20 | D | upbringing | 30 | A | storeroom | 40 | A | blackout |

### Practice Test 16

| | | | | | | | |
|---|---|---|---|---|---|---|---|
| 1 | al | 11 | ad | 21 | be | 31 | be |
| 2 | ox | 12 | af | 22 | ar | 32 | by |
| 3 | en | 13 | ag | 23 | at | 33 | as |
| 4 | de | 14 | be | 24 | dr | 34 | in |
| 5 | no | 15 | af | 25 | de | 35 | bl |
| 6 | in | 16 | al | 26 | di | 36 | im |
| 7 | be | 17 | es | 27 | dr | 37 | in |
| 8 | re | 18 | ad | 28 | as | 38 | im |
| 9 | sp | 19 | as | 29 | bl | 39 | in |
| 10 | en | 20 | ap | 30 | di | 40 | in |

### Practice Test 17

| | | | | | | | |
|---|---|---|---|---|---|---|---|
| 1 | top | 11 | cut | 21 | mis | 31 | non |
| 2 | pit | 12 | day | 22 | god | 32 | mis |
| 3 | man | 13 | dis | 23 | por | | |
| 4 | air | 14 | gun | 24 | air | | |
| 5 | bee | 15 | air | 25 | lay | | |
| 6 | gar | 16 | geo | 26 | per | | |
| 7 | air | 17 | dis | 27 | top | | |
| 8 | par | 18 | law | 28 | mis | | |
| 9 | saw | 19 | eye | 29 | dis | | |
| 10 | bed | 20 | dis | 30 | gas | | |

### Practice Test 18

| | | | | | | | |
|---|---|---|---|---|---|---|---|
| 1 | over | 11 | anti | 21 | door | 31 | down |
| 2 | hair | 12 | over | 22 | book | 32 | fore |
| 3 | free | 13 | over | 23 | down | 33 | fool |
| 4 | aero | 14 | cock | 24 | anti | 34 | lady |
| 5 | anti | 15 | back | 25 | fire | 35 | life |

PRACTICE TESTS IN VERBAL REASONING

| 6 | back | 16 | copy | 26 | door | 36 | fire |
| 7 | over | 17 | band | 27 | back | 37 | king |
| 8 | bare | 18 | corn | 28 | flag | 38 | land |
| 9 | bull | 19 | anti | 29 | band | 39 | main |
| 10 | back | 20 | back | 30 | fore | 40 | moon |

## Practice Test 19

| 1 | blind | 11 | night | 21 | under |
| 2 | after | 12 | cross | 22 | cross |
| 3 | block | 13 | black | 23 | house |
| 4 | mouth | 14 | water | 24 | green |
| 5 | table | 15 | cross | 25 | tooth |
| 6 | heart | 16 | house | 26 | inter |
| 7 | night | 17 | grand | 27 | light |
| 8 | inter | 18 | heart | 28 | night |
| 9 | house | 19 | after | 29 | inter |
| 10 | match | 20 | micro | 30 | photo |

## Practice Test 20

| 1 | murdrum | c | 11 | deified | a | 21 | refer | d | 31 | radar | c |
| 2 | level | d | 12 | dewed | a | 22 | Hannah | d | 32 | madam | c |
| 3 | rotator | a | 13 | reifier | d | 23 | detartrated | d | 33 | deleveled | b |
| 4 | evitative | a | 14 | tenet | d | 24 | ewe | a | 34 | civic | d |
| 5 | redder | a | 15 | kayak | a | 25 | repaper | a | 35 | racecar | a |
| 6 | devoved | b | 16 | minim | b | 26 | solos | a | 36 | keek | b |
| 7 | terret | c | 17 | peeweep | c | 27 | alula | a | 37 | testset | a |
| 8 | reviver | c | 18 | redder | b | 28 | wow | b | 38 | sexes | c |
| 9 | stats | c | 19 | sagas | b | 29 | malayalam | b | 39 | rotor | a |
| 10 | aibohphobia | c | 20 | lemel | d | 30 | refer | b | 40 | pop | b |

## Practice Test 21

| 1 | backbone | 11 | brush | 21 | bald |
| 2 | autumn | 12 | luck | 22 | howl |
| 3 | bacteria | 13 | kiwi | 23 | funfair |
| 4 | bomb | 14 | adequate | 24 | admiral |
| 5 | bulb | 15 | machine | 25 | hyena |
| 6 | acorn | 16 | breakfast | 26 | maize |
| 7 | brittle | 17 | inhale | 27 | gander |
| 8 | compass | 18 | anchovy | 28 | bonfire |
| 9 | iceberg | 19 | ladder | 29 | garlic |
| 10 | lounge | 20 | comic | 30 | alphabet |

# PRACTICE TESTS IN VERBAL REASONING

## Practice Test 22

| | | | | | |
|---|---|---|---|---|---|
| 1 | altar | 11 | different | 21 | arithmetic |
| 2 | majesty | 12 | cottage | 22 | chorus |
| 3 | examination | 13 | armadillo | 23 | aluminum |
| 4 | chameleon | 14 | football | 24 | gorilla |
| 5 | Buddhist | 15 | almond | 25 | chopsticks |
| 6 | bacteria | 16 | example | 26 | background |
| 7 | awesome | 17 | convenient | 27 | glimpse |
| 8 | article | 18 | handwriting | 28 | fraction |
| 9 | albatross | 19 | glider | 29 | isolated |
| 10 | exhibition | 20 | good-bye | 30 | glutton |

## Practice Test 23

| | | | | | |
|---|---|---|---|---|---|
| 1 | b | 11 | c | 21 | c |
| 2 | b | 12 | b | 22 | b |
| 3 | b | 13 | d | 23 | c |
| 4 | b | 14 | a | 24 | a |
| 5 | c | 15 | d | 25 | d |
| 6 | b | 16 | d | 26 | b |
| 7 | d | 17 | a | 27 | c |
| 8 | a | 18 | c | 28 | d |
| 9 | d | 19 | a | 29 | a |
| 10 | c | 20 | b | 30 | a |

## Practice Test 24

| | | | | | |
|---|---|---|---|---|---|
| 1 | d | 11 | c | 21 | a |
| 2 | a | 12 | a | 22 | a |
| 3 | c | 13 | a | 23 | c |
| 4 | a | 14 | c | 24 | a |
| 5 | c | 15 | b | 25 | a |
| 6 | a | 16 | d | 26 | a |
| 7 | b | 17 | a | 27 | c |
| 8 | a | 18 | b | 28 | b |
| 9 | a | 19 | a | 29 | b |
| 10 | a | 20 | d | 30 | c |

## Practice Test 25

| | | | | | | | |
|---|---|---|---|---|---|---|---|
| 1 | dependants | 2 | affected | 3 | mail | 4 | dual |
| 5 | three | 6 | brake | 7 | dairy | 8 | deserts |
| 9 | access | 10 | caught | 11 | write | 12 | loan |
| 13 | bee | 14 | flower | 15 | their | 16 | discrete |
| 17 | dye | 18 | broach | 19 | allowed | 20 | mourning |

PRACTICE TESTS IN VERBAL REASONING

| 21 | dam | 22 | uninterested | 23 | due | 24 | hiss |
| 25 | flaw | 26 | byte | 27 | stationery | 28 | detracted |
| 29 | aisle | 30 | knead | | | | |

## Practice Test 26

| 1 | hole | 2 | blue | 3 | did | 4 | still |
| 5 | sit | 6 | by | 7 | read | 8 | too |
| 9 | aunt | 10 | boar | 11 | sole | 12 | course |
| 13 | peak | 14 | cheek | 15 | new | 16 | site |
| 17 | steak | 18 | role | 19 | dear | 20 | meet |
| 21 | sweet | 22 | bored | 23 | current | 24 | deed |
| 25 | insure | 26 | advice | 27 | route | 28 | pries |
| 29 | principal | 30 | stimulant | | | | |

## Practice Test 27

| 1 | D | learned | 16 | C | lingering |
| 2 | A | consistent | 17 | C | disagreement |
| 3 | C | credentials | 18 | C | consider |
| 4 | B | challenging | 19 | C | entertained |
| 5 | B | arduous | 20 | C | speculating |
| 6 | B | disenchanted | 21 | B | scenario |
| 7 | D | challenge | 22 | D | compensated |
| 8 | C | indulging | 23 | C | tactics |
| 9 | C | compassionate | 24 | C | collapsed |
| 10 | C | improvement | 25 | C | ambiguous |
| 11 | A | entitled | 26 | B | representative |
| 12 | A | consolidate | 27 | C | intriguing |
| 13 | D | successor | 28 | D | applauded |
| 14 | D | aggressive | 29 | C | balance |
| 15 | C | executive | 30 | C | exceptional |

## Practice Test 28

| 1 | C | essential | 16 | B | relations |
| 2 | C | conversational | 17 | B | taxidermist |
| 3 | B | reliable | 18 | B | exquisite |
| 4 | C | hospitalized | 19 | B | flabbergasted |
| 5 | B | credibility | 20 | D | anticipation |
| 6 | C | appalled | 21 | C | frequently |
| 7 | B | plummeting | 22 | B | off-putting |
| 8 | A | financial | 23 | B | brazenly |
| 9 | B | discussing | 24 | B | fatherhood |
| 10 | C | neighborhood | 25 | B | revelation |
| 11 | B | resolution | 26 | B | monogamous |

PRACTICE TESTS IN VERBAL REASONING

| 12 | B | training | 27 | D | prime |
| 13 | D | discovered | 28 | D | ulterior |
| 14 | B | individual | 29 | A | unprecedented |
| 15 | D | picturesque | 30 | C | exaggerated |

**Practice Test 29**

1  as proud as a peacock
2  as plain as day
3  as old as hills
4  as quick as lightning/a wink
5  as slippery as an eel
6  as slow as a snail/tortoise
7  as sound as a bell
8  as solid as a rock/the ground we stand on
9  as thin as a rake
10 as smooth as silk
11 as white as ghost/sheet/snow
12 as pure as snow
13 as sharp as a razor
14 as wise as Solomon/an owl
15 as sour as vinegar
16 as tall as giraffe
17 as mad as a hatter/hornet
18 as poor as dirt/a church mouse
19 as scarce as hen's teeth
20 as quiet as a church mouse
21 as safe as houses
22 as timid as a rabbit
23 as tough as nails/leather
24 as strong as an ox
25 as busy as a bee/beaver/cat on a hot tin roof roof
26 as calm as a millpond
27 as bald as a coot
28 as blind as bat/mole
29 as clear as crystal/a bell/mud
30 as deaf as a post
31 as dry as a bone/dust
32 as easy as A-B-C./apple pie
33 as hard as nails
34 as hungry as a bear/wolf
35 as innocent as a lamb
36 as light as air/a feather
37 as large as life
38 as brave as a lion
39 as bright as a button/a new pin
40 as stubborn as a mule

**Practice Test 30**

1  a babble of barbers
2  an ostentation of peacocks
3  an army of ants/caterpillars or frogs
4  an ambush of tigers
5  an aurora of polar bears
6  a band of men/brothers/pirates/gorillas
7  a battery of barracudas
8  an ascension of larks
9  a barrel of monkeys
10 a bask of crocodiles
11 a barn of animals
12 a bew of partridges
13 a bevy of beauties/larks/quails/roe deer/swans
14 a bike of bees
15 a bloodstock of thoroughbred horses
16 a blessing of unicorns
17 a chaos of children
18 a cask of hawks
19 a bunch of lies/widgeon/grapes
20 a bushel of corn/crabs
21 a crackle of hyenas
22 a caravan of camels
23 a business of ferrets
24 a choir of singers
25 a chatter of budgerigars
26 a chime of wrens
27 a coalition of cheetahs
28 a cloud of grasshoppers/gnats/seafowl

PRACTICE TESTS IN VERBAL REASONING

29  a colony of ants/bats/frogs/gulls/penguins/ beavers
30  a colony of penguins
31  a congregation of crocodiles/eagles/plovers
32  a diligence of messengers
33  a cuddle of aunts
34  a dazzle of zebras
35  a field of racehorses
36  a flamboyance of flamingoes
37  a drift of bees/swans
38  a drove of asses/oxen
39  a fever of stingrays
40  a flight of birds
41  an exaltation of larks/angles
42  a flock of parrots/sheep/swifts
43  a hive of bees
44  a host of sparrows
45  a huddle of bricklayers/penguins
46  a litter of cubs/kittens/puppies
47  a parliament of owls/rooks
48  a pride of lions/sheep/peacocks
49  a school of dolphins/fish/whale
50  a shoal of fish

## Practice Test 31

1   a squadron of flying fish/swans
2   a swarm of ants/bees/flies
3   a tuft of grass/hair
4   a walk of snipes
5   a board of directors
6   a yoke of oxen
7   a zeal of zebras
8   a zoo of animals
9   a caravan of gypsies
10  a company of soldiers/actors
11  a crowd of people/spectators
12  a class of students/pupils
13  a crew of sailors
14  a dynasty of kings
15  a batch of bread
16  an album of autographs/photographs/stamps
17  an archipelago of islands
18  a basket of fruit
19  a bouquet of flowers
20  a bunch of bananas/flowers/grapes/keys/
21  a block of flats
22  a bowl of rice
23  a cloud of dust
24  a bundle of hay/old clothes/firewood/hay/ sticks/joy
25  a chest of drawers
26  a cloud of dust
27  a constellation of stars
28  a column of smoke
29  a compendium of games
30  a flight of steps/airplanes
31  a clump of trees/bushes
32  a harvest of wheat/corn
33  a grove of trees
34  a hedge of bushes
35  a fall of snow/rain
36  a necklace of pearls
37  a mass of ruin/hair
38  a list of names
39  a library of books
40  a heap of rubbish/stones/ruins
41  a fleet of cars/taxi
42  a quiver of arrows
43  a pencil of rays
44  a range of hills/mountains
45  a row of houses
46  an outfit of clothes
47  a ream of paper
48  a suite of furniture/rooms
49  a series of events
50  a set of china/clubs/tools

# PRACTICE TESTS IN VERBAL REASONING

Practice Test 32

| | | | | | | | |
|---|---|---|---|---|---|---|---|
| 1 | Wrong | 11 | Right | 21 | Right | 31 | Right |
| 2 | Wrong | 12 | Right | 22 | Wrong | 32 | Wrong |
| 3 | Wrong | 13 | Right | 23 | Wrong | 33 | Wrong |
| 4 | Wrong | 14 | Right | 24 | Wrong | 34 | Wrong |
| 5 | Wrong | 15 | Right | 25 | Wrong | 35 | Wrong |
| 6 | Wrong | 16 | Right | 26 | Right | 36 | Wrong |
| 7 | Wrong | 17 | Right | 27 | Wrong | 37 | Right |
| 8 | Right | 18 | Right | 28 | Wrong | 38 | Right |
| 9 | Right | 19 | Right | 29 | Wrong | 39 | Wrong |
| 10 | Right | 20 | Wrong | 30 | Wrong | 40 | Right |

**Practice Test 33**

1  Sticks and stones may break my bones.
2  There is a new film about the life of the famous ballet dancer.
3  The payment was credited to the account.
4  A lynx is a predatory cat.
5  Those people were treated badly for doing right.
6  All the pirates invaded the Spanish galleon.
7  Hammerhead sharks are carnivorous.
8  We all watched in amazement as he won the race.
9  Don't tie your laces in a revolving door.
10  The president is being inaugurated at the annual parade.
11  Never take a chance at a level crossing.
12  I told him not to give into peer pressure when he goes.
13  Maths is my absolute favorite subject.
14  The opticians gave me designer glasses for my eyes.
15  We are required to attend lectures if we expect to pass.
16  I need help with the extremely complicated quiz.
17  The Volkswagen really needed an MOT at the mechanic.
18  Chess is an extremely intricate game.
19  Hyphenation can help with complicated writing.
20  The trip to the zoo was a memorable experience.
21  Gatwick airport was overcrowded by late passengers.
22  A dictionary is used for finding definitions of words.
23  I know wildebeests live in the area close to where we went on the African safari
24  Emerald is a priceless green jewel.
25  Santa's grotto is a child-friendly and fun experience.
26  Carbon monoxide is a poisonous gas.
27  Fulham played a football match against Arsenal.
28  Kingston is the capital city of Jamaica, a Caribbean country.
29  James birthday celebration was a complete success.
30  A parrot is an intelligent bird that can mimic speech.

PRACTICE TESTS IN VERBAL REASONING

**Practice Test 34**

| Question | Answer | How to work out the answer |
|---|---|---|
| 1 | 3 c | Letters increment by one every second letter. |
| 2 | 4 e | ccd . . . eef . . . ggh |
| 3 | 5 y | First letter of alphabet, then last, second, second last, third, third last |
| 4 | 3 j | Two interspersed sequences. First decreasing by one: fedc and second increasing by one: ghi j |
| 5 | 4 r | Letters are in triplets decreasing by one: rqp . . . rqp . . . rqp |
| 6 | 3 q | Letters go up by three each time. Second letter of alphabet, fifth, eighth, etc. |
| 7 | 1 s | Two interspersed sequences again. First one decrementing by two, second incrementing by two. |
| 8 | 5 t | Letters decrement by four each time. |
| 9 | 4 m | The gap between letters increases by one each time: 0, 1, 2, 3, 4. |
| 10 | 1 h | Letters are in triplets that decrement by three, but starting letter of each triplet increments by one: 10, 7, 4 . . . 11, 8, 5. |
| 11 | 5 p | Letters double each time: 1, 2, 4, 8, 16 = n |
| 12 | 4 f | Two sequences interspersed, both incrementing by two each time |
| 13 | 1 p | Sequence of squares according to place in alphabet: 1, 4, 9, 16 = p |
| 14 | 4 h | Take out the d's, and you get a simple alphabetical sequence! |
| 15 | 1 r | Letters are in triplets: letter, letter+1, letter+1, then triplet repeats but incremented by two. |
| 16 | 2 s | Letters are in pairs that increment by four places in the alphabet each time. |
| 17 | 1 m | The odd letters decrement by four each time. |
| 18 | 3 x | Each whole triplet increments by one while the letters in the triplet decrease by three. |
| 19 | 1 f | Take out the k's and you have a simple alphabetical sequence. |
| 20 | 5 g | Each third letter descends by one. |
| 21 | 2 l | Each letter increments by seven; the alphabet wraps round. |
| 22 | 3 n | Each third letter increments by two. |
| 23 | 1 l | The even letters decrement by one each time. |
| 24 | 3 f | These are triplets; the first and the last letter of the triplet increments by one each triplet. |
| 25 | 4 h | Every second letter increments by two. |
| 26 | 2 m | Getting hard now! Prime numbers. |
| 27 | 5 o | One m, two n's, three o's, four p's |

**Practice Test 35**

| | | | | | |
|---|---|---|---|---|---|
| 1 | cat, dog, fox | 11 | event, order, waste | 21 | jewel, naught, sky |
| 2 | bull, humane, pig | 12 | earth, golden, text | 22 | caught, love, possess |
| 3 | choir, place, south | 13 | emerge, paste, wrap | 23 | bite, hurt, nip |
| 4 | lose, scale, vote | 14 | data, first, view | 24 | hip, shoot, vow |

249

# PRACTICE TESTS IN VERBAL REASONING

| | | | | | |
|---|---|---|---|---|---|
| 5 | center, future, town | 15 | horn, reason, styles | 25 | long, regular, short |
| 6 | horrid, locust, mean | 16 | firm, king, lode | 26 | cry, heat, sweat |
| 7 | ghosts, months, zenith | 17 | camel, fooled, snoop | 27 | dumb, pole, struck |
| 8 | advice, flood, help | 18 | lined, loop, pull | 28 | arise, greet, hello |
| 9 | about, public, reason | 19 | lecture, light, snip | 29 | call, car, stomp |
| 10 | chart, month, thump | 20 | antler, cart, fine | 30 | fast, homely, lovely |

## Practice Test 36

| | | | | | |
|---|---|---|---|---|---|
| 1 | den, liquid, rainbow | 11 | hear, poor, ways | 21 | commerce, purpose, trademark |
| 2 | child, poem, story | 12 | eyes, feet, part | 22 | electric, remember, verbal |
| 3 | enjoy, little, whale | 13 | hill, mountain, trees | 23 | divulge, involve, union |
| 4 | ark, night, sleep | 14 | arise, bless, thank | 24 | international, piano, quest |
| 5 | angel, drowsy, soft | 15 | accept, divide, words | 25 | floor, keyboard, string |
| 6 | creep, gentle, peace | 16 | copy, match, north | 26 | base, bath, string |
| 7 | attend, breath, delight | 17 | publish, quote, whole | 27 | bag, lamp, violin |
| 8 | daily, guardian, leave | 18 | radio, television, video | 28 | abide, sack, trunk |
| 9 | goodness, grow, teach | 19 | permit, reserve, write | 29 | keep, jacket, log |
| 10 | dust, friend, life | 20 | adapt, cubic, draw | 30 | hair, pencil, tickle |

## Practice Test 37

| | | | | | | | | | |
|---|---|---|---|---|---|---|---|---|---|
| 1 | d | 11 | c | 21 | a | 31 | b | 41 | b |
| 2 | a | 12 | d | 22 | d | 32 | a | 42 | b |
| 3 | a | 13 | a | 23 | a | 33 | d | 43 | d |
| 4 | a | 14 | b | 24 | b | 34 | a | 44 | a |
| 5 | d | 15 | c | 25 | d | 35 | d | 45 | a |
| 6 | c | 16 | b | 26 | c | 36 | a | 46 | c |
| 7 | d | 17 | a | 27 | a | 37 | a | 47 | c |
| 8 | b | 18 | b | 28 | c | 38 | c | 48 | a |
| 9 | c | 19 | d | 29 | c | 39 | c | 49 | c |
| 10 | a | 20 | b | 30 | d | 40 | c | 50 | a |

## Practice Test 38

| | | | | | | | | | |
|---|---|---|---|---|---|---|---|---|---|
| 1 | d | 11 | b | 21 | a | 31 | b | 41 | c |
| 2 | b | 12 | d | 22 | a | 32 | a | 42 | d |
| 3 | a | 13 | c | 23 | d | 33 | a | 43 | b |
| 4 | c | 14 | b | 24 | d | 34 | d | 44 | c |
| 5 | a | 15 | c | 25 | a | 35 | b | 45 | a |
| 6 | c | 16 | a | 26 | d | 36 | d | 46 | d |
| 7 | d | 17 | c | 27 | c | 37 | a | 47 | a |
| 8 | b | 18 | a | 28 | c | 38 | b | 48 | b |
| 9 | c | 19 | a | 29 | a | 39 | c | 49 | d |
| 10 | c | 20 | b | 30 | b | 40 | a | 50 | a |

PRACTICE TESTS IN VERBAL REASONING

**Practice Test 39**

1  i    l  e  a  d  e  r
   ii   e  l  d  e  r
   iii  r  e  e  d
   iv   r  e  d
   v    d  r
   vi   r

2  i    a  r  r  e  s  t
   ii   s  t  a  r  e
   iii  s  e  a  t
   iv   s  e  a
   v    a  s
   vi   s

3  i    s  t  r  i  p  e
   ii   s  t  r  i  p
   iii  s  p  i  t
   iv   s  i  t
   v    i  t
   vi   i

4  i    p  a  r  t  l  y
   ii   p  a  r  t  y
   iii  p  a  r  t
   iv   t  a  r
   v    a  t
   vi   t

5  i    m  a  n  g  e  r
   ii   r  a  n  g  e
   iii  n  e  a  r
   iv   e  a  r
   v    r  e
   vi   e

**Practice Test 40**

1  i    p  l  a  n  e  t
   ii   p  l  a  n  e
   iii  l  a  n  e
   iv   a  l  e
   v    l  e
   vi   l

2  i    d  r  a  g  o  n
   ii   g  r  o  a  n
   iii  n  o  r  a
   iv   o  a  r
   v    o  r
   vi   r

3  i    s  o  l  e  m  n
   ii   l  e  m  o  n
   iii  n  o  e  l
   iv   l  e  o
   v    n  e
   vi   e

4  i    g  r  a  i  n  s
   ii   g  r  a  i  n
   iii  r  i  n  g
   iv   n  a  g
   v    a  n
   vi   n

5  i    r  e  g  g  a  e
   ii   e  a  g  e  r
   iii  r  a  g  e
   iv   a  g  e
   v    e  a
   vi   e

**Practice Test 41**

1  i    e  s  c  a  p  e
   ii   c  a  p  e  s
   iii  p  e  a  s
   iv   s  e  a
   v    p  a
   vi   a

3  i    s  t  r  o  n  g
   ii   s  n  o  r  t
   iii  t  o  r  n
   iv   n  o  r
   v    n  o
   vi   o

5  i    r  e  g  r  e  t
   ii   g  r  e  e  t
   iii  t  r  e  e
   iv   t  e  e
   v    e  e
   vi   e

251

PRACTICE TESTS IN VERBAL REASONING

2  i   i s l a n d        4  i   m o b i l e
   ii  s l a i n             ii  l i m b o
   iii n a i l               iii l i m o
   iv  n i l                 iv  o i l
   v   i s                   v   l o
   vi  i                     vi  l

**Practice Test 42**

1  i   s c a r c e        3  i   a n s w e r        5  i   s o n n e t
   ii  s c a r e             ii  s w e a r             ii  n o t e s
   iii c a r e               iii w e a r               iii t o n e
   iv  c a r                 iv  r a w                 iv  o n e
   v   r e                   v   w r                   v   n o
   vi  r                     vi  w                     vi  n

2  i   r e g i m e        4  i   p e r s o n
   ii  g r i m e             ii  p r o s e
   iii g r i m               iii p o r e
   iv  r i m                 iv  p e r
   v   m r                   v   r p
   vi  m                     vi  p

**Practice Test 43**

| 1  | XY | 11 | LK |
|----|----|----|----|
| 2  | CA | 12 | KJ |
| 3  | YZ | 13 | EV |
| 4  | TP | 14 | WD |
| 5  | DW | 15 | TU |
| 6  | OQ | 16 | ID |
| 7  | WU | 17 | LD |
| 8  | ST | 18 | OT |
| 9  | UP | 19 | WK |
| 10 | JO | 20 | HG |

**Practice Test 44**

1  10, 12
2  10, 15
3  54, 61
4  6, 48
5  24, 40

252

PRACTICE TESTS IN VERBAL REASONING

| 6 | 37, 53 |
|---|---|
| 7 | 68, 60 |
| 8 | 17, 29 |
| 9 | 83, 67 |
| 10 | 69, 77 |
| 11 | 26, 72 |
| 12 | 47, 62 |
| 13 | 18, 9 |
| 14 | 15, 29 |
| 15 | 83, 71 |
| 16 | 28, 1 |
| 17 | 9, 14 |
| 18 | 76, 85 |
| 19 | 27, 36 |
| 20 | 34, 26 |

**Practice Test 45**

| 1 | a and d | 11 | a and e | 21 | b and c | 31 | b and e | 41 | b and e |
|---|---|---|---|---|---|---|---|---|---|
| 2 | b and e | 12 | c and e | 22 | b and d | 32 | b and d | 42 | a and c |
| 3 | a and c | 13 | b and d | 23 | b and d | 33 | a and e | 43 | a and e |
| 4 | a and e | 14 | a and c | 24 | b and e | 34 | c and e | 44 | b and d |
| 5 | b and d | 15 | b and e | 25 | b and e | 35 | b and d | 45 | a and c |
| 6 | a and c | 16 | a and e | 26 | b and d | 36 | a and c | 46 | c and e |
| 7 | b and e | 17 | b and d | 27 | b and d | 37 | a and e | 47 | b and e |
| 8 | a and c | 18 | a and c | 28 | a and d | 38 | b and d | 48 | a and c |
| 9 | b and d | 19 | b and d | 29 | a and e | 39 | a and c | 49 | b and d |
| 10 | c and e | 20 | b and e | 30 | a and d | 40 | b and d | 50 | a and c |

**Practice Test 46**

| 1 | dental | % | ? | £ | $ | ! | & | | |
| 2 | taunt | $ | ! | # | £ | $ | | | |
| 3 | mental | \ | ? | £ | $ | ! | & | | |
| 4 | timid | $ | @ | \ | @ | % | | | |
| 5 | men | \ | ? | £ | | | | | |
| 6 | emotion | ? | \ | ^ | $ | @ | ^ | £ | |

253

# PRACTICE TESTS IN VERBAL REASONING

| 7 | tidal | $ | @ | % | ! | & | | | |
| 8 | dime | % | @ | \ | ? | | | | |
| 9 | limit | & | @ | \ | @ | $ | | | |
| 10 | tide | $ | @ | % | ? | | | | |
| 11 | medal | \ | ? | % | ! | & | | | |
| 12 | ultimate | # | & | $ | @ | \ | ! | $ | ? |
| 13 | monument | / | ^ | £ | # | \ | ? | £ | $ |
| 14 | dame | % | ! | \ | ? | | | | |
| 15 | mention | \ | ? | £ | $ | @ | ^ | £ | |
| 16 | moat | \ | ^ | ! | $ | | | | |
| 17 | out | ^ | # | $ | | | | | |
| 18 | limitation | & | @ | \ | @ | $ | ! | $ | @ | ^ |
| 19 | mule | \ | # | & | ? | | | | |
| 20 | mental | \ | ? | £ | $ | ! | & | | |
| 21 | date | % | ! | $ | ? | | | | |
| 22 | imminent | @ | \ | \ | @ | £ | ? | £ | $ |
| 23 | ale | ! | & | ? | | | | | |
| 24 | dimension | % | @ | \ | ? | £ | ] | @ | ^ | £ |
| 25 | mansion | \ | ! | £ | ] | @ | ^ | £ | |
| 26 | allude | ! | & | & | # | % | ? | | |
| 27 | motion | \ | ^ | $ | @ | ^ | £ | | |
| 28 | dominate | % | ^ | \ | @ | £ | ! | $ | ? |
| 29 | stem | ] | $ | ? | \ | | | | |
| 30 | stile | ] | $ | @ | & | ? | | | |

## Practice Test 47

| 1 | C | 11 | E | 21 | E |
| 2 | A | 12 | C | 22 | C |
| 3 | D | 13 | E | 23 | C |
| 4 | A | 14 | A | 24 | A |
| 5 | E | 15 | D | 25 | D |
| 6 | B | 16 | B | 26 | C |
| 7 | A | 17 | D | 27 | D |
| 8 | D | 18 | D | 28 | E |
| 9 | C | 19 | E | 29 | A |
| 10 | C | 20 | B | 30 | E |

## Practice Test 48

| 1 | D | 11 | C | 21 | B |
| 2 | B | 12 | A | 22 | A |
| 3 | B | 13 | B | 23 | D |
| 4 | A | 14 | D | 24 | C |
| 5 | B | 15 | D | 25 | A |
| 6 | A | 16 | C | 26 | B |

PRACTICE TESTS IN VERBAL REASONING

| 7 | A | 17 | E | 27 | D |
| 8 | C | 18 | D | 28 | C |
| 9 | C | 19 | B | 29 | B |
| 10 | E | 20 | C | 30 | A |

## Practice Test 49

Please note that it is sometimes possible for your layout to differ from those given in these answers.

**1**
| c | o | l | o | n |
|---|---|---|---|---|
| r |   |   |   | o |
| e |   |   |   | b |
| a |   |   |   | l |
| t | r | a | d | e |

**8**
| g | r | e | e | d |
|---|---|---|---|---|
| r |   |   |   | r |
| e |   |   |   | e |
| a |   |   |   | a |
| t | r | e | a | d |

**15**
| m | o | u | s | e |
|---|---|---|---|---|
| o |   |   |   | x |
| u |   |   |   | u |
| n |   |   |   | d |
| t | h | e | m | e |

**2**
| t | r | e | a | t |
|---|---|---|---|---|
| r |   |   |   | r |
| u |   |   |   | a |
| n |   |   |   | c |
| k | n | o | c | k |

**9**
| s | c | o | r | e |
|---|---|---|---|---|
| c |   |   |   | x |
| i |   |   |   | a |
| z |   |   |   | c |
| o | v | e | r | t |

**16**
| d | r | i | n | k |
|---|---|---|---|---|
| r |   |   |   | i |
| e |   |   |   | t |
| s |   |   |   | e |
| s | i | x | e | s |

**3**
| s | a | u | n | a |
|---|---|---|---|---|
| t |   |   |   | p |
| a |   |   |   | p |
| t |   |   |   | l |
| e | l | a | t | e |

**10**
| o | v | a | r | y |
|---|---|---|---|---|
| z |   |   |   | o |
| o |   |   |   | k |
| n |   |   |   | e |
| e | m | e | n | d |

**17**
| b | o | a | r | d |
|---|---|---|---|---|
| r |   |   |   | e |
| i |   |   |   | p |
| n |   |   |   | o |
| g | r | e | e | t |

**4**
| d | w | a | r | f |
|---|---|---|---|---|
| o |   |   |   | e |
| n |   |   |   | t |
| o |   |   |   | c |
| r | e | a | c | h |

**11**
| b | l | u | n | t |
|---|---|---|---|---|
| a |   |   |   | e |
| k |   |   |   | a |
| e |   |   |   | c |
| r | o | u | g | h |

**18**
| v | a | l | u | e |
|---|---|---|---|---|
| a |   |   |   | r |
| l |   |   |   | a |
| e |   |   |   | s |
| t | h | e | r | e |

**5**
| d | r | i | f | t |
|---|---|---|---|---|
| r |   |   |   | r |
| i |   |   |   | a |
| n |   |   |   | d |
| k | n | i | f | e |

**12**
| a | s | i | a | n |
|---|---|---|---|---|
| r |   |   |   | o |
| o |   |   |   | n |
| m |   |   |   | e |
| a | r | i | e | s |

**19**
| t | r | i | c | e |
|---|---|---|---|---|
| e |   |   |   | n |
| n |   |   |   | t |
| o |   |   |   | r |
| r | o | c | k | y |

PRACTICE TESTS IN VERBAL REASONING

6
| w | r | o | n | g |
| r |   |   |   | r |
| i |   |   |   | e |
| s |   |   |   | a |
| t | w | i | s | t |

13
| p | o | l | y | p |
| a |   |   |   | l |
| i |   |   |   | a |
| n |   |   |   | i |
| t | r | a | i | n |

20
| o | c | e | a | n |
| l |   |   |   | o |
| i |   |   |   | i |
| v |   |   |   | s |
| e | v | a | d | e |

7
| s | w | e | e | t |
| c |   |   |   | r |
| o |   |   |   | a |
| t |   |   |   | i |
| s | m | a | l | l |

14
| t | r | i | p | e |
| o |   |   |   | r |
| w |   |   |   | u |
| e |   |   |   | p |
| l | e | a | s | t |

**Practice Test 50**

Please note that it is sometimes possible for your layout to differ from those given in these answers.

1
| s | p | e | c | k |
| p |   |   |   | n |
| a |   |   |   | i |
| c |   |   |   | f |
| e | v | o | k | e |

8
| w | a | f | e | r |
| e |   |   |   | e |
| i |   |   |   | e |
| g |   |   |   | v |
| h | o | r | s | e |

15
| s | n | a | k | e |
| h |   |   |   | e |
| o |   |   |   | r |
| p |   |   |   | i |
| s | h | i | n | e |

2
| k | n | e | l | t |
| o |   |   |   | h |
| a |   |   |   | e |
| l |   |   |   | i |
| a | c | t | o | r |

9
| r | e | a | c | t |
| a |   |   |   | a |
| d |   |   |   | b |
| a |   |   |   | o |
| r | a | d | i | o |

16
| f | o | y | e | r |
| o |   |   |   | i |
| r |   |   |   | d |
| g |   |   |   | g |
| e | m | p | t | y |

3
| f | a | i | r | y |
| r |   |   |   | e |
| u |   |   |   | a |
| i |   |   |   | s |
| t | r | u | s | t |

10
| d | r | a | f | t |
| o |   |   |   | a |
| u |   |   |   | n |
| g |   |   |   | g |
| h | a | p | p | y |

17
| t | o | u | g | h |
| h |   |   |   | u |
| r |   |   |   | s |
| o |   |   |   | s |
| w | o | r | r | y |

4
| b | a | s | i | c |
| r |   |   |   | a |
| a |   |   |   | b |
| s |   |   |   | l |
| h | a | l | v | e |

11
| m | a | m | m | a |
| a |   |   |   | l |
| n |   |   |   | p |
| i |   |   |   | h |
| c | e | d | a | r |

18
| h | y | d | r | o |
| u |   |   |   | v |
| n |   |   |   | a |
| c |   |   |   | r |
| h | u | m | p | y |

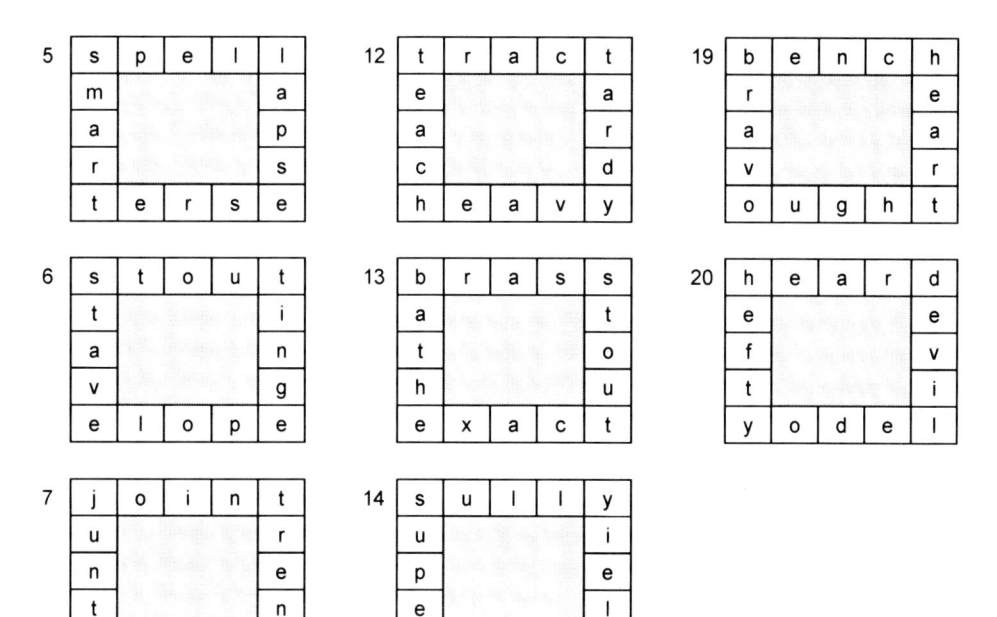

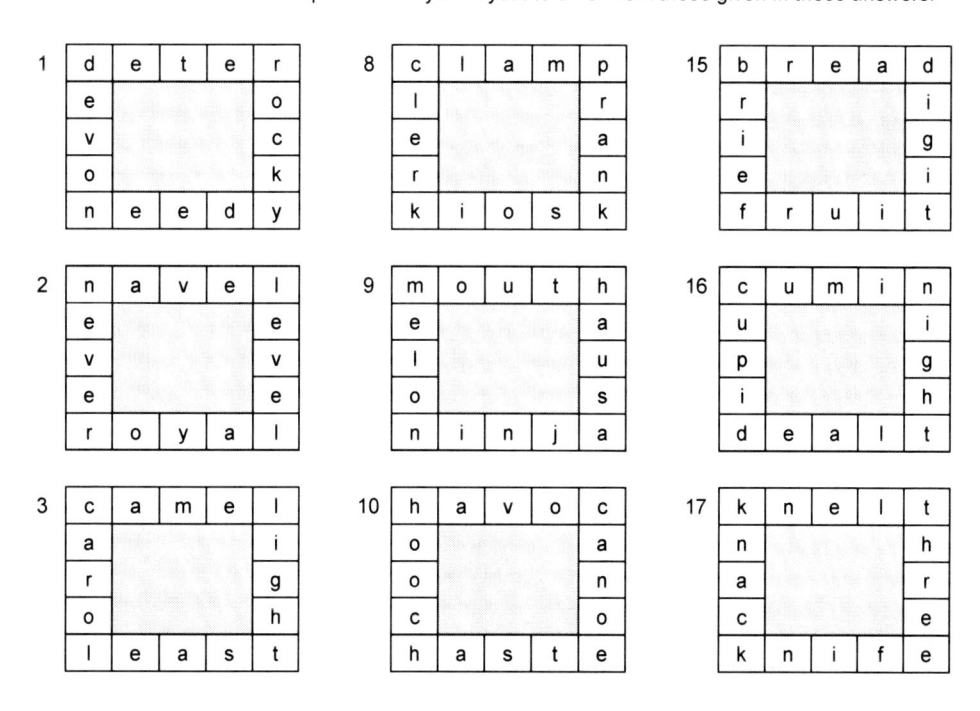

PRACTICE TESTS IN VERBAL REASONING

5. spell / smart / terse / lamps
6. stout / stave / elope / outing
7. joint / junta / award / trend
12. tract / teach / heavy / tardy
13. brass / bathe / exact / stout
14. sully / supe / raked / yield
19. bench / brave / ought / heart
20. heard / hefty / yodel / devil

**Practice Test 51**
Please note that it is sometimes possible for your layout to differ from those given in these answers.

1. deter / devon / needy / rocky
2. navel / evere / royal / level
3. camel / caro / least / light
8. clamp / clerk / kiosk / prank
9. mouth / melon / ninja / haus
10. havoc / hooc / haste / cano
15. bread / brief / fruit / digit
16. cumin / cupid / dealt / night
17. knelt / knack / knife / three

257

PRACTICE TESTS IN VERBAL REASONING

4
| a | r | r | o | w |
|---|---|---|---|---|
| r |   |   |   | h |
| m |   |   |   | i |
| o |   |   |   | t |
| r | a | i | s | e |

11
| c | a | r | g | o |
|---|---|---|---|---|
| a |   |   |   | l |
| r |   |   |   | d |
| o |   |   |   | e |
| b | r | o | w | n |

18
| s | t | i | n | g |
|---|---|---|---|---|
| o |   |   |   | h |
| u |   |   |   | o |
| n |   |   |   | s |
| d | r | a | f | t |

5
| r | i | p | e | r |
|---|---|---|---|---|
| a |   |   |   | a |
| p |   |   |   | n |
| i |   |   |   | c |
| d | i | t | c | h |

12
| c | o | u | g | h |
|---|---|---|---|---|
| a |   |   |   | a |
| r |   |   |   | r |
| a |   |   |   | s |
| t | r | a | s | h |

19
| w | h | e | a | t |
|---|---|---|---|---|
| a |   |   |   | o |
| t |   |   |   | a |
| e |   |   |   | d |
| r | i | d | e | s |

6
| g | a | u | n | t |
|---|---|---|---|---|
| u |   |   |   | r |
| e |   |   |   | e |
| s |   |   |   | a |
| s | t | e | a | d |

13
| h | o | v | e | l |
|---|---|---|---|---|
| o |   |   |   | i |
| n |   |   |   | p |
| o |   |   |   | i |
| r | a | p | i | d |

20
| r | o | v | e | r |
|---|---|---|---|---|
| a |   |   |   | o |
| d |   |   |   | u |
| a |   |   |   | t |
| r | i | f | l | e |

7
| f | r | a | n | k |
|---|---|---|---|---|
| e |   |   |   | i |
| n |   |   |   | t |
| c |   |   |   | t |
| e | d | i | f | y |

14
| s | t | a | m | p |
|---|---|---|---|---|
| m |   |   |   | o |
| a |   |   |   | w |
| l |   |   |   | e |
| l | o | w | e | r |

### Practice Test 52

| 1 | 136 | + | 235 | = | 371 |
|---|-----|---|-----|---|-----|
| 2 | 140 | + | 670 | = | 810 |
| 3 | 340 | + | 123 | = | 463 |
| 4 | 450 | + | 177 | = | 627 |
| 5 | 532 | + | 421 | = | 953 |
| 6 | 987 | + | 12  | = | 999 |
| 7 | 876 | + | 121 | = | 997 |
| 8 | 647 | + | 213 | = | 860 |
| 9 | 323 | + | 334 | = | 657 |
| 10 | 431 | + | 171 | = | 602 |
| 11 | 181 | + | 90  | = | 271 |
| 12 | 271 | + | 177 | = | 448 |

### Practice Test 53

| 1 | 947 | − | 20 | = | 927 |
|---|-----|---|-----|---|-----|
| 2 | 302 | − | 4 | = | 298 |
| 3 | 786 | − | 32 | = | 754 |
| 4 | 543 | − | 140 | = | 403 |
| 5 | 777 | − | 327 | = | 450 |
| 6 | 549 | − | 119 | = | 430 |
| 7 | 763 | − | 57 | = | 706 |
| 8 | 899 | − | 67 | = | 832 |
| 9 | 294 | − | 420 | = | −126 |
| 10 | 367 | − | 583 | = | −216 |
| 11 | 739 | − | 254 | = | 485 |
| 12 | 652 | − | 373 | = | 279 |

PRACTICE TESTS IN VERBAL REASONING

| 13 | 121 | + | 231 | = | 352 |
|---|---|---|---|---|---|
| 14 | 643 | + | 111 | = | 754 |
| 15 | 222 | + | 343 | = | 565 |
| 16 | 189 | + | 511 | = | 700 |
| 17 | 444 | + | 221 | = | 665 |
| 18 | 342 | + | 134 | = | 476 |
| 19 | 161 | + | 231 | = | 392 |
| 20 | 141 | + | 321 | = | 462 |
| 21 | 432 | + | 211 | = | 643 |
| 22 | 423 | + | 101 | = | 524 |
| 23 | 356 | + | 169 | = | 525 |
| 24 | 258 | + | 237 | = | 495 |

| 13 | 450 | − | 13 | = | 437 |
|---|---|---|---|---|---|
| 14 | 380 | − | 239 | = | 141 |
| 15 | 984 | − | 674 | = | 310 |
| 16 | 320 | − | 13 | = | 307 |
| 17 | 289 | − | 321 | = | −32 |
| 18 | 602 | − | 17 | = | 585 |
| 19 | 270 | − | 160 | = | 110 |
| 20 | 891 | − | 136 | = | 755 |
| 21 | 671 | − | 589 | = | 82 |
| 22 | 749 | − | 881 | = | −132 |
| 23 | 679 | − | 345 | = | 334 |
| 24 | 459 | − | 123 | = | 336 |

**Practice Test 54**

|  | Test answers plus process |
|---|---|
| 1. Kimi | Debbie, Kimi, and Michael have Ferraris. Michael also has a Reliant Robin. Jensen has a Mercedes and a Model T. Rubens also has a Mercedes. Debbie also has a Bugatti Veyron. Rubens has just bought a Toyota Prius. Who has the least cars?<br><br>Debbie: Ferrari, Bugatti Veyron<br>**Kimi: Ferrari**<br>Michael: Ferrari, Reliant Robin,<br>Jensen: Mercedes, Model T,<br>Rubens: Mercedes, Toyota Prius |
| 2. 66 | One-third of a number is 4 times 11. What is half of that number?<br><br>1/3 = 44<br>number = 132<br>half of 132 = **66** |
| 3. Jensen doesn't qualify | Jensen, Lewis, and Mika need to be able to run 100 meters in under 12.5 seconds to qualify for a championship. Lewis and Mika run faster than Jensen. Jensen's best time for the 100 meters is 13.1 seconds. Which of these *must* be true:<br><br>▪ Only Lewis qualifies<br>▪ **Jensen doesn't qualify**<br>▪ Lewis and Mika both qualify<br>▪ Jensen qualifies<br>▪ No one qualifies |

# PRACTICE TESTS IN VERBAL REASONING

| | |
|---|---|
| 4. 7 | Wayne is double the age of Fernando and one third as old as Didier, who will be 48 years old in 6 years. How old is Fernando?<br><br>- Didier is 48 - 6 = 42 years old<br>- Wayne is 1/3 of 42 years old = 14<br>- Fernando is half of 14 years old = **7 years old** |
| 5. Hilary | Hanif, Horace, Hilary, and Hannah are polyglots. Hanif and Horace speak Chinese, whereas the others speak Arabic. Horace and Hannah speak Albanian. Everyone except Hanif speaks Esperanto.<br><br>Hanif speaks Chinese.<br>Horace: Chinese, Albanian, and Esperanto.<br>Hilary: Arabic and Esperanto.<br>Hannah: Arabic, Albanian, and Esperanto.<br><br>Who only speaks Arabic and Esperanto? **Hilary** |
| 6. Horace | Who speaks more than one language but not Arabic? **Horace** |
| 7. 13 | Josh, the postman, has eleven red rubber bands, he gives Sunita 3 bands. Sunita now has twice the amount of bands Josh has left. How many bands did Sunita have at the beginning?<br><br>11 - 3 = 8<br>Sunita: 2 × 8 = 16<br>16 - 3 = **13** |
| 8. 4:15 p.m. | Simon, Cheryl, and Dannii are all going by train to London to watch a singing competition. Cheryl gets the 2.15 pm train. Simon's train journey takes 50% longer than Dannii's. Simon catches the 3:00 train. Dannii leaves 20 minutes after Cheryl and arrives at 3:25 pm. When will Simon arrive?<br><br>Dannii leaves at 2:35 and arrives at 3:25; therefore, he has 50-meter journey<br>Simon's journey takes 75 meters; therefore, he **arrives at 4:15 p.m.** |
| 9. 9 | If 5 bricklayers can lay a total of 50 bricks in 30 minutes, how many bricklayers are required to lay a total of 60 bricks in 20 minutes?<br><br>1 bricklayer lays 10 bricks in 30 minutes = 1 brick every 3 minutes<br>60 bricks would take 1 bricklayer 180 minutes<br>Therefore 180/20 bricklayers are required to lay these in 20 minutes = **9** |

PRACTICE TESTS IN VERBAL REASONING

| | |
|---|---|
| 10. North | An old treasure map has the following instructions:<br><br>Stand next to the black rock and face west. Walk 20 yards and then turn 90 degrees clockwise. Walk another 10 yards and then turn 45 degrees anticlockwise. Walk another 15 yards, reverse your direction, and walk 5 yards back. Turn 135 degrees clockwise and walk another 10 yards. In which direction are you now facing? **North**<br><br>Ignore the distances (these are red herrings); the direction you face is all that matters!<br>W, N, NW, SE, **N** |
| 11. Skoda and Fiat Uno | You are the head of purchasing for a company and have to buy the following 9 cars for the company pool in the next 3 months. The company is very bureaucratic and has a rule that exactly £60,000 must be spent in each of the 3 months, and you are only allowed to buy 3 cars each month. In the first month, you buy the Fiat Uno. Which other two cars must you buy that month?<br>You must spend £60,000 each month the Fiat accounts for £8,000 of this, leaving £52,000 to be spent on two more cars. The only way of achieving this is to buy the BMW and Skoda.<br><br>- **BMW Series 3 £40,000**<br>  - Lexus £36,000<br>  - Volvo Estate £32,000<br>  - Ford Focus £14,000<br>  - Ford Focus £14,000<br>  - Ford Focus £14,000<br>- **Skoda Octavia £12,000**<br>  - Ford Car £10,000<br>- **Fiat Uno £8,000** |
| 12. Athos | Athos, Portos, and Aramis live in three adjoining houses. Aramis has a black cat called d'Artagnan, Portos has a white dog, whereas Athos has a red herring. Portos has a neighbor with a red door. The owner of a four-legged animal has a blue door. Either a feline or fish owner has a green door. Aramis and Portos are not neighbors. Whose door is red?<br><br>Portos, white dog, blue door<br>**Athos,** red herring, **red door**<br>Aramis, black cat, green door |

# PRACTICE TESTS IN VERBAL REASONING

| | |
|---|---|
| 13. Mr. Bumpem and Mr. Parker | Mrs. Krashem, a driving instructor, has to arrange booking for a number of her pupils. She has 8 new pupils who wish to book either a morning or afternoon of a particular day. As these are two-hour introductory lessons, she only sees one pupil each morning or afternoon.<br><br>- Miss Banger is only available Tuesday mornings<br>- Mr. Bumpem can make any time on a Wednesday<br>- Mrs. Exhaust is free on Tuesdays all day<br>- Mr. Hilstart is only free Wednesday afternoons<br>- Miss Boot is only available Friday mornings<br>- Miss Bonnet can only make Saturday afternoons<br>- Mrs. Speed is available all day Fridays<br>- Mr. Parker can make any time on a Saturday<br><br>Which must both have morning appointments?<br><br>- Mr. Bumpem—a.m.<br>- Mrs. Exhaust—p.m.<br>- Mr. Parker—a.m.<br>- Mrs. Speed—p.m.<br>- **Mr. Bumpem and Mr. Parker—am** |
| 14. Mrs. Exhaust and Mrs. Speed | Which must both have morning appointments?<br><br>**Mrs. Exhaust and Mrs. Speed** |
| 15. 15 degrees | How many degrees are there between clock hands at 6:30 a.m.?<br><br>Minute hand is at 180 degrees<br><br>Hour hand is at 180 + 360/24 degrees as it has moved half an hour further = 180 +15 degrees.<br><br>Therefore, difference in angle = **15 degrees** |

| | |
|---|---|
| 16. Magician and ball games | You are holding a children's party for 7 children and have asked the children what activities they would like at the party. Because of time constraints, you will only have time for two activities but want to make sure that everyone gets either their first or second choice. The children and activity preferences are as follows:<br><br>| **Rachel** | face painting | magician | bouncy castle | ball games | disco |<br>|---|---|---|---|---|---|<br>| **Debbie** | bouncy castle | ball games | face painting | magician | disco |<br>| **Sunita** | magician | face painting | magician | disco | ball games |<br>| **Ben** | ball games | face painting | disco | magician | bouncy castle |<br>| **Mia** | disco | magician | face painting | bouncy castle | ball games |<br>| **Jo** | magician | bouncy castle | disco | face painting | ball games |<br>| **Amel** | face painting | ball games | bouncy castle | magician | disco |<br><br>Which two activities should you choose? **Magician and ball games** |
| 17. 16 Pounds | You spend 56 pounds in total on a cactus, a stuffed porcupine, and a pack of bandages. The cactus costs twice as much as the bandages and the stuffed porcupine double the price of the cactus. How much did the porcupine cost?<br><br>Using simple algebra, say cost of bandages = $x$, then cost of cactus is $2x$, and cost of porcupine is $4x$<br>Therefore, total cost = $x + 2x + 4x = 7x$<br>$7x = 56$ pounds<br>Therefore $x = 8$ pounds<br>The cactus costs $2x$, which is **16 pounds**. |

# PRACTICE TESTS IN VERBAL REASONING

| | |
|---|---|
| 18. Kitten | You take seven children to a toy shop to buy each a soft toy. The toy shop only has one of each type, so you ask the children their preferences. You decide to give each child one of their preferred toys.<br><br>| **James** | wombat | panda | gorilla | kitten | rat | |<br>|---|---|---|---|---|---|---|<br>| **Josh** | panda | donkey | dog | | | |<br>| **Jezebel** | panda | donkey | kitten | dog | | |<br>| **Jamelia** | panda | donkey | dog | | | |<br>| **Janine** | wombat | gorilla | donkey | kitten | rat | |<br>| **Jasbeet** | panda | dog | | | | |<br>| **Jason** | wombat | gorilla | dog | rat | kitten | |<br><br>Which animal will you give Jezebel? **Kitten**<br><br>The trick here is to realize that you can ignore the children with more than four choices.<br><br>Josh, Jamelia, and Jasbeet all have only two or three choices, and all want a panda, donkey, or dog, so they must each get one of these.<br><br>Jezebel also wants a panda, donkey, or dog, but she would also accept a kitten, so she must be given this if each child is to be allowed a preferred animal. |
| 19. Run | A crofter has to get to his herd of sheep quickly as he has been told they are being attacked by a dog. His sheep are on the other side of a steep hill. He can run over the hill (3 miles) at 4 miles an hour or take his tractor via an old dirt track that is 5 miles at an average of 6 miles an hour or he can drive his car along a very narrow winding road but this is 14 miles, and he can only go at 18 miles an hour on average. Which method should he choose?<br><br>Running 3 miles at 4 mph takes 45 minutes.<br>Driving the tractor for 5 miles at 6 mph takes 50 minutes.<br>Driving the car for 14 miles at 18 mph takes 47 minutes.<br>Therefore, he should **run**. |
| 20. 66 | If 42 is 7 times a particular number, what is 11 times that number?<br><br>$7 \times 6 = 42$<br>$1 \times 6 = 66$ |

**Practice Test 55**

| 1 | a | 11 | a | 21 | a | 31 | a | 41 | b |
|---|---|---|---|---|---|---|---|---|---|
| 2 | a | 12 | b | 22 | a | 32 | c | 42 | a |
| 3 | a | 13 | b | 23 | b | 33 | a | 43 | b |
| 4 | b | 14 | b | 24 | a | 34 | c | 44 | b |

PRACTICE TESTS IN VERBAL REASONING

| | | | | | | | | | |
|---|---|---|---|---|---|---|---|---|---|
| 5 | b | 15 | a | 25 | c | 35 | a | 45 | a |
| 6 | c | 16 | a | 26 | a | 36 | b | 46 | a |
| 7 | a | 17 | a | 27 | a | 37 | c | 47 | c |
| 8 | a | 18 | a | 28 | a | 38 | a | 48 | b |
| 9 | b | 19 | c | 29 | c | 39 | a | 49 | a |
| 10 | b | 20 | b | 30 | a | 40 | c | 50 | a |

**PracticeTest 56**

| | | | | | | | | | |
|---|---|---|---|---|---|---|---|---|---|
| 1 | c | 11 | b | 21 | c | 31 | a | 41 | a |
| 2 | a | 12 | b | 22 | c | 32 | b | 42 | b |
| 3 | a | 13 | a | 23 | a | 33 | b | 43 | b |
| 4 | b | 14 | b | 24 | a | 34 | b | 44 | b |
| 5 | b | 15 | b | 25 | b | 35 | a | 45 | a |
| 6 | b | 16 | a | 26 | a | 36 | b | 46 | c |
| 7 | a | 17 | b | 27 | a | 37 | b | 47 | c |
| 8 | b | 18 | b | 28 | c | 38 | a | 48 | c |
| 9 | b | 19 | b | 29 | a | 39 | b | 49 | a |
| 10 | a | 20 | a | 30 | c | 40 | a | 50 | a |

**Practice Test 57**

| | | | | | | |
|---|---|---|---|---|---|---|
| 1 | cipher | crack | 21 | tongue | taste |
| 2 | law | anarchy | 22 | England | England |
| 3 | nib | pen | 23 | draper | cloth |
| 4 | helmet | injury | 24 | week | days |
| 5 | employed | unemployed | 25 | milliner | hat |
| 6 | circle | sphere | 26 | bone | horse |
| 7 | spinach | tomato | 27 | push | pull |
| 8 | king | throne | 28 | eyes | vision |
| 9 | color | spectrum | 29 | rockies | america |
| 10 | pension | retirement | 30 | apple | cabbage |
| 11 | Liberia | Austria | 31 | fragment | bone |
| 12 | bed | sleep | 32 | lawn tennis | racket |
| 13 | college | university | 33 | income | expenditure |
| 14 | extort | obtain | 34 | monarch | subject |
| 15 | footballer | pitch | 35 | driver | car |
| 16 | train | track | 36 | linen | summer |
| 17 | stern | boat | 37 | feet | sole |
| 18 | start | finish | 38 | sermon | priest |
| 19 | slice | bread | 39 | teeth | chew |
| 20 | pestle | mortar | 40 | summer | winter |

# PRACTICE TESTS IN VERBAL REASONING

## Practice Test 58

| | | | | | | |
|---|---|---|---|---|---|---|
| 1 | landlord | tenant | | 21 | school | pupils |
| 2 | utensils | kitchen | | 22 | lad | masculine |
| 3 | Brussels | Belgium | | 23 | cinema | audience |
| 4 | ring | finger | | 24 | kettle | boil |
| 5 | pen | paintbrush | | 25 | pottery | shard |
| 6 | belt | waist | | 26 | boy | father |
| 7 | urban | rural | | 27 | go | depart |
| 8 | ink | pen | | 28 | princess | queen |
| 9 | church | mosque | | 29 | hat | head |
| 10 | orange | juice | | 30 | thirst | drink |
| 11 | few | common | | 31 | clap | hand |
| 12 | egg | chicken | | 32 | sunrise | sunset |
| 13 | dark | light | | 33 | south pole | north pole |
| 14 | kitten | cat | | 34 | attach | separate |
| 15 | actor | stage | | 35 | sun | day |
| 16 | lyrics | songs | | 36 | mountain | valley |
| 17 | story | tell | | 37 | motion | still |
| 18 | Kilimanjaro | Tanzania | | 38 | car | sea |
| 19 | plane | air | | 39 | chill | fridge |
| 20 | hammer | anvil | | 40 | tragedy | cry |

## Practice Test 59

| | | | | | | | | | | |
|---|---|---|---|---|---|---|---|---|---|---|
| 1 | d | | 11 | c | | 21 | d | | 31 | a |
| 2 | a | | 12 | a | | 22 | c | | 32 | c |
| 3 | c | | 13 | a | | 23 | a | | 33 | d |
| 4 | d | | 14 | b | | 24 | a | | 34 | c |
| 5 | b | | 15 | d | | 25 | a | | 35 | b |
| 6 | d | | 16 | b | | 26 | c | | 36 | b |
| 7 | b | | 17 | b | | 27 | a | | 37 | d |
| 8 | c | | 18 | a | | 28 | d | | 38 | b |
| 9 | a | | 19 | b | | 29 | b | | 39 | d |
| 10 | d | | 20 | d | | 30 | c | | 40 | c |

## Practice Test 60

| | | | | | | | | | | |
|---|---|---|---|---|---|---|---|---|---|---|
| 1 | a | | 11 | b | | 21 | b | | 31 | d |
| 2 | a | | 12 | c | | 22 | b | | 32 | c |
| 3 | c | | 13 | a | | 23 | d | | 33 | b |
| 4 | b | | 14 | a | | 24 | c | | 34 | b |
| 5 | c | | 15 | d | | 25 | b | | 35 | a |
| 6 | d | | 16 | d | | 26 | a | | 36 | d |
| 7 | d | | 17 | c | | 27 | b | | 37 | c |
| 8 | d | | 18 | c | | 28 | c | | 38 | a |

| 9  | a | 19 | c | 29 | d | 39 | d |
| 10 | b | 20 | a | 30 | a | 40 | c |

**Practice Test 61**

| 1  | c | 11 | c | 21 | c | 31 | e |
| 2  | a | 12 | d | 22 | e | 32 | d |
| 3  | e | 13 | a | 23 | a | 33 | a |
| 4  | a | 14 | e | 24 | a | 34 | e |
| 5  | c | 15 | b | 25 | c | 35 | b |
| 6  | a | 16 | d | 26 | e | 36 | d |
| 7  | d | 17 | e | 27 | d | 37 | b |
| 8  | b | 18 | d | 28 | b | 38 | d |
| 9  | e | 19 | c | 29 | c | 39 | c |
| 10 | a | 20 | a | 30 | a | 40 | a |

**Practice Test 62**

| 1  | b | 11 | b | 21 | b | 31 | c |
| 2  | e | 12 | c | 22 | e | 32 | d |
| 3  | d | 13 | e | 23 | c | 33 | a |
| 4  | b | 14 | c | 24 | a | 34 | e |
| 5  | d | 15 | d | 25 | e | 35 | c |
| 6  | c | 16 | c | 26 | a | 36 | a |
| 7  | a | 17 | a | 27 | d | 37 | d |
| 8  | e | 18 | e | 28 | b | 38 | b |
| 9  | a | 19 | b | 29 | c | 39 | e |
| 10 | d | 20 | d | 30 | a | 40 | a |

**Practice Test 63**

| 1  | d | 11 | a | 21 | e | 31 | a |
| 2  | b | 12 | c | 22 | a | 32 | c |
| 3  | e | 13 | a | 23 | c | 33 | a |
| 4  | a | 14 | d | 24 | a | 34 | d |
| 5  | c | 15 | b | 25 | d | 35 | e |
| 6  | d | 16 | e | 26 | e | 36 | d |
| 7  | a | 17 | a | 27 | d | 37 | c |
| 8  | c | 18 | c | 28 | c | 38 | e |
| 9  | a | 19 | c | 29 | a | 39 | d |
| 10 | e | 20 | a | 30 | e | 40 | b |

# PRACTICE TESTS IN VERBAL REASONING

## Practice Test 64

| | | | | | | | |
|---|---|---|---|---|---|---|---|
| 1 | c | 11 | c | 21 | c | 31 | a |
| 2 | a | 12 | a | 22 | a | 32 | e |
| 3 | e | 13 | b | 23 | d | 33 | d |
| 4 | d | 14 | e | 24 | e | 34 | a |
| 5 | a | 15 | d | 25 | d | 35 | e |
| 6 | e | 16 | b | 26 | c | 36 | b |
| 7 | b | 17 | d | 27 | e | 37 | d |
| 8 | d | 18 | a | 28 | d | 38 | b |
| 9 | b | 19 | e | 29 | b | 39 | d |
| 10 | d | 20 | a | 30 | c | 40 | c |

## Practice Test 65

| | | | | | | | |
|---|---|---|---|---|---|---|---|
| 1 | a | 11 | c | 21 | c | 31 | a |
| 2 | d | 12 | b | 22 | d | 32 | d |
| 3 | d | 13 | b | 23 | d | 33 | c |
| 4 | c | 14 | a | 24 | d | 34 | b |
| 5 | d | 15 | b | 25 | c | 35 | a |
| 6 | c | 16 | d | 26 | b | 36 | c |
| 7 | d | 17 | c | 27 | b | 37 | b |
| 8 | c | 18 | b | 28 | a | 38 | c |
| 9 | c | 19 | a | 29 | d | 39 | c |
| 10 | a | 20 | b | 30 | c | 40 | d |

## Practice Test 66

| | | | | | | | |
|---|---|---|---|---|---|---|---|
| 1 | d | 11 | c | 21 | c | 31 | a |
| 2 | a | 12 | b | 22 | a | 32 | b |
| 3 | b | 13 | a | 23 | a | 33 | d |
| 4 | c | 14 | b | 24 | b | 34 | d |
| 5 | a | 15 | a | 25 | a | 35 | c |
| 6 | a | 16 | c | 26 | c | 36 | a |
| 7 | a | 17 | d | 27 | b | 37 | a |
| 8 | d | 18 | b | 28 | d | 38 | a |
| 9 | d | 19 | d | 29 | b | 39 | c |
| 10 | c | 20 | b | 30 | b | 40 | a |

## Practice Test 67

| | | | | | | | | | |
|---|---|---|---|---|---|---|---|---|---|
| 1 | d | 11 | d | 21 | d | 31 | b | 41 | d |
| 2 | a | 12 | a | 22 | b | 32 | c | 42 | b |
| 3 | d | 13 | b | 23 | c | 33 | a | 43 | d |
| 4 | c | 14 | d | 24 | d | 34 | c | 44 | a |
| 5 | d | 15 | a | 25 | b | 35 | d | 45 | b |

PRACTICE TESTS IN VERBAL REASONING

| 6 | a | 16 | a | 26 | a | 36 | a | 46 | d |
| --- | --- | --- | --- | --- | --- | --- | --- | --- | --- |
| 7 | d | 17 | c | 27 | d | 37 | b | 47 | b |
| 8 | d | 18 | c | 28 | c | 38 | d | 48 | c |
| 9 | c | 19 | c | 29 | d | 39 | b | 49 | a |
| 10 | d | 20 | a | 30 | a | 40 | c | 50 | b |

**Practice Test 68**

| 1 | c | 11 | a | 21 | b | 31 | a | 41 | d |
| --- | --- | --- | --- | --- | --- | --- | --- | --- | --- |
| 2 | d | 12 | c | 22 | d | 32 | c | 42 | b |
| 3 | b | 13 | d | 23 | b | 33 | d | 43 | c |
| 4 | d | 14 | d | 24 | c | 34 | d | 44 | c |
| 5 | d | 15 | b | 25 | a | 35 | b | 45 | d |
| 6 | b | 16 | c | 26 | d | 36 | c | 46 | c |
| 7 | d | 17 | a | 27 | d | 37 | a | 47 | a |
| 8 | b | 18 | c | 28 | c | 38 | b | 48 | c |
| 9 | c | 19 | a | 29 | a | 39 | a | 49 | d |
| 10 | d | 20 | c | 30 | c | 40 | b | 50 | b |

**Practice Test 70**

| 1 | ink | pill | 20 | lip | flame | 39 | ore | pinch |
| --- | --- | --- | --- | --- | --- | --- | --- | --- |
| 2 | hose | tear | 21 | pay | late | 40 | pace | plot |
| 3 | arm | wit | 22 | hen | warm | 41 | fight | timer |
| 4 | pant | place | 23 | robe | pact | 42 | due | sting |
| 5 | grim | cheap | 24 | ear | those | 43 | arrow | thank |
| 6 | bush | trip | 25 | ore | pride | 44 | rain | pleat |
| 7 | on | hotels | 26 | brow | taken | 45 | cane | beak |
| 8 | hop | seat | 27 | lobe | glass | 46 | fight | camel |
| 9 | hoe | pant | 28 | oil | charm | 47 | art | table |
| 10 | fee | health | 29 | bated | paint | 48 | hose | then |
| 11 | at | hash | 30 | ore | box | 49 | at | peel |
| 12 | bank | lace | 31 | ink | pear | 50 | old | path |
| 13 | tall | sink | 32 | bank | plan | | | |
| 14 | not | tear | 33 | payer | flight | | | |
| 15 | pant | lice | 34 | heath | flee | | | |
| 16 | of | fold | 35 | lame | blow | | | |
| 17 | ear | hat | 36 | bush | card | | | |
| 18 | all | tact | 37 | pace | least | | | |
| 19 | art | pant | 38 | love | cup | | | |

**Practice Test 71**

| 1 | Cannot say | 11 | Cannot say | 21 | Cannot say | 31 | True |
| --- | --- | --- | --- | --- | --- | --- | --- |
| 2 | True | 12 | Cannot say | 22 | False | 32 | True |
| 3 | True | 13 | True | 23 | True | 33 | False |

## PRACTICE TESTS IN VERBAL REASONING

| | | | | | | | |
|---|---|---|---|---|---|---|---|
| 4 | True | 14 | Cannot say | 24 | Cannot say | 34 | Cannot say |
| 5 | False | 15 | True | 25 | False | | |
| 6 | Cannot say | 16 | Cannot say | 26 | Cannot say | | |
| 7 | Cannot say | 17 | False | 27 | True | | |
| 8 | False | 18 | False | 28 | False | | |
| 9 | True | 19 | True | 29 | True | | |
| 10 | True | 20 | False | 30 | False | | |

**Practice Test 72**

| | | | | | |
|---|---|---|---|---|---|
| 1 | Cannot say | 11 | Cannot say | 21 | True |
| 2 | True | 12 | True | 22 | False |
| 3 | False | 13 | True | 23 | True |
| 4 | True | 14 | False | 24 | Cannot say |
| 5 | Cannot say | 15 | False | 25 | True |
| 6 | False | 16 | Cannot say | 26 | True |
| 7 | Cannot say | 17 | False | 27 | Cannot say |
| 8 | False | 18 | False | 28 | Cannot say |
| 9 | False | 19 | Cannot say | | |
| 10 | False | 20 | True | | |

# SECTION 4

# FURTHER INFORMATION

## Hints on Improving Your Performance

The following hints and tips provide useful information to you in your quest for success. It will help you ace your test.

### VERBAL USAGE AND VERBAL COMPREHENSION

- Have a small notebook to write the words you spell incorrectly or any new words you have learned. Refer to this book periodically, and add new words to it. Your word power will surely increase, and you will become more articulate.
- Read books, newspapers, and read general interest and professional magazines. You will find it very helpful to own a good dictionary and thesaurus. Use them to learn new words.
- All verbal reasoning tests are timed, so work quickly and accurately.
- If you are not sure of any questions, go through a process of elimination. You can also guess if you need to. Do not leave any question unanswered.

### VERBAL APPLICATION

- Speed and accuracy are very important to your success, so be diligent.
- Look for the required sequence in the letters, words, or numbers.

## VERBAL ANALYSIS

- The hints stated above are also relevant.
- Read the question carefully, and make notes to help you with your analysis. These questions may not be multiple choice in format, so accuracy is essential.

## VERBAL ANALOGIES

- The hints provided in the sections above also apply.
- Always remember that you are required to identify a specific relationship between words.
- Think of an answer to the question before reading all the options available.
- Words have different meanings, so choose the appropriate meaning of the word as an answer.
- These questions are usually quite straightforward and are generally easier to answer. They are somewhat easier to do; therefore, under test conditions, you can do them first to boost your confidence.

## CRITICAL VERBAL REASONING

- Read the questions before you read the passage you are given because it will save you time and help you understand the passage and what you are required to do.
- Learn to read and understand passages quickly.
- Only use the information provided when deciding on the answer.
- Answer the questions you know first and then go back to those you are less certain of.
- Finish all the questions because they generally carry equal marks, and leaving any unanswered means you automatically lose marks.

## 1. PREPARATION: BEFORE THE TEST

### a. Practice Is Essential

Success in anything requires knowing what the objective is and why you are aiming for it. You should have a clear and concise mental picture of your goal. Your objective is to pass verbal reasoning tests for either college admission or employment purposes. It is therefore essential to practice as many tests as possible. Ensure that you furnish yourself with sample and practice questions at an early stage so that you can start taking the practice tests as soon as possible. You can request past question papers from colleges or download them from their websites. Test providers also have sample tests on their websites, which you will also find useful.

When practicing the tests, ensure that you simulate exam conditions and have an action plan so that you have a structured approach to your preparation. Make time for both your social and study time so that you have a balanced life. After taking each practice test, mark and take time to review your performance, and make a note of the areas that need attention. Focus on how you can improve your performance and then take some more practice tests. You will find that keeping a record of your performance is helpful in assessing your progress.

A good dictionary is a necessary resource. Reading novels, newspapers, magazines, and other periodicals will also contribute to increasing your word power. You can buy books from the internet and bookshops, or you can simply borrow the books from public and institutional libraries. Having a little notebook where you record new words you have learned will help you.

## b. Health and Well-being Is Essential

The saying "Health is wealth" is so true. It is important that you eat well and look after yourself if you are to be your best. Nutritionists and other health practitioners provide us with guidelines, which include the following:

- Drink a lot of water, and keep hydrated as this can contribute to your ability to learn and concentrate. Eat the right amount of nutritional food.
- Adequate rest is required to make you effective in life. Plan and ensure that you have enough rest so that you can be and stay your best. It is also essential to include exercise and leisure activities in your daily activities. Make time to go for short walks, read, listen to music, pamper yourself, and play games you enjoy.
- Keep well away from the use of stimulants that could adversely affect your sleep patterns and your performance.

## c. Know Yourself

In the words of Ralph Waldo Emerson, "Each mind has its own method." Knowing your learning style is important. Some of the tools used by human resource specialists include Myers-Briggs Type Inventory (MBIT), Gardner's Multiple Intelligences, Honey and Mumford's Learning Styles, and Flemming's VARK. While an in-depth knowledge of these tools is not the focus of this book, you might find it useful to read more about them on the Internet or refer to some of the books on the list of references at the back of this book. The knowledge gained from understanding your learning style will assist you to make the most of your time and energy. When preparing for the tests, make sure you take the time to put yourself in the best learning space, free from what makes it difficult for you to learn and take in new information.

### d. Be Confident

Confidence is gained by being well prepared, and this book aims to help you to be as well prepared as you can be. Do not allow self-doubt and negative thoughts to get the better of you. Remember that you cannot change anything in the past that may cause insecurity, but you can make constructive decisions to influence your future. Try your best to control the feeling of anxiety that is common to us all. Remember that since you have taken the trouble to practice, there is no real reason to worry. Worrying will not change anything. Focus on passing the tests and the opportunities the success can give you. Try to visualize it, and be motivated by the objective so you can do your best.

### e. Test Materials

Ensure that you have all the necessary materials for the tests. You may be provided with a list, which may include pencils, rulers, erasers, and other stationery. Buy and have them ready for the test. This is a very important aspect of being prepared. If you are unsure what to bring or what test stationery will be provided, contact the relevant organization for information on the requirement.

### f. Location

Make sure that you know where to go and how long it will take you to get there. Get there early so that you are not rushed and can relax before the test and focus of the passing the test. This will contribute to reducing the negative elements of anxiety

## 2. PERFORMANCE: DURING THE TEST

### a. Be Adaptive

Always remember that no matter how much you prepare, you will come across questions and scenarios that you have not come across before. In such a situation, make sure you understand what is being asked of you so that you can provide the answer without panicking. . This mindset and game plan is key to you performing well.

## b. Do Your Best

What are you like when you are at your best? What are the indicators that you are working at your best? Be aware of these so that you can know when you need to take a moment to get yourself there. This is better than simply plodding along, burdened by something that is stopping you from being the best you can be during the exam. Relax so that you are able to understand the questions and respond appropriately.

## c Seek Clarification If Required

If you are uncertain of anything, you must seek assistance from the test administrators. Remember to ask for help from the test administrators, if necessary.

## d. Be Diligent

Make sure that your name and reference details are on the relevant answer paper. Your details may have been pre-printed, but check that they are correct. You must also carefully read the instructions for each test. The layout of the questions may be similar to some you have practiced before, but the requirement may be different. Do not assume that you know what the question is asking.

## e. Time Management

It is common knowledge that we cannot manage time because time does not wait for anyone. How you use your time is crucial to your success because it is not what you know but what you can demonstrate that you know during the test that matters. Have a quick glance at the questions so that you have a good understanding of what is expected. Time yourself so that you can finish all the questions. Aim to have a few minutes' spare to review your work. Generally, these questions are multiple choice, so don't spend too long on any one question that you are finding difficult because this means you will have less time to complete the ones you may know. Do as many as possible so that you can increase your chance of success.

## f. Have a Strategy

You can use mnemonics to jog your memory, should you require it. The most common format of these questions is multiple choice. If you are unsure of the answer, you should eliminate the option that is obviously wrong then intelligently choose your answer from the other options. You must also make sure that, having read the instructions, you spend your time wisely, making sure you get as high a score as possible. This might mean leaving questions and coming back to them if you have time.

### g. Be Focused

The aim is to pass the test, so do not be distracted by looking at what other candidates are doing. You have to mind your own business and remember why you are doing the test. Stay motivated, focused, and confident. It is during the exam that your confidence will reap rewards.

### 3. AFTER THE TEST

### a. Assessing your failings

Unless you are going to take the exam again very soon, there is very little benefit in looking into what you did wrong on an exam. Review your approach, and make improvements if you were not properly prepared for the test.

### b. Confidence

Remember that while tests are an effective methodology in assessing the readiness of a candidate for a job or position, they do not test everything. You can still have a great influence over final results and decisions in other ways. In addition, you may have other tests to do, and you need to be confident.

# Guide to Writing an Effective CV

The purpose of the CV is to obtain an interview. It will also be used as a "talking point" for that interview. Ensure that your CV is clear, concise with a positive tone, and with an emphasis on your accomplishments. The following tips will help you write an effective CV.

1. Conserve space at the top (e.g., large font for name, spread out details along longer lines, omit CV designation).
2. Remain positive in profile with dynamic and engaging words such as *highly experienced* or *highly qualified*, especially if pursuing a senior position. If pursuing a more junior position as indicated by your qualifications, play it down slightly to avoid being classed as overqualified.

3. If enthusiastic, this should be carried through the tone of the CV (e.g., selective word choice, not such words as *able*).
4. Profile sentences should be clear andconcise.
5. Utilize bullet points for clarity whenever possible (e.g., skills and achievements).
6. Use bullet points to effectively highlight achievements, duties and recent positions and duties..
7. Use action verbs (i.e., ending in -ed) at the beginning of your skills and also accomplishments (e.g. *structured, managed, initiated*). Avoid using *I*.
8. Avoid repeating action verbs in accomplishments in succession (e.g., *managed, managed*).
9. Limit submission to two pages.
10. For fonts, use Arial 10 or 11 or Times Roman. This will help with clarity and limit the space of the CV (i.e., remember, no more than two pages).
11. Personal information is an unnecessary use of space (e.g., birth date, marital status).
12. Interests are valuable as a talking point, but again, use action verbs, and consider something physical (but not extremely dangerous!), social,and intellectual.
13. No need for "References available upon request" (it uses up space) because employer will make this assumption.
14. Be conscious of key words used in your industry and include utilise jargon, but be clear.
15. Print and read the hard copy as best form of review.

# Useful Powerful Action Verbs

Powerful words answer the concerns of potential employers, such as:

- Works on a team
- Learns and adapts to new ways of doing things and thinking
- Engages and motivates others through leadership
- Understands how profits are generated
- Manages change
- Has business acumen or savvy
- Maintains high professional standards

Here is a list of powerful action verbs to consider and add to your CV:

| A | C | D |
|---|---|---|
| ☐ Achieved | ☐ Completed | ☐ Delivered |
| ☐ Acquired | ☐ Conducted | |

- ☐ Administered
- ☐ Advised
- ☐ Analyzed

**E**
- ☐ Evaluated

**I**
- ☐ Identified
- ☐ Implemented
- ☐ Improved
- ☐ Increased
- ☐ Initiated
- ☐ Instructed

**O**
- ☐ Organized

**S**
- ☐ Solved
- ☐ Supervised

- ☐ Constructed
- ☐ Coordinated
- ☐ Created

**F**
- ☐ Facilitated
- ☐ Founded

**L**
- ☐ Launched
- ☐ Led

**P**
- ☐ Performed
- ☐ Produced

**T**
- ☐ Trained

- ☐ Developed
- ☐ Diagnosed
- ☐ Directed
- ☐ Drafted
- ☐ Drove
- ☐ Designed

**M**
- ☐ Maintained
- ☐ Managed

**N**
- ☐ Negotiated

**R**
- ☐ Reduced (losses)
- ☐ Renewed
- ☐ Researched
- ☐ Reviewed

# APPENDIX A

# List of Test Publishers and Suppliers

Caliper UK, New Broad Street House, 35 New Broad Street, London EC2M 1NH
  www.caliper.co.uk
CDA, Oak House, 1 Limewood Way, Limewood Business Park, Seacroft, Leeds LS14 1AB
  www.cdaq.co.uk
Centre For Corporate Culture, Folville Lodge, Church Street, Bodicote, Oxon OX15 4DW
  www.centreforcorporatculture.com
Consulting Tools Ltd., 5 Caxton House, Broad Street, Great Cambourne, Cambridge CB3 6JN
  www.consultingtools.com
Criterion Partnership Ltd., Unthought Corner, 85 Gloucester Road, Brighton BN1 4AP
  www.criterionpartnership.co.uk
Eras Ltd., Providence Court, 104-106 Denmark Street, DISS, Norfolk IP22 4WW
  www.eras.co.uk
Eysenck Cripps Cook Occupational Scales, Yarner, Darlington, Totnes, Devon TQ9 6JH
  www.eccoc.co.uk
GL Assessment, The Chiswick Centre, 414 Chiswick High Road, London W4 5TF
  www.gl-assessment.co.uk
Hogrefe, Burgner House, 4630 Kingsgate, Oxford Business Park, Oxford OX4 2SU
  www.hogrefe.co.uk
Husdon, Moustraat 56, 9000 Gent, Belgium
  http://belgium.hudson.com
Human Factors UK Ltd., 8 Staple Inn, High Holborn, London WC1V 7QH
  www.hfi.com
Insights Learning and Development Ltd., Global Head Office, Jack Martin Way, Claverhouse Old House, Dundee DD4 9BZ
  www.insights.com
JCA (Occupational Psychologists) Ltd., Spa House, 17 Royal Crescent, Cheltenham, Glos. GL50 3DA
  www.jca.eu.com
Kenexa, Hygeia Building, 66-68 College Road, Harrow, Middlesex HA1 1BE
  www.kenexa.com

Knight Chapman Psychological Limited, 1 High Street, Lewes, East Sussex BN7 2DA
www.kcpltd.com
Lafayette Instrument Company, 4 Park Road, Sileby, Loughborough, Leicester LE12 7TJ
www.lafayetteinstrumenteurope.com
Master Management International A/S, Gydevang 39-41, DK-3450, Allerod, Denmark
www.master-hr.com
MHS (UK), 39a Kingfisher Court, Hambridge Road, Newbury, Berkshire RG14 5SJ
www.mhs.com
Mindmill, 22 Joymount, Carrickfergus, Co. Antrim BT28 7DN
www.censeo-services.com
Occupational Research Centre, Cornerways, Cardigan Street, Newmarket, Suffolk CB8 8HZ
www.kaicentre.com
OPP Ltd, Elsfield Hall, 15-17 Elsfield Way, Oxford OX2 8EP
www.opp.eu.com
Pario Innovations Ltd., 9 Laurel Close, Prestwood, Great Missenden, Bucks HP16 9DX
Pearson Assessment, 80 Strand, London WC2R 0RL
www.talentlens.co.uk
Previsor (ASE), Arlington Square, Downshire Way, Bracknell, Berks RG12 1WA
www.ase-solutions.co.uk
Profiles International Inc., 5205 Lakeshore Drive, Waco TX, 76710 USA
www.profilesinternational.com
Psychological Consultancy Ltd., 8 Mount Ephraim, Tunbridge Wells TNa 8AS
http://www.psychological-consultancy.com
Psytech International Ltd., The Grange, Church Road, Pulloxhill, Bedfordshire MK45 5HE
www.psytech.co.uk
Quest Partnership Ltd., Lakeside Business Park, South Cerney, Cirencester, Glos. GL7 5XE
www.questpartnership.co.uk
Selby & Mills Ltd, Prospect House, Prospect Place, Beechen Cliff, Bath BA2 4QP
www.selbymills.co.uk
SHL Group Ltd., The Pavillion, 1 Atwell Place, Thames Ditton, Surrey KT7 0NE
www.shlgroup.com

# APPENDIX B

# List of Useful Websites (in alphabetical order)

http://backtowork.direct.gov.uk/job-coach.html
http://en.wikipedia.org/wiki/Myers-Briggs_Type_Indicator
http://shop.gl-assessment.co.uk/home.php?cat=377&gclid=CIyB9tfipJ8CFVtn4wodyD8plw
http://www.agcas.org.uk/search_tags?from_controller=events&tag=Psychometric
http://www.allthetests.com/
http://www.bath.ac.uk/careers/catalogue/skills.html
http://www.bournemouth.ac.uk/careers/applying_for_jobs/resources_interviews.html
http://www.career-paths.co.uk/phdi/p1.nsf/supppages/0975?opendocument&part=4
http://www.careerpsychologycentre.com/solutions.html
http://www.careers.stir.ac.uk/documents/psych_tests09.pdf
http://www.challengeconsulting.com.au/people_services/psychometric_testing.htm
http://www.civilservice.gov.uk/jobs/faststream/index.aspx
http://www.employment360.com/career-aptitude-test.html
http://www.georgianaheadrecruitment.co.uk/advice-resources/psychometric-testing/
http://www.humanresourcesmagazine.com.au/articles/10/0C055010.asp
http://www.job-application-and-interview-advice.com/job-aptitude-test.html
http://www.jobtestprep.co.uk/jtpsite/content/English_UK/home/PsychometricTestOnline.aspx
http://www.kenexa.com/assessments/what-we-assess
http://www.lboro.ac.uk/service/careers/section/applications/psych_tests.html
http://www.ncirl.ie/Careers/Students_&_Graduates/Selection_and_Psychometric_Testing
http://www.nottingham.ac.uk/careers/graduates/applications/psychometric/
http://www.pantesting.com/products/Psychcorp/DAT_Verbal.asp
http://www.potential-unlimited.co.za/psychometric.htm
http://www.professional-cv-writingservices.co.uk/psychometric-test/psychometric-personality-aptitude-testing.html
http://www.profilingforsuccess.com/kogan-page/
http://www.psyasia.com/swift_comprehension_aptitude.php

http://www.psychometricadvantage.co.uk/personalityprofiling.html
http://www.psychometricassessment.com/swift_comprehension_aptitude.php
http://www.psychometricinstitute.com.au/Psychometric-Test-Guide/Verbal-Reasoning-Test-Guide.html
http://www.readytomanage.com/downloads/LMATsamplereport.pdf
http://www.secondpost.com/news-careers-advice/1043/How-to-approach-psychometric-testing/careers-advice
http://www.shef.ac.uk/careers/students/gettingajob/psychometric.html
http://www.ukcat.ac.uk/pages/details.aspx?page=practiceQuestions
http://www.uowdubai.ac.ae/ss/career/recruitment_selection_tests.pdf
http://www.verbal-reasoning.com/
http://www.westherts.ac.uk/
http://www2.surrey.ac.uk/careers/current/work/psychometrictests/
ww.ReedGlobal.com
www.admissiontests.cambridgeassessment.org.uk/adt/
www.aptitudeonline.co.uk
www.aptitudetestsonline.co.uk
www.assessmentcentral.com
www.assessmentday.co.uk
www.barcap.com/graduatecareers/barcap_test.pdf
www.businessballs.com › self/personal development
www.careerpsychologycentre.com/solutionsadvanced.html
www.careers-uk.com
www.cipd.org.uk
www.CivilServicePrep.co.uk
www.deloite.co.uk/index.asp
www.doctorjob.com/testingzone
www.englishforum
www.englishtogo
www.gl-assessment.co.uk
www.howtobooks.co.uk/.../psychometric-testing/free.asp
www.hrmagazine.co.uk/.../Technology-E-recruitment-psychometric-testing/
www.kent.ac.uk/careers/psychotests.htm
www.kent.ac.uk/careers/tests/verbaltest.htm
www.kogan-page.co.uk
www.mensa.org.uk
www.Morrisby.com
www.MyersBriggsReports.com
www.mypotential.net
www.oneclickhr.com
www.practicalfinancialdetox.co.uk
www.prospects.ac.uk

www.psychometricsonline.com
www.psytech.co.uk
www.psytech.com
www.publicjobs.ie/en/careers/advice/sample_tests.htm
www.puzz.com
www.reedglobal.com/Consulting
www.shldirect.com
www.shlgroup.com
www.skillstudio.co.uk
www.TalentLens.co.uk
www.testagency.co.uk
http://www.testpreppractice.net/GRE/Default.aspx

# APPENDIX C

# General Careers Information: Useful Links and Resources

**Careers Information**

www.business.com – list of informative resources on career assessments
www.prospects.ac.uk – undergraduate and graduate careers website
www.learndirect.co.uk – general career information and advice, 0-800-00-900 (toll-free phone)
www.careersa-z.co.uk – general career information
www.connexions-direct.com – information and advice for young people and general careers information
www.direct.gov.uk – general careers, employment, course information, and funding information
www.jobs.guardian.co.uk – general information on careers, advice, and progression
www.cascaid.co.uk – adult directions and other career quizzes to find out what work you are suited to
www.channel4.com/life/microsites/B/brilliantcareers/ – career assessment for young people

**Course Information**

www.hotcourses.com – general course information and searches
www.learndirect.co.uk – general course information and searches
www.floodlight.co.uk – course search in London
www.ucas.com – full-time university degrees, diplomas, and foundation degrees
www.prospects.ac.uk – post-graduate courses
www.hero.ac.uk – course search for university
www.push.co.uk – information on university and degrees
www.timesonline.co.uk – university league tables by subject
www.isc.co.uk – list of UK independent private schools
www.ukprivateschools.com – list of UK private schools
www.unistats.com – ompare UK universities

## Qualifications

www.naric.org.uk – find out how your qualifications compare to UK or overseas qualifications
www.direct.gov.uk – find out what each qualification and level means

## Funding for Courses

www.egas-online.org – Search for charities that can provide grants toward further study.
www.direct.gov.uk – Information on funding toward courses.
Career Development Loan (Provided by Barclays, RBS, and the Cooperative Bank)
If you have graduated in the last two or three years, you may be able to get assistance from your university.
www.learndirect.co.uk – career advice over the telephone (free)
www.icg-uk.org – Find a career adviser (probably paid for.
www.nextstep.org.uk – Contact Next Step for face-to-face advice if you are over twenty and do not have a level 2 qualification. (free)
www.careers.lon.ac.uk –graduate career advice (paid)
www.connexions-direct.com – career advice for young people (free)
www.prospects.ac.uk – one hundred twenty-one online interactive career advice (paid)

## Job Search

www.monster.com – general job search and e-mail alerts
www.jobs.guardian.co.uk – Search by sector or employer, including media, public sector, graduate, and IT positions.
www.fish4jobs.co.uk – general job search and recruitment
www.workthing.com
vso.org.uk/volunteering
www.jobserve.com – Search over fifty thousand permanent, contract, temporary jobs advertised weekly, covering jobs in all industry sectors.
www.jobsearch.co.uk – general job search
www.jobcentreplus.gov.uk – general job search and advice
www.totaljobs.com – Search over one hundred thirty jobs in the United Kingdom.
www.jobs.telegraph.co.uk – thousands of jobs in London and across the United Kingdom. Executive and senior job search online.
www.jobs.independent.co.uk – A recruitment website with thousands of vacancies in job sectors including accountancy, teaching, secretarial, banking, legal, it, marketing, sales, human resources, etc.
www.jobsite.co.uk – job search and job email service

www.newscientistjobs.com – Find global science jobs on New Scientist Jobs. Search to find the latest jobs in science.

www.jobs.ac.uk – Search thousands of science-, research-, and academic-related vacancies in the United Kingdom and abroad.

www.redgoldfish.co.uk – general job search

www.ukjobsnet.co.uk – general job search

www.londonjobs.co.uk – various jobs in construction, marketing, accounting, banking, etc.

www.jobs1.co.uk – UK job search and recruitment agency resource

www.exec-appointments.com – global executive jobs, executive search, and management jobs

www.reed.co.uk – Covers the United Kingdom and all job sectors. Includes vacancy search, CV builder, and labour market information.

**CV, Interview Techniques, Application Forms, and Job Search Advice**

www.prospects.ac.uk – CV and cover letter advice (graduate)

www.jobs.guardian.co.uk – CV, application forms, interview techniques, and cover letters

www.monster.com – CV, application forms, cover letter advice

www.workthing.com – CV and cover letter advice

www.learndirect.co.uk – job search, CV, and interview techniques advice

# APPENDIX D

## Additional Answer Sheet
## Practice Test Number_____

| | | | | | | | |
|---|---|---|---|---|---|---|---|
| 1 | ☐ | 14 | ☐ | 27 | ☐ | 40 | ☐ |
| 2 | ☐ | 15 | ☐ | 28 | ☐ | 41 | ☐ |
| 3 | ☐ | 16 | ☐ | 29 | ☐ | 42 | ☐ |
| 4 | ☐ | 17 | ☐ | 30 | ☐ | 43 | ☐ |
| 5 | ☐ | 18 | ☐ | 31 | ☐ | 44 | ☐ |
| 6 | ☐ | 19 | ☐ | 32 | ☐ | 45 | ☐ |
| 7 | ☐ | 20 | ☐ | 33 | ☐ | 46 | ☐ |
| 8 | ☐ | 21 | ☐ | 34 | ☐ | 47 | ☐ |
| 9 | ☐ | 22 | ☐ | 35 | ☐ | 48 | ☐ |
| 10 | ☐ | 23 | ☐ | 36 | ☐ | 49 | ☐ |
| 11 | ☐ | 24 | ☐ | 37 | ☐ | 50 | ☐ |
| 12 | ☐ | 25 | ☐ | 38 | ☐ | | |
| 13 | ☐ | 26 | ☐ | 39 | ☐ | | |

### Record Your Progress

| Number of Times You Have Taken the Test | Record | | | Record Your Completion Time |
|---|---|---|---|---|
| | Number of Questions Completed | Your Total Score | Total No. of Questions | |
| 1 | | | | |
| 2 | | | | |
| 3 | | | | |
| 4 | | | | |
| 5 | | | | |

PRACTICE TESTS IN VERBAL REASONING

# Additional Answer Sheet
# Practice Test Number_____

| 1  |  | 14 |  | 27 |  | 40 |  |
|----|--|----|--|----|--|----|--|
| 2  |  | 15 |  | 28 |  | 41 |  |
| 3  |  | 16 |  | 29 |  | 42 |  |
| 4  |  | 17 |  | 30 |  | 43 |  |
| 5  |  | 18 |  | 31 |  | 44 |  |
| 6  |  | 19 |  | 32 |  | 45 |  |
| 7  |  | 20 |  | 33 |  | 46 |  |
| 8  |  | 21 |  | 34 |  | 47 |  |
| 9  |  | 22 |  | 35 |  | 48 |  |
| 10 |  | 23 |  | 36 |  | 49 |  |
| 11 |  | 24 |  | 37 |  | 50 |  |
| 12 |  | 25 |  | 38 |  |    |  |
| 13 |  | 26 |  | 39 |  |    |  |

| Record Your Progress ||||
|---|---|---|---|---|
| Number of Times You Have Taken the Test | Record ||| Record Your Completion Time |
| | Number of Questions Completed | Your Total Score | Total No. of Questions | |
| 1 | | | | |
| 2 | | | | |
| 3 | | | | |
| 4 | | | | |
| 5 | | | | |

## Additional Answer Sheet
## Practice Test Number_____

| | | | | | | | |
|---|---|---|---|---|---|---|---|
| 1 | ☐ | 14 | ☐ | 27 | ☐ | 40 | ☐ |
| 2 | ☐ | 15 | ☐ | 28 | ☐ | 41 | ☐ |
| 3 | ☐ | 16 | ☐ | 29 | ☐ | 42 | ☐ |
| 4 | ☐ | 17 | ☐ | 30 | ☐ | 43 | ☐ |
| 5 | ☐ | 18 | ☐ | 31 | ☐ | 44 | ☐ |
| 6 | ☐ | 19 | ☐ | 32 | ☐ | 45 | ☐ |
| 7 | ☐ | 20 | ☐ | 33 | ☐ | 46 | ☐ |
| 8 | ☐ | 21 | ☐ | 34 | ☐ | 47 | ☐ |
| 9 | ☐ | 22 | ☐ | 35 | ☐ | 48 | ☐ |
| 10 | ☐ | 23 | ☐ | 36 | ☐ | 49 | ☐ |
| 11 | ☐ | 24 | ☐ | 37 | ☐ | 50 | ☐ |
| 12 | ☐ | 25 | ☐ | 38 | ☐ | | |
| 13 | ☐ | 26 | ☐ | 39 | ☐ | | |

| \multicolumn{5}{c|}{**Record Your Progress**} |
|---|---|---|---|---|
| Number of Times You Have Taken the Test | \multicolumn{3}{c|}{Record} | Record Your Completion Time |
| | Number of Questions Completed | Your Total Score | Total No. of Questions | |
| **1** | | | | |
| **2** | | | | |
| **3** | | | | |
| **4** | | | | |
| **5** | | | | |

PRACTICE TESTS IN VERBAL REASONING

**LAST ONE—MAKE A COPY IF YOU NEED MORE!**

# Additional Answer Sheet
# Practice Test Number_____

| 1  | | 14 | | 27 | | 40 | |
|----|-|----|-|----|-|----|-|
| 2  | | 15 | | 28 | | 41 | |
| 3  | | 16 | | 29 | | 42 | |
| 4  | | 17 | | 30 | | 43 | |
| 5  | | 18 | | 31 | | 44 | |
| 6  | | 19 | | 32 | | 45 | |
| 7  | | 20 | | 33 | | 46 | |
| 8  | | 21 | | 34 | | 47 | |
| 9  | | 22 | | 35 | | 48 | |
| 10 | | 23 | | 36 | | 49 | |
| 11 | | 24 | | 37 | | 50 | |
| 12 | | 25 | | 38 | |    | |
| 13 | | 26 | | 39 | |    | |

| Record Your Progress ||||
|---|---|---|---|---|
| Number of Times You Have Taken the Test | Record ||| Record Your Completion Time |
| | Number of Questions Completed | Your Total Score | Total No. of Questions | |
| 1 | | | | |
| 2 | | | | |
| 3 | | | | |
| 4 | | | | |
| 5 | | | | |

# APPENDIX E

# Personal Study Planner

| Time | Mon | Tue | Wed | Thurs | Fri | Sat | Sun |
|---|---|---|---|---|---|---|---|
| 7:00 | | | | | | | |
| 8:00 | | | | | | | |
| 9:00 | | | | | | | |
| 10:00 | | | | | | | |
| 11:00 | | | | | | | |
| 12:00 | | | | | | | |
| 1:00 | | | | | | | |
| 2:00 | | | | | | | |
| 3:00 | | | | | | | |
| 4:00 | | | | | | | |
| 5:00 | | | | | | | |
| 6:00 | | | | | | | |
| 7:00 | | | | | | | |
| 8:00 | | | | | | | |
| 9:00 | | | | | | | |
| 10:00 | | | | | | | |
| 11:00 | | | | | | | |
| | | | | | | | |
| | | | | | | | |

Reminder Notes

# APPENDIX F

# Spelling Practice Sheet

| 1st Attempt | 2nd Attempt | 3rd Attempt | 4th Attempt |
|---|---|---|---|
|  |  |  |  |
|  |  |  |  |
|  |  |  |  |
|  |  |  |  |
|  |  |  |  |
|  |  |  |  |
|  |  |  |  |
|  |  |  |  |
|  |  |  |  |
|  |  |  |  |
|  |  |  |  |
|  |  |  |  |
|  |  |  |  |
|  |  |  |  |
|  |  |  |  |
|  |  |  |  |
|  |  |  |  |
|  |  |  |  |
|  |  |  |  |
|  |  |  |  |
|  |  |  |  |
|  |  |  |  |
|  |  |  |  |
|  |  |  |  |
|  |  |  |  |
|  |  |  |  |
|  |  |  |  |
|  |  |  |  |
|  |  |  |  |

# NOTES

# REFERENCES

Parkinson, Mark. 3rd ed. 2004. *How To Master Psychometric Tests*
Barrett, Jim. 2003. *The Aptitide Test Workbook*
Honey, Peter. *The Learning Styles Questionnaire*
Hamilton-Phillips, Siobhan. *Expert Guidance For Career Development and Changing Careers*
Barrett, Jim. 2002. *How to Pass Advance Aptitude Tests*
Everett, Lesley. *Walking Tall: Key Steps to Total Image Impact*
Johnson, Spencer Dr. *Who Moved My Cheese*
Byron, Mike, 2004. *How to Pass Secondary School Selection Tests*,
Chappell, Cherry. *Minding Your Own Business*
Nuga, Simbo. 2004. *Succeed at Psychometric Test- Practice Tests Tor Verbal Reasoning (Intermediate)*
Nuga, Simbo. 2008. *Succeed at Psychometric Test- Practice Tests Tor Verbal Reasoning (Intermediate)*
Coaley, Keith. *An Introduction to Psychological Assessment and Psychometrics*
Shavick, Andrea. *Practice Psychometric Tests: How To Familiarise Yourself With Genuine Recruitment Tests And Get The Job You Want*
Daughtrey, Susan. J. *Verbal Reasoning Technique and Practice: Volume 1*
Walmsley, Beatrice. *Succeed at Psychometric Testing Practice Tests for the Armed Forces*
Thomas, Ken., Tolley, Harry. *How to Pass Verbal Reasoning Tests*
Byron, Mike. *How to Pass Advanced Verbal Reasoning Tests*
Parkinson, Mark.
Byron, Mike. *How to Pass Graduate Psychometric Tests*
Barrett, Jim. *The Aptitude Test Workbook*
Byron, Mike. *How to Pass the Civil Service Qualifying* Tests
Deluca, Matthey J. *Best Answers to the 201 Most Frequently Asked Interview Questions*

Hodgson, Susan. *Brilliant Tactics to Pass Aptitude Tests: Psychometric, Numeracy, Verbal Reasoning and Many More*
Corfield, Rebecca. *How You Can Get That Job: Application Forms and Letters Made Easy*
Davidshofer, Charles O., Murphy, Kevin R. *Psychological Testing Principles and Applications*
Yate, Martin John, *Great Answers to Tough Interview Questions*
Matton, Caroline R., Williamson, Pauline R., Hill, Kevin. *The Ultimate Guide to Verbal Reasoning: Further Practice Bk.2* I
Hansen, Katharine., Hansen Randall S. *Dynamic Cover Letters: How to Write the Letter That Gets You the Job*
Baron, Renee. *What Type am I?: Discover Who You Really are*
Hornby, Malcolm. *Get That Job: Easy Steps to the Job You Want*
Edenborough, Robert. *Assessment Methods in Recruitment Selection and Performance*
Taylor, Felicity., Hutton, Rosalie., Hutton, Glenn. 2009 *Passing the UK Clinical Aptitude Test (UKCAT) and BMAT*
Jeffries, Williams C. *True to Type: Answers the Most Commonly Asked Questions About Interpreting the Myers-Briggs Type Indicator*
Gregory, O.B. *Essentials of Verbal Reasoning*
Keirsey, D. *Please Understand ME: 2*
Carter, Philio. *The IQ and Psychometric Test Workbook*
Mills, Lorraine. *How To Get That Job!*
Barrett, Jim. *Career Aptitude and Selection Tests*
Pelshenke, Paul. *How to Win at Aptitude Tests*
Rhodes, Peter. *Succeed at Psychometric Testing - Practice Tests for Critical Verbal Reasoning*
Daughtrey, Susan J. *Verbal Reasoning: Graded Test Papers No. 1*
Myers, Isabel., Myers, Peter B. *Gifts Differing: Understanding Personality Type*
Kay, Philip. *Step by Step Verbal Reasoning: Preparation for Selection Tests*
Redman, Alan. *Practice and Pass - Professional: Verbal Reasoning Tests: Practice questions and expert commentary to help you pass verbal reasoning tests and achieve your personal best*
King, Graham. *Collins Wordpower Vocabulary Expander*
King, Graham. *Collins Wordpower Good Grammar*
Tumelty, Sue. *Which Essential Guides CV and Interview Handbook*
McMillan, Kathleen., Weyers, Jonathan. *How to succeed in Exams and Assessments*
Shavick, Andrea. *Passing Psychometric Tests*
Corfield, Rebecca. *Preparing Your Own CV*